# Fighting Poverty with Microcredit

# Fighting Poverty with Microcredit

*Experience in Bangladesh*

———

Shahidur R. Khandker

*Published for the World Bank*

Oxford University Press

*Oxford University Press*

OXFORD  NEW YORK  ATHENS  AUCKLAND  BANGKOK
BOGOTA  BUENOS AIRES  CALCUTTA  CAPE TOWN  CHENNAI
DAR ES SALAAM  DELHI  FLORENCE  HONG KONG  ISTANBUL
KARACHI  KUALA LUMPUR  MADRID  MELBOURNE  MEXICO CITY
MUMBAI  NAIROBI  PARIS  SAO PAULO  SINGAPORE
TAIPEI  TOKYO  TORONTO  WARSAW

and associated companies in
BERLIN  IBADAN

Published by Oxford University Press, Inc.
198 Madison Avenue, New York, N.Y. 10016

Oxford is a registered trademark of Oxford University Press.

Manufactured in the United States of America
First Printing October 1998

The findings, interpretations, and conclusions expressed in this study are
entirely those of the author and should not be attributed in any manner to
the World Bank, to its affiliated organizations, or to members of its Board of
Executive Directors or the countries they represent.

*Cover:* Woman at chalkboard and woman holding jug by Kay
Chernush/The World Bank. Woman weaving basket by Salahudin Azizee,
used with permission from Grameen Bank.

*Library of Congress Cataloguing-in-Publication Data*

Khandker, Shahidur R.
   Fighting poverty with microcredit : experience in
Bangladesh / Shahidur R. Khandker.
   p. cm.
Includes bibliographical references and index.
ISBN 0-19-521121-9
1. Microfinance—Bangladesh. 2. Microfinance. I. Title .
HG178.33.B3 K49 1998
332.7—dc21

                                  98-37303
                                     CIP

# Contents

Foreword                                                                ix
Acknowledgments                                                         xi

1 Poverty Alleviation and Microcredit Programs                          1

2 The Evolution of Microcredit Programs
   in Bangladesh                                                       16

3 Socioeconomic Impacts of Microcredit Programs                        37

4 Growth Potential of Activities Financed
   through Microcredit                                                 63

5 Institutional and Financial Viability of Microcredit
   Programs                                                            84

6 Microcredit Programs and Rural Financial
   Markets                                                            110

7 Cost-Effectiveness of Alternative Poverty
   Alleviation Programs                                               133

8 Conclusions and Policy Implications: What Have
   We Learned?                                                        145

Appendixes
A Statistical Tables                                                  159
B Description of the Sample Used in the Bangladesh
   Institute of Development Studies–World Bank 1991/92 Survey         180
C Evaluating Microcredit Programs                                     182
D Resolving the Problem of Endogeneity in Estimating
   the Impact of Credit                                               205

Bibliography                                                          209

Index                                                                 219

Tables

2.1 Features of the Food-for-Work and Vulnerable Group
Development Programs in Bangladesh                          22
2.2 Features of Three Microcredit Programs in Bangladesh      24
2.3 Codes of Conduct for Members of Microcredit Programs      26
3.1 Rates of Poverty and Net Worth Accumulation before
and after Program Participation                              58
4.1 Sectoral Distribution of Loans, 1990–94                   68
4.2 Size and Type of Loans by Formal, Microfinance,
and Informal Lenders                                        71
4.3 Size and Type of Loans by Program Participation Status    72
4.4 Estimated Marginal Returns to Labor and Capital
for Selected Activities                                     74
4.5 Capital-Labor Ratios by Activity                          74
4.6 Capital-Labor Ratios by Program Participation Status      75
4.7 Marginal Returns to Capital and Labor for Nonfarm
Activities by Length of Program Participation               76
4.8 Credit Constraints and Loan Amounts by Sources of Credit  77
4.9 Sources of Start-Up Capital for Rural Nonfarm
Activities by Program Participation Status                  78
4.10 Marginal Returns to Capital and Capital-Labor Ratios
by Primary Sources of Finance                               78
4.11 Marginal Returns to Capital and Labor and Capital-Labor
Ratios for Purely Rural Areas and Rural Growth Centers      80
5.1 Villages Covered and Number of Village-Based
Organizations of Grameen Bank, BRAC, and RD-12,
1989–94                                                     87
5.2 Members and Borrowers of Grameen Bank, BRAC,
and RD-12, 1989–94                                          88
5.3 Loan Disbursements, Loans Outstanding, and Member
Savings at Grameen Bank, BRAC, and RD-12, 1990–94           89
5.4 Funds Received by Grameen Bank and BRAC, 1986–94          90
5.5 Staff Size and Dropout Rates for Grameen Bank,
BRAC, and RD-12, 1990–94                                    93
5.6 Staff Productivity at Grameen Bank, BRAC,
and RD-12, 1990–94                                          94
5.7 Annual Member Dropout Rates for Grameen Bank,
BRAC, and RD-12, 1986–94                                    96
5.8 Cost Structure of Lending and Break-Even Interest
Rates at Grameen Bank and BRAC, 1990–94                     98
5.9 Financial Margins and Profits at Grameen Bank
and BRAC, 1991–94                                           98
5.10 Interest Rates and Subsidies for Grameen Bank
and BRAC, 1990–94                                          103

5.11 Extent of Subsidies and Subsidy Dependence
by Grameen Bank and BRAC, 1990–94 ............ 104
5.12 Nominal and Real Lending Rates Charged on Regular
Loans by Grameen Bank, 1989–94 ............ 107
5.13 Landlessness and Poverty in Target Households, 1991/92 ... 107
6.1 Agricultural GDP and Formal Agricultural Credit
in Bangladesh, 1983–94 ............ 113
6.2 Loan Recovery on Agricultural Loans by Formal Lenders,
1981–93 ............ 115
6.3 Recovery Rates on Agricultural Loans by Formal Lenders,
July 1, 1994, to June 30, 1995 ............ 116
6.4 Performance of Major Financial Institutions, 1990–94 ... 120
6.5 Subsidy Dependence of Formal Finance and Microfinance
Institutions, 1994 ............ 121
6.6 Average Loan Size and Distribution of Loans by Sector ... 126
6.7 Average Loan Size and Distribution of Loans by Landholding 128
7.1 Costs of Delivering Services of Alternative Credit
Programs, 1991/92 ............ 135
7.2 Cost-Effectiveness of Alternative Credit Programs, 1991/92 136
7.3 Cost-Effectiveness of the Food-for-Work
and Vulnerable Group Development Programs, 1991–92 ... 139
7.4 Cost-Effectiveness of Infrastructure Development ... 141
A3.1 Bivariate Tobit Fixed-Effect Estimates of Demand
for Credit by Gender ............ 159
A3.2 Impact of Credit on Selected Household Outcomes ... 160
A3.3 Joint Significance of Various Credit Variables
on Socioeconomic Outcomes ............ 162
A3.4 Thana-Level Fixed-Effect Estimates of Impacts
of Credit on Selected Anthropometric Measures
of Children ............ 162
A3.5a Estimates of the Impact of Credit on the Seasonality
of Consumption ............ 163
A3.5b Estimates of the Impact of Credit on the Seasonality
of Labor Supply ............ 163
A3.6 Village-Level Impacts of Microcredit Program Intervention 164
A3.7 Microcredit Program Impact on Village-Level Poverty ... 166
A4.1 Determinants of Participation in Rural Nonfarm
Activities ............ 167
A4.2 Cobb-Douglas Production Function Estimates
for Rural Nonfarm Activities ............ 168
A5.1 Determinants of Branch Manager Salaries at Grameen Bank,
BRAC, and RD-12 ............ 170
A5.2 Determinants of Member Dropout Rates for Grameen
Bank and BRAC ............ 171

A5.3   Determinants of Branch-Level Loan Recovery Rates
       for Grameen Bank and RD-12                                    172
A5.4   Estimated Marginal Cost of Membership, Lending,
       and Savings Mobilization for Grameen Bank, BRAC,
·      and RD-12                                                     172
A6.1   Determinants of Individual Borrowing                         173
A6.2   Determinants of Informal Interest Rates at Village Level     174
A6.3   Determinants of Informal Interest Rates on Individual
       Loans                                                        175
A6.4   Determinants of Interhousehold Transfers in Taka             176
A6.5   Determinants of Sources of Borrowing for Agricultural
       Loans                                                        177
A7.1   Effects of Education and Test Scores on Individual
       Participation in Microcredit Programs                        178
A7.2   Effects of Education and Test Scores on Individual
       Participation in Wage Employment                             179

Figures
3.1    Program Participation among Target Households                 39
3.2    Length of Program Participation                               40
3.3    Distribution of Agricultural Landholding among
       Program Participants                                          41
4.1    Distribution of Rural Nonfarm Activities, 1991–92             66
4.2    Distribution of Sources of Employment and Income
       in Bangladesh, 1991–92                                        67
6.1    Sources of Rural Loans, 1985 and 1991/92                      114
6.2    Productivity of Agricultural Development Banks
       and Microfinance Institutions, 1990–94                        118

# Foreword

Microcredit programs are of great interest to policymakers because of their potential for reducing poverty, particularly among women. Programs based on the Grameen Bank model of group-based lending have flourished in Bangladesh and elsewhere, and microcredit institutions have emerged in dozens of other countries as well. Past research has examined specific measures of program performance, such as subsidy dependence and loan recovery rates, but the efficiency of these programs as instruments for reducing poverty has not been evaluated. This study assesses for the first time the cost-effectiveness of microcredit programs as instruments for poverty reduction.

Based on extensive survey data from Bangladesh, this study shows that microcredit programs are an effective policy instrument for reducing poverty among poor people with the skills to become self-employed. It also shows that such programs are more cost-effective than some other types of antipoverty programs. Microcredit programs were found to be particularly important for Bangladeshi women, many of whom are restricted by social custom from seeking wage employment. Their only source of income is self-employment, and they face difficulty in accessing individual lending programs. Defying traditional wisdom, women (who constitute 94 percent of Grameen Bank members) have proved to be excellent credit risks, with a rate of default that is less than one-third that of men. For all three of the microcredit programs studied, the impact on household consumption was twice as great when the borrowers were women. Women who participated in microcredit programs also increased their net wealth and their status within the household, and improved the lives of their children as well.

The policy implications of the book's findings will be of particular interest to government decisionmakers, international donors, and practitioners of microfinance. Researchers will also benefit from the book's rigorous technical analysis, much of which is presented in the appendixes. All readers will come away with a new appreciation of the value of microcredit.

*Joseph E. Stiglitz*
*Senior Vice President, Development Economics*
*and Chief Economist*
*The World Bank*

# Acknowledgments

This book is based on analysis of a rich data set collected in Bangladesh for the research project "Credit Programs for the Poor: Household and Intrahousehold Impacts and Program Sustainability." The project was funded under the Research Support Budget of the World Bank, and the data collection and analysis were conducted by researchers from the World Bank and other organizations. The book also draws on my additional research using the same data. I am indebted to my collaborators on the research project—Mark Pitt, Baqui Khalily, Abdul Latif, Omar Chowdhury, Osman Chowdhury, Rushidan Rahman, Zahed Khan, and Syed Ahsan—for their invaluable contributions to the book. Barbara Herz, Martin Karcher, and Roger Slade provided guidance at the initial stage of the research project, without which the study would never have materialized. I am also indebted to Minhchau Nguyen for her support and encouragement throughout the study—support that was instrumental in bringing the book to fruition.

I am thankful to the World Bank's Research Committee, especially Gregory Ingram and Clara Else, for funding the research project and its dissemination, including an international workshop in Dhaka at which preliminary findings were discussed. I would also like to thank officials of the Ford Foundation and the U.S. Agency for International Development in Dhaka for providing financial help to the Bangladesh Institute of Development Studies (BIDS) for data analysis and the hosting of the Dhaka workshop. Officials of the three programs studied—Grameen Bank, the Bangladesh Rural Advancement Committee (BRAC), and the Rural Development Project-12 (RD-12) of the Bangladesh Rural Development Board—were extremely cooperative in providing us with program-level and selected branch-level data. They were also helpful in extending support to the BIDS field interviewers who conducted the household surveys. I am ever grateful to Muhammad Yunus of Grameen Bank, Fazle H. Abed of BRAC, and Daudur Rahman of RD-12 for their enthusiastic support of the study. I am also thankful to Salahuddin Ahmad, Shafiqul Islam, and M.G. Sattar of BRAC and Dipal Barua and Masud Isa of Grameen Bank for their help during the branch-level data collection. BIDS administrative staff and research officers, especially Bashir Ahmed, Hosne Ara Begum, Abdus Salam, and dozens of enumerators, provided invaluable assistance with data collection. I am grateful to Shahana Iqbal of the World Bank field office in Dhaka, who acted as a liaison between BIDS and others in Bangladesh to facilitate the collection and processing of the monumental data set. I am also thankful to the men and women in the 87 villages in Bangladesh who gave generously of their time during the three phases of interviews carried out in 1991–92.

I would like to thank Harold Alderman, George Clarke, Gershon Feder, Andrew Foster, Ishrat Husain, Martin Ravallion, Orlando Sacay, Khalid Siraj, Chris Udry, Muhammad Yunus, and four anonymous reviewers chosen by the Bank's editorial committee for detailed comments on earlier drafts of this book. The book reflects the constructive and insightful comments of all the reviewers. The book also benefited from earlier comments of participants in the workshop "Credit Programs for the Poor," held in Dhaka, on March 19–22, 1995. In particular, Abu Abdullah, Lynn Bennett, Rashid Faruqee, Mahabub Hossain, Mosharraf Hossain, Nurul Islam, N.J. Kurian, Pierre Landell-Mills, Wahid Mahmud, Richard Meyer, Sarfraz Qureshi, Joanne Salop, and Khaled Shams provided helpful comments and suggestions on preliminary findings of various studies presented at the workshop. Thanks are also due to Hussain Samad for excellent research assistance; Meta de Coquereaumont, Barbara Karni, and Ilyse Zable for editorial assistance; and Dawn Ballantyne, Stella David, Thierry Debaille, and Carrie Palma for production support.

# 1

# Poverty Alleviation and Microcredit Programs

Providing the poor with access to financial services is one of many ways to help increase their incomes and productivity. In many countries, however, traditional financial institutions have failed to provide this service (Adams, Graham, and von Pischke 1984; Braverman and Guasch 1986, 1989; Hoff and Stiglitz 1990; World Bank 1975, 1993). Microcredit and cooperative programs have been developed to fill this gap. Their purpose is to help the poor become self-employed and thus escape poverty. Many of these programs provide credit using social mechanisms, such as group-based lending, to reach the poor and other clients, including women, who lack access to formal financial institutions (Huppi and Feder 1990; Holt and Ribe 1991; Stiglitz 1990; Varian 1990; von Pischke, Adams, and Donald 1983; Yaron 1994). With increasing assistance from the World Bank and other donors, microfinance is emerging as an instrument for reducing poverty and improving the poor's access to financial services in low-income countries (World Bank 1990; Binswanger and Landell-Mills 1995).[1]

## How Can Microcredit Reduce Poverty?

The appropriateness of microcredit as a tool for reducing poverty depends on local circumstances. Poverty is often the result of low economic growth, high population growth, and extremely unequal distribution of resources. The proximate determinants of poverty are unemployment and the low productivity of the poor. When poverty results from unemployment, reducing poverty requires creating jobs; when poverty results from low productivity and low income, reducing poverty requires investing in human and physical capital to increase workers' productivity. In many countries, such as Bangladesh, poverty is caused by lack of both physical and human capital. Consequently, the best way to reduce poverty is to deal with both problems: increasing productivity by creating employment and developing human capital.

One way to increase the productivity of the poor is through broad-based economic growth. Such growth ensures more inclusive participation in development by providing widespread employment

1

opportunities. Agricultural development provides opportunities for broad-based economic growth. But substantial job expansion within agriculture may not be feasible, since agriculture already provides more than 70 percent of employment in many low-income countries. If rural poverty is the result of seasonal agricultural unemployment, Food-for-Work and targeted wage employment schemes can smooth consumption by the poor (Ravallion 1991). If unemployment is chronic rather than seasonal, however, sustainable employment generation is needed.

Lack of savings and capital make it difficult for many poor people who want jobs in the farm and nonfarm sectors to become self-employed and to undertake productive employment-generating activities. Providing credit seems to be a way to generate self-employment opportunities for the poor. But because the poor lack physical collateral, they have almost no access to institutional credit. Informal lenders play an important role in many low-income countries (Adams and Fitchett 1992; Ghate 1992), but they often charge high interest rates, inhibiting poor rural households from investing in productive income-increasing activities. Moreover, although informal groups, such as rotating savings and credit associations, can meet the occasional financial needs of rural households in many societies, they are not reliable sources of finance for income-generating activities (Webster and Fidler 1995). Microcredit programs are able to reach the poor at affordable cost and can thus help the poor become self-employed.

Still, views differ on the role of microfinance and microcredit programs. Detractors view such programs as a social liability, consuming scarce resources without significantly affecting long-term outcomes. Critics argue that the small enterprises supported by microcredit programs have limited growth potential and so have no sustained impact on the poor. Instead, they contend, these programs make the poor economically dependent on the program itself (Bouman and Hospes 1994). Microcredit programs also depend on donors, as they are often highly subsidized (Adams and von Pischke 1992). Thus even if microcredit programs are able to reach the poor, they may not be cost-effective and hence worth supporting as a resource transfer mechanism.

Proponents of microcredit consider increasing the poor's access to institutional credit an important means of ending poverty (Yunus 1983). They argue that by virtue of their design such programs can reach the poor and overcome problems of credit market imperfections. In their view improved access to credit smoothes consumption and eases constraints in production, raising the incomes and productivity of the poor. Empirical studies support this view to some extent: credit market interventions improve both the consumption and production of the poor who otherwise lack access to credit (Feder and others 1988; Foster 1995; Rosenzweig and Wolpin 1993). According to proponents of microcredit, when traditional banks and financial institutions fail to meet the needs of women and the poor, alternative institutions should be developed to meet these groups' demand for financial services.

## Global Experience with Microcredit

Many countries have established microcredit programs with the explicit objective of reducing poverty by providing small amounts of credit to the poor to generate self-employment in income-earning activities. Bangladesh is a leader among low-income countries offering microcredit. Using a group-based approach to lending, the country's small-scale microcredit programs provide more credit than do traditional financial institutions in rural areas (World Bank 1996a).[2]

Grameen Bank, founded in 1976 as a project and transformed into a specialized bank in 1983, is the best-known microcredit program. By 1994 it had mobilized more than 2 million members, 94 percent of them women, and achieved a loan recovery rate of more than 95 percent.

The bank's group-based lending scheme has two important features that attract the poor: borrowers are allowed to deal with a financial institution through a group and members self-select their own group. Group-based lending also reduces Grameen's loan default costs by exerting peer pressure to repay loans. It also allows Grameen Bank to pool resources and diversify the risks of lending by lending across communities and groups, thus enabling it to provide loans at an affordable price.

Grameen's group-based lending approach is the guiding principle for more than 750 nongovernmental organizations (NGOs) operating small-scale microcredit programs in Bangladesh. Two other large microcredit programs in Bangladesh are the Bangladesh Rural Advancement Committee (BRAC), with more than 1 million members, and the Rural Development Project-12 (RD-12) of the Bangladesh Rural Development Board (BRDB), with about 0.5 million members. BRAC is an NGO; RD-12 is a government program. Both programs use group-based credit schemes to target women and the poor.

Grameen Bank's success in recovering loans and reaching the poor has attracted worldwide attention (Binswanger and Landell-Mills 1995). The bank's group-based approach to lending has been replicated in more than 45 countries, including the United States (Khandker, Khalily, and Khan 1995). Accion International and Women's World Banking are working to expand microcredit programs in many countries (Otero and Rhyne 1994; Webster and Fidler 1995; Christen,

Rhyne, and Vogel 1994; Binswanger and Landell-Mills 1995). In addition, donors such as U.S. Agency for International Development (USAID), International Fund for Agricultural Development (IFAD), Norwegian Agency for International Development (NORAD), Canadian International Development Agency (CIDA), and Swedish International Development Authority (SIDA) are playing major roles in the development of microcredit institutions in many countries. By 1994 more than 33 million microenterprise loans were outstanding, financed by more than 56 million savings deposits accounts, with a total value of more than $16 million.

The World Bank's contribution to microfinance growth has been relatively modest. In 1995 it provided grant funding of $30 million to establish the Consultative Group to Assist the Poorest (CGAP) fund of $100 million to directly support and spread microcredit programs in developing countries. CGAP seeks to strengthen microcredit programs by providing grants to support efforts to extend banking to the poor. It also identifies best practices, develops guidelines for microcredit programs, and channels funds to women and the poor through microcredit programs. The World Bank is also financing microcredit programs directly as well as indirectly through various social fund projects in different countries. Since 1987 it has provided more than $1 billion in loans to 87 microcredit projects, including social funds that are components of larger projects (CGAP 1997).

The practice of microfinance worldwide is as diverse as its source of finance. A worldwide inventory of microfinance programs prepared by the World Bank documents more than 1,000 microfinance institutions—commercial banks, savings banks, credit unions, and NGOs—providing microcredit to women and the poor in 101 developing countries (World Bank 1996d). More than 90 percent of these institutions have more than 1,000 clients. The 206 microfinance institutions studied closely by the World Bank had more than $7 billion in outstanding loans and $19 billion in deposits in 1995. More than 55 percent of these institutions served more women than men, and more than 60 percent practiced group-based lending. Commercial banks and savings banks disbursed more than 80 percent of the total microcredit loans, with NGOs disbursing just 9 percent. Commercial banks and credit unions drew more than half their loanable funds for microcredit programs from deposit mobilization, while NGOs received most of their funds (70 percent) from donors.

Microfinance funding is regionally concentrated, with nearly 76 percent of total loans disbursed in Asia, 21 percent in Latin America and 3 percent in Africa. The share of donor funding also varies regionally, with donors providing 55 percent of funds in Latin America, 47 percent in Asia, and 39 percent in Africa.

## What Do We Know about Microcredit Programs?

An extensive literature exists on microcredit programs. Rather than analyze the effect of these programs on poverty reduction and their cost-effectiveness, however, this research has focused on four areas: their role as credit delivery mechanisms, their effectiveness at outreach (the extent of program coverage), their dependence on subsidies, and their social and economic consequences.

### Credit Delivery Mechanism

Credit market imperfections can create inefficiency in both production and consumption, a problem that disproportionately affects the poor in rural areas (Foster 1995; Townsend 1994). Government-directed financial institutions have been developed in order to provide the poor with access to credit. In many countries directed credit programs have been heavily subsidized. Much of the literature on institutional credit concludes that directed rural credit programs have rarely created viable financial institutions (Adams, Graham, and von Pischke 1983, 1984; Feder, Huppi, and Yaron 1989; Sacay and Randhawa 1995; USAID 1973, 1991; von Pischke, Adams, and Donald 1983).[3] Moreover, because the poor lack the physical capital necessary as collateral, credit subsidies have reached the better-off, who often fail to repay their loans, thereby undermining the repayment morale of all borrowers (Binswanger and Khandker 1995).

Many directed credit programs set interest rates below the market rate and deliver credit without mobilizing savings (Adams, Graham, and von Pischke 1984). Policymakers have been urged to liberalize financial markets and to design credit programs that engage in true financial intermediation rather than merely delivering credit from government or donor funds (Cho and Khatkhate 1989). Some analysts argue that even if financial institutions began practicing financial intermediation or raising interest rates to cover costs, such measures would not necessarily resolve credit market or sustainability problems. A small body of theoretical research has shown that if asymmetric information and imperfect enforcement plague rural credit markets, raising interest rates will not necessarily improve loan recovery rates, and targeted loans may fail to reach target households even if the price of the loan is right (Stiglitz and Weiss 1981, 1983). Thus, as researchers argue, financial institutions may need to address concerns of imperfect information and imperfect enforcement (Hoff and Stiglitz 1990).

Microcredit programs have been more successful than traditional financial institutions at reaching the poor, and they have managed to reduce loan default costs. Many microcredit programs rely on group-based lending and other methods to resolve the problems of imperfect information and imperfect enforcement of lending. By relying on peer pressure to monitor and enforce contracts, group-based lending provides an incentive for borrowers to repay and helps avoid adverse selection of borrowers, thereby improving loan recovery rates (Stiglitz 1990; Varian 1990). While group-based lending does not always improve loan recovery (Besley and Coate 1995), it constitutes a powerful incentive for repayment when it helps create "social collateral" that works against loan default.[4] But social collateral cannot be the sole reason for adopting a group-based lending scheme. Social collateral can also be harnessed through individual-based lending—by involving community leaders, for example, as Indonesia's Badan Kredit Kecamatan (BKK) has done (Yaron 1992a, b). Group lending may help identify target households better than individual lending. Individual lending can "perpetuate and reinforce the existing socioeconomic inequities and access to scarce financial resources" (Yaron 1992a, p.12). In contrast, group lending can help the poor self-select programs, making it a powerful instrument of identification and targeting (Khandker, Khalily, and Khan 1995). Microcredit programs that adopt group lending practices can benefit from better targeting and better loan repayment if group lending results in self-selection, peer monitoring, and creation of social collateral.

Some programs that do not rely on group mechanisms have also been successful in reaching small borrowers and recovering loans. What accounts for their success is their reliance on social pressure through village leaders (Chaves and Gonzalez-Vega 1996; Patten and Rosengard 1991; Riedinger 1994; Yaron 1994). For example, Indonesia's success in rural finance rests on the networks of semiautonomous units of Badan Kredit Kecamatan and Bank Rakyat Indonesia, which use local information to enforce loan contracts. In Africa, which has no rural financial institutions, some rural credit programs have also become successful through the use of local networks to reduce asymmetric information (Christen, Rhyne, and Vogel 1994; Gurgand, Pederson, and Yaron 1994; Webster and Fidler 1995).

## Outreach and Loan Recovery

Many microcredit programs have attained the outreach objective of reaching a large number of clients with small amounts of resources (Bennett, Goldberg, and Hunte 1996; Dessing 1990; Hossain 1988; Hulme and Mosley 1996; Yaron 1992a, b). But studies of outreach fail to indicate who has benefited from microcredit. In many countries women are the main participants in microcredit programs. Yet many women lack enough power within households to use their loans to improve productivity and welfare (Goetz and Gupta 1996). It is thus important to explore how women benefit from participation in microcredit programs. A related issue is determining which poor and small borrowers actually participate in these programs.

The extent of benefits accruing to borrowers also needs to be identified. Many researchers contend that the high loan recovery rates of microcredit programs imply that programs are benefiting participants. But loan recovery rates cannot be used as the sole determinant of a program's success since many microcredit programs rely on social, peer, and other forms of pressure to maintain high loan recovery rates. Moreover, in many programs high loan recovery rates are often achieved only by repeat or rollover loans, so high loan recoveries do not necessarily reflect high benefits.

Loans for self-employment can be self-sustaining only if they generate sufficient income to support the borrowers' livelihood and to allow borrowers to repay the loans. The emphasis on outreach fails to distinguish between productive loans and unproductive loans. If loan repayment is not an issue and the financial sustainability of microfinance and microcredit programs is not an achievable objective, such programs become merely mechanisms for transferring resources to the poor. If microfinance programs represent nothing more than transfer mechanisms, they must be compared with other programs, such as wage employment schemes, that also aim at reaching the poor.

## Subsidy Dependence

Although microcredit programs have improved loan repayment rates and seem to be better targeted than other programs aimed at the poor, they have high transactions costs. Many of the activities that are critical to maintaining high loan recovery rates and identifying the poor are costly. Group lending, for example, involves social intermediation, including group formation, training, and other noncredit activities. Group activities that are sometimes necessary to create a sense of individual responsibility can be considered a social investment for poverty reduction. But these high transactions costs may make microcredit programs dependent on subsidized resources. An important concern in the literature about microcredit programs is the extent of this subsidy dependence.

Microcredit programs rely heavily on subsidies. Although microcredit programs usually do not provide interest subsidies to their borrowers (that is, interest rates are generally at or above market levels), many programs depend on donor or subsidized resources for on-lending and institutional development and cannot break even at the market cost of these resources. The literature concludes that subsidy dependence is so high that with few exceptions even microcredit programs that have been operating for years are unable to function on their own (Bennett and Cuevas 1996; Yaron 1992a, b; Christen, Rhyne, and Vogel 1994; Webster and Fidler 1995). Although many microcredit programs are better able than formal credit institutions to reach the poor (as shown by their outreach indicators) and to recover loans (as shown by their loan recovery rates), they are unable to fully cover their operational costs, at least early on. To become fully financially self-sustainable, microcredit programs would need to charge rates of interest that would be too high for borrowers to bear given the level of profit they can expect to generate from their loans.

To what extent do microcredit programs require subsidization? Should governments and donors continue to subsidize these schemes? There is an ongoing debate in the current literature about how much subsidy microcredit programs should receive from donors (Morduch 1998). To answer these questions, the full costs of microcredit programs must be determined. The ability of microcredit programs to eliminate subsidies depends not only on interest rate policies and cost efficiency but also on the growth and income generation potential of the activities they support. The growth potential of microenterprises largely determines the rate of return to capital financed by these programs and hence influences their long-run sustainability and that of their clients. The literature on subsidy dependence has not examined the benefits that accrue to borrowers or whether these benefits justify the full pricing of loans and financial services to microcredit clients.

The influence of agroclimate conditions on subsidy dependence also needs to be quantified. A small body of literature on rural finance shows that rural credit transactions suffer not only from behavioral loan default risk (because of asymmetric information) but also from the material risk caused by the unfavorable agroclimate and production conditions in rural areas (Binswanger and Rosenzweig 1986). Traditional financial institutions do not place programs in areas that are flood-prone, have pronounced seasonality, have poorly developed infrastructure, or suffer from other unfavorable production conditions, because production risks and transport costs are too high (Binswanger, Khandker, and Rosenzweig 1993). In some locations, such as Bangladesh, loan recovery rates are highly conditional on weather, and financial intermediation is costly in areas with poorly developed infrastructure. The literature has ignored the possibility that subsidy or donor dependency may be due in part to these areas' vulnerability to material risk caused by poor and risky agroclimate conditions.

A useful aspect of microcredit program evaluation would be to investigate whether the group lending feature of a microcredit scheme is sufficient to guarantee high loan recovery in poor agroclimate regions. If production risk is an important component of loan default risk, a group-based credit delivery scheme that accounts only for the behavioral risk of loan default cannot guarantee full loan recovery. Risk-efficient lending (that is, lending with low loan default costs) would then require additional means, such as mandatory insurance schemes, to protect lenders against the material risk of lending. Indeed, programs such as Grameen Bank, which operate in highly risky areas that are subject to frequent floods and cyclones, have relied on such instruments as mandatory savings and insurance schemes.

## Social and Economic Benefits

Determining whether programs can charge interest rates high enough to cover their full costs requires identification of the social and private benefits of microcredit programs. If microcredit programs were based on financial sustainability and poverty reduction were not a goal, these benefits would not need to be assessed. Many programs are targeted to the poor and are subsidized by governments and donors, however. Their benefits in terms of net worth must thus be calculated, so that policy-makers can determine whether their support of microcredit programs is warranted.

Many studies have attempted to measure the benefits of microcredit in terms of income, employment, and other socioeconomic outcomes (BIDS 1990; J. Alam 1988; M. Alam 1989; Amin and others 1994; Amin and Pebley 1990; Hossain 1988; Hulme and Mosely 1996; Schuler and Hashemi 1994). The analysis has largely failed to indicate whether the measured benefits are due to program participation, however.

The literature on the impacts of microcredit programs considers only participant-level impacts. Such estimates fail to consider the self-selection process involved in program participation and the nonrandomness of program placement. Measurement of causal impacts requires participant-level analysis that accounts for both why a microcredit institution places its program in a particular area and why a particular person or household participates in a program.

The literature measuring the socioeconomic impacts of microcredit programs has also failed to document whether microcredit programs benefit borrowers at the cost of others in society. Introducing a microcredit program in an area in which there is no economic growth may hurt those who are already in business, with the benefits that accrue to program participants coming at the expense of their competitors. The only way to determine the net effect of a program is to evaluate economywide impacts by identifying the benefits to both program participants and nonparticipants. A recent study in India shows that targeted agricultural credit programs contributed to the growth of rural nonfarm income even though their impact on farm productivity and investment was slight. Even a conservative estimate shows that the overall benefit of targeted farm credit exceeded the cost to the government by 13 percent (Binswanger and Khandker 1995). Because funds are fungible, the impact of farm credit has to be evaluated not only in terms of farm production and investment (participant-level impact) but also in terms of rural nonfarm production and employment (economywide impacts).

Microcredit programs could benefit society overall by overcoming the liquidity, consumption smoothing, and unemployment problems associated with highly imperfect credit markets. The impacts could be so large that the social benefits exceed the social cost of program placement, even for microcredit programs that are not viable without sustained support from government and donors. To determine whether this is the case, microcredit programs must be evaluated against other programs (such as agricultural and industrial development banks or targeted wage employment schemes) that also rely on government and donor funds. The cost-effectiveness of these alternative programs must be evaluated to determine whether society would benefit from a reallocation of resources.

## Purpose and Organization of the Book

Microcredit programs are intended to alleviate poverty. Evaluation of these programs thus requires analysis of how effective these programs have been at reducing poverty, something that previous research has failed to do. Program-level cost analysis must be performed that takes account of both the operational costs and the economic costs of subsidized operations. Evaluation of microcredit programs must also assess their self-sustainability—that is, their financial, economic, and institutional viability and the viability of their borrowers.

Program evaluation begins with an assessment of the impact on program participants in terms of household welfare, including changes in per capita consumption, household net worth, assets, schooling of male and female children, contraceptive use, and fertility. Impact analysis also gauges the level of women's participation to determine if women benefit from targeted credit programs. Village-level effects are also assessed to measure the total net effect of these programs.

Funds allocated to microcredit programs could be allocated to other antipoverty programs, such as targeted food interventions or infrastructure development. To justify continued support of microcredit programs, policymakers must be able to compare the cost-effectiveness of all of these programs. To allow them to do so, cost-benefit ratios of various antipoverty schemes are calculated.

Bangladesh's microcredit programs are the pioneers of microfinance, and an extensive network of these programs is in place in Bangladesh. Evaluation of these programs should thus yield important policy lessons about the strengths and weaknesses of microcredit programs as a tool for reducing poverty. Lessons about the effectiveness of these programs in providing financial services to women and the poor in rural areas should also emerge from this analysis.

This book examines the experiences of the Grameen Bank and two other major microcredit programs in Bangladesh in order to quantify the potential and limitations of microcredit programs as an instrument for reducing poverty and delivering financial services to the poor. Specifically, it addresses whether microcredit alleviates poverty, whether microfinance is a cost-effective way of transferring resources to the poor (even if it fails to reduce poverty), and whether microfinance is a cost-effective way of providing financial services to the poor when formal financial institutions fail to meet their needs. It also examines who among the poor benefits from microfinance and how. The analysis, based on household survey and program-level data, suggests that when these programs attain a certain level of operation they are cost-effective. The programs reduce poverty on a sustained basis and are well targeted, with more than 80 percent of borrowers owning less than half an acre of land.

Although microfinance generates benefits for women and the poor, it seems to benefit only that portion of the poor that is able to use loans productively. Some eligible poor do not join microfinance programs because they lack either the ability to use loans productively or the land (a source of employment and an important form of economic security) needed to bear the risk of self-employment. Eligible individuals who are ultrapoor (the poorest of the poor) and lack human capital tend not to borrow from microcredit programs.

Although the accrued benefits to borrowers and society justify microcredit program interventions, Bangladeshi programs are highly subsidized. Over time, however, some programs, such as Grameen Bank, have reduced subsidy dependence without attaining full self-sustainability, that is, the ability to provide self-sustainable financial services to clients without help from donors. Even if microcredit programs are worth supporting, they should not be the sole instrument for poverty reduction. The ultrapoor may not join such programs even if they are eligible because they lack human capital. Other targeted programs (such as Food-for-Work) as well as broad-based economic growth are required for the left-out groups to become productive and able to escape poverty.

The three microcredit programs in Bangladesh selected for in-depth study are described in chapter 2. Grameen Bank was selected because of its size and prominence both within and outside Bangladesh. BRAC was chosen because it is the largest NGO in Bangladesh providing financial services to the poor through a group-based approach to lending; it also provides significant social development and skills development services. RD-12 was selected because it is a government program that uses a small group–based approach within the government bureaucratic structure as well as a large group–based cooperative framework. The chapter reviews program design, targeting, delivery mechanisms, and management structure. To put the evolution of microcredit programs in Bangladesh in proper perspective, chapter 2 also discusses alternative poverty alleviation programs (such as Food-for-Work and other targeted schemes) and their strengths and weaknesses in reaching the poor.

Chapter 3 uses cross-sectional household survey data to document the impact of these microcredit programs on poverty reduction and other welfare measures. It examines who benefits from program participation, looking specifically at whether women benefit. It finds that program participation is endogenously determined by the same individual and household characteristics that determine household and intrahousehold behavioral outcomes (consumption, assets, ownership, labor supply, fertility, contraceptive use, and children's schooling enrollment). For many of the outcomes examined, credit to women has a larger impact than credit to men. Women also benefit from program participation through the cash income generated by self-employment and the assets they acquire in the process. Estimates indicate that microfinance reduces poverty among program participants and reduces aggregate poverty in program villages (even after controlling for observable village characteristics that partially determine the extent of village poverty).

Chapter 4 examines long-run issues, such as whether the program benefits that accrue to participants and society are sustainable. The long-run sustainability of benefits is important because half of microcredit borrowers are engaged in rural nonfarm activities, such as trade and commerce, that have low growth potential. Activities with high growth potential include manufacturing and processing, which attract the second largest concentration of microcredit borrowers. Because Grameen Bank provides more credit than BRAC and RD-12, it seems to have a larger overall impact on rural nonfarm production. But repeat borrowers from BRAC have higher returns to capital, suggesting that the program's skills development training is effective. These findings suggest that microcredit programs may need to provide skills development and other ancillary services to poor and unskilled borrowers to sustain their benefits. Provision of such inputs may be necessary for the long-run viability of microcredit programs and their borrowers. Public provision of infrastructure, such as roads, marketing facilities, and electrification, also seems important for sustaining long-run benefits in microenterprises.

Once the benefits of microcredit programs have been identified, the cost of delivering financial services to the poor must be determined. Chapter 5 analyzes the cost structure, subsidy dependence, and institutional development of microcredit programs to evaluate a program's sustainability—its financial, economic, and institutional viability. Although subsidy dependence has declined in recent years, all three programs remain subsidized. These programs could become subsidy free by raising interest rates. The rate of return to capital in microenterprises seems to be higher than the cost of funds borrowed from microcredit programs, suggesting that borrowers could profitably borrow more at the current cost of borrowing. Raising interest rates would increase capital costs and could reduce the impact on poverty reduction. But market expansion as a result of technological improvement could enhance the profitability of microenterprises, allowing them to bear higher borrowing rates.

Subsidized funds have been crucial for the institutional development of microcredit programs because of the high costs of group-based lending, of mobilizing and training the poor to make them creditworthy, and of placing programs in poor agroclimate areas. Subsidy reduction depends on greater cost efficiency through learning and a decentralized management structure. High staff productivity and morale may also contribute to institutional cost-effectiveness. No single measure is adequate, however. Subsidy dependency should be reduced using a combination of policies—raising interest rates, reducing administrative costs, and improving staff productivity.

Chapter 6 focuses on the impact of microcredit programs on rural financial markets in terms of their effects on the sources and extent of borrowing, lending rates, and interfamily transfers. It also explores their cost-effectiveness as financial intermediaries compared with that of other institutions, such as agricultural development banks. The chapter also examines the financing of small and medium-size farmers, who seem to be excluded from both formal finance and microfinance institutions. The main findings are that Grameen Bank increased borrowing from microfinance institutions, reduced borrowing from informal sources, lowered the informal lending rate, and reduced interfamily transfers.

Microfinance programs were found to be more cost-effective in delivering financial services than agricultural development banks. Improving efficiency in government-subsidized banks is an important step toward efficient rural financial intermediation. Group-based credit delivery has been applied on a pilot basis by several commercial banks to finance small and medium-size farmers. The institutional costs of small loans are high, however, and expansion of such group-based programs is constrained by a lack of institutional support from commercial banks, the government, and donors. Since small and medium-size farmers constitute more than 45 percent of the population in rural Bangladesh and cultivate more than 55 percent of the land there, development of financial instruments to meet this group's needs will have a far-reaching impact on poverty and economic growth.

Chapter 7 examines the cost-effectiveness of alternative poverty alleviation programs. It compares the cost-effectiveness of microcredit programs with that of targeted food intervention programs and nontargeted programs aimed at promoting broad-based economic growth. The main finding is that the microfinance programs of Grameen Bank appear to be more cost-effective both in delivering services and in generating benefits than all other targeted credit and noncredit programs. This does not mean that all resources earmarked for poverty alleviation should go to microfinance programs. Analysis of household data indicates that participants in microfinance programs have special abilities (oral accounting skills, for example) that enable them to use loans to generate income. Those who are eligible but do not participate in microfinance programs lack these skills, which may explain why they do not participate. Wage employment or other types of schemes are more appropriate for this group.

Chapter 8 summarizes what has been learned from the experiences of microfinance programs in Bangladesh. The small group–based lending approach developed by Grameen Bank has been successfully replicated by hundreds of NGOs in Bangladesh. Replication of such group–based schemes in other countries may, however, be a formidable task without dedicated and committed leadership. This chapter discusses some of the other attributes of group–based lending that may be relevant for replication in other countries. This chapter also discusses the limitations of microfinance.

Appendix A includes the results of various regressions. Appendix B describes the sample used in the study. Appendix C discusses the appropriate methods for evaluating the cost-effectiveness of microcredit programs and examines the methods used to estimate costs and benefits. Appendix D provides a technical explanation of the issues involved in resolving the problem of endogeneity in estimating the impact of credit.

## Notes

1. Microfinance refers to the loans and savings services provided by microcredit institutions and programs. Some microcredit programs also provide other services, such as training and organizational help.

2. The loan-savings ratio is 1.2 for microcredit programs, six times the 0.2 ratio for traditional financial institutions. In 1994/95 traditional financial insti-

tutions provided about $370 million in credit while microcredit programs provided about $540 million, 71 percent of which was provided by Grameen Bank alone.

3. Only Thailand's Bank of Agriculture and Agricultural Cooperatives (BAAC) and Indonesia's Badan Kredit Kecamatan (BKK) are financially viable.

4. Group lending can have both positive and negative effects on loan repayments. The positive effect results from the possibility that successful borrowers may make the loan payments of less successful borrowers who are not able to repay the loan. The negative effect arises when the entire group defaults (that is, when some borrowers who would have paid default because of the liabilities of other group members).

# 2

# The Evolution of Microcredit Programs in Bangladesh

Providing credit is one way of enabling the poor to acquire assets and become productive. Targeted credit programs for the poor were first tried in 1976, when Muhammad Yunus, a Bangladeshi economics professor, introduced an experimental project to test whether the poor were creditworthy and whether credit could be provided without physical collateral. With the help of some Bangladeshi banks, Yunus conducted an innovative experiment emphasizing group delivery of credit and exploring what constituted a manageable group size for effective financial intermediation. The central bank of Bangladesh later facilitated Yunus' work by arranging for funding from the International Fund for Agricultural Development (IFAD). In Yunus' experiment, group collateral substituted for physical collateral. The group guarantee to repay individual loans became the hallmark of microlending. Using the mechanism, poor people with no physical collateral were able to form groups to gain access to institutional credit. The mechanism also allowed credit to reach the poor, especially poor women.

The central premise of this targeted credit approach is that lack of access to credit is the greatest constraint on the economic advancement of the rural poor. Yunus believes that with appropriate support, the poor can be productively employed in income-generating activities, including processing and manufacturing, transport, storage and marketing of agricultural products, and poultry and livestock raising. After almost seven years of experimentation with a variety of group–based mechanisms, his idea took formal shape as a bank with its own charter. With the government holding about 90 percent of the shares in paid-up capital, Grameen Bank was established in 1983 to work exclusively with the poor, defined as individuals owning less than half an acre of land.

Where Grameen Bank believes that the most immediate need of the poor is credit to create and expand self-employment opportunities, the Bangladesh Rural Advancement Committee (BRAC) believes that the poor need skills development and other organizational inputs. BRAC was established in 1972 as a charitable organization to help resettle households displaced during the 1971 war. BRAC's founder, F. H. Abed, soon realized that relief simply maintained the status quo; it was inadequate to alleviate poverty. BRAC's relief experience helped it under-stand the causes of rural poverty and develop a framework for poverty alleviation.

BRAC's approach has been to combine lending with the delivery of organizational inputs, such as skills promotion and consciousness-raising (Lovell 1992). It has never viewed credit as a central instrument for poverty alleviation. Rather it believes that economic dependency on exploitative village economic structures is the ultimate cause of persistent poverty. As revealed in many anthropological studies (BRAC 1984; Chowdhury 1982; Islam 1974), landholding and command of financial resources are still the major determinants of rural social class. While the wealthiest households dominate the rural society, the rural poor, lacking access to alternative resources and an awareness of their situation, maintain the dominance of each faction by associating themselves with a particular faction for protection and security. As a result, the poor remain poor and become the victims of exploitative forces.

Over time BRAC and Grameen Bank have learned from one another. BRAC has learned that credit must be provided along with skills development training; Grameen Bank has realized that credit alone is not enough, that the poor need social development and organizational inputs to become more disciplined and productive. BRAC continues to provide skills training and other inputs before disbursing credit, however, while Grameen Bank continues to disburse credit before providing social development and organizational inputs.

Following the examples of Grameen Bank and BRAC, the government of Bangladesh introduced a group–based targeted credit approach based on the Comilla model of two-tier cooperatives. The Comilla model of rural development was designed and implemented by Akhter Hamid Khan in the 1960s at the Academy for Rural Development in Comilla, Bangladesh. The idea involves organizing farmers into cooperative societies in order to distribute modern inputs, such as high-yielding crop varieties, fertilizer, pesticides, irrigation, and subsidized credit. The organizational approach, which established primary farmers' cooperative societies that were federated into central cooperative societies at the *thana* (a thana is the administrative center for a number of villages) level, was found to be effective in reaching farmers.

Following Bangladesh's independence in 1971, the government adopted the Comilla model as the basis for national development. This strategy led to the creation of the two-tier cooperative system. The Comilla model was adopted throughout the nation as part of the Integrated Rural Development Program (IRDP). The Bangladesh Rural Development Board (BRDB), a semiautonomous government agency under the Ministry of Local Government, Rural Development and Cooperatives, was established in 1982 to replace the IRDP. Like the

IRDP, it was based on two-tier cooperatives, but it employed credit as its main input and included a component that specifically targeted the rural poor. The BRDB experimented with a number of projects to increase income and employment opportunities for the rural poor by setting up a separate system of primary cooperatives. The eligible poor were men and women who owned less than half of an acre of land and depended on manual labor as their main source of income. These cooperatives, called Bittaheen Samabay Samity for men and Mohila Bittaheen Samaby Samity for women, provided members with skills development, training in group leadership and management, and access to credit. Savings mobilization was also part of the program. With funds from the Canadian International Development Agency, this program was strengthened in 1988 and renamed the Rural Development Project-12 (RD-12).

RD-12 was based on the model of a two-tier cooperative structure with solidarity groups of five to six members, following the credit delivery model of Grameen Bank. This small group–targeted approach was more successful than the large group approach of the BRDB in reaching the poor and recovering loans. Along with the small group delivery approach of Grameen Bank, RD-12 adopted BRAC's skill development approach for promoting productivity of the poor.

## Sources of Poverty

Bangladesh is a predominantly rural economy. The labor force has been growing by 2.4 percent a year, while the agriculture, industry, and service sectors can accommodate no more than 1.7 percent annual growth of the labor force. Agriculture provides 78 percent of employment and is unable to provide additional employment because of technical constraints. Increasing the productivity of the unemployed and the poor is thus an important policy concern. Because the modern urban sector is too small to absorb additional labor, increasing productivity and income through self-employment in the informal sector and improving human capital are the only viable ways to alleviate poverty and promote economic growth (World Bank 1997).

The incidence of poverty is high in Bangladesh, and it is higher in rural areas than in urban areas (Rahman and Hossain 1995). Although poverty has fallen in recent years (Ravallion and Sen 1995), more than 50 percent of the rural population still lives below the poverty line. Poverty in Bangladesh is a manifestation of increasing landlessness, high unemployment, low literacy, and high population growth. More than half of all rural households are landless, and population pressure has reduced the average size of farms continuously over the past several decades (the average farm size fell from 3.5 acres in 1977 to 2.4 acres in 1984, for example). With limited land, the 1.8 percent annual growth in the population has increasingly marginalized farmers. Only 45 percent of the active labor force is gainfully employed.

Although more than 90 percent of cultivable land is used for food-grain production, the low agricultural growth rate in Bangladesh (less than 2 percent) means that the country does not produce enough to meet its requirements. Malnutrition is serious among the poor, especially among women and children. The infant mortality rate is 78 per 1,000 live births—higher than the average rate of 72 for low-income countries. Wages for unskilled labor are so low (about $1 a day per person) that they do not cover even basic needs. Literacy rates are also low (about 41 percent for men and 19 percent for women).

The extreme pressure on land in Bangladesh forces a large labor force to find marginal activities within the rural economy to survive. About 29 percent of the labor force was involved in marginal activities (those having very low productivity) in 1989–90 (Hossain and Rashid 1991). Projections show that poverty-driven low-productivity employment will increase by only 25 percent during the 1990s. Even if the economy grows 5 percent a year, as much as 15 percent of the labor force will remain in marginal low-productivity activities by 2000.

Arresting poverty in Bangladesh means reducing the population pressure on land by creating off-farm employment opportunities. But workers enter the labor force every year without adequate human capital. So arresting poverty also means slowing population growth and reducing illiteracy, malnutrition, and poor health, which hurt the productivity of the poor. Any attempt to alleviate poverty must therefore address the problem of how to effectively augment the productive means of the poor in terms of both gainful employment and human resource development.

## Attempts to Alleviate Poverty

Like many other countries, Bangladesh pursued growth-oriented development strategies in the 1960s to increase both employment and productivity through higher economic growth. Issues of distribution and poverty alleviation were considered peripheral, because it was thought that the trickle-down effect would raise living standards among all strata of society. The basic thrust of the growth-oriented development strategy was that economic growth could be achieved through modernization in both industry and agriculture. In industry this meant higher capital intensity in production, with higher profitability and, consequently, higher investment for further growth. In agriculture this strategy meant supporting and implementing Green Revolution technology, which relied more heavily on irrigation and modern cultivation methods. The growth strategy required that the government supply subsidized inputs such as credit, fertilizer, irrigation equipment, and pesticides. Proponents of this strategy believed that improved agricultural production would reduce poverty by creating new demand and employment opportunities.

Bangladesh's experience with Green Revolution technology has been mixed. New and improved varieties of crops and increased use of fertilizer and pesticides helped to increase production. Rice production increased at least fourfold, leading to near self-sufficiency in rice by 1990. Bangladesh's agriculture-led growth strategy was articulated through the IRDP, which used two-tier cooperatives to promote the Green Revolution in agriculture. About 50-60 farmers were formed into cooperatives, which were federated into thana-level central cooperative societies. Although the idea was to help farmers gain access to modern inputs, including subsidized credit, the cooperatives were dominated by the rural elite and large landowners (Khan 1971). Some researchers have observed that the Comilla-type cooperatives were critical in initiating the transition to a more productive method of production, improving agricultural yields, and increasing infrastructural growth (Abdullah, Hossain, and Nations 1974). Later studies, however, showed that the early optimism over Comilla cooperatives as a new way to achieve agricultural growth and social equity was unfounded (Jones 1979). The agricultural growth strategy failed to make the rural poor productive and self-supporting because subsidized inputs encouraged capital-intensive methods of agricultural production and hence discouraged a demand-induced growth strategy. Moreover, growth achieved through such capital-intensive methods of production was not sustainable. Bangladesh's historical growth rate of about 5 percent per year is sluggish. Because of a lack of strong intersectoral linkages and a demand-induced pattern of growth, institutions established to implement government policies and programs were not self-sustainable and continued to receive huge subsidies from the government (World Bank 1987).

The supply-based approach is based on the idea that there is a latent demand for inputs such as credit and schooling and that households with access to such inputs can improve their welfare through increased production, consumption, and investment. A classic example is the government credit programs that were introduced with the help of bilateral and multilateral donor agencies through government-controlled banking and cooperative institutions. The poor farm households that needed subsidized credit the most were excluded from these institutions' loans. Only about 7 percent of landless households (defined as those owning less than half an acre of land) had access to institutional credit (Hossain 1988). Most poor households were excluded because they did not have adequate resources to offer as collateral. In contrast, 20 percent of medium-size and large farmers were able to obtain subsidized credit. According to the 1987 Rural Credit Survey of Bangladesh, land and immovable property are the dominant forms of collateral, accounting for 74 percent of the credit transactions of formal financial institutions (Bangladesh Bureau of Statistics 1989). Insufficient mortgaged land (33 percent) followed by high transactions costs (26 percent) were reported to be the main reasons why needy households did not apply for bank loans. In short, the supply-based strategies, which were designed to create conditions for the alleviation of poverty, did not directly address the income and employment problems of the poor.

A targeted wage employment approach was introduced in the 1970s, when policymakers realized that the homogeneous community-based approach had bypassed the poor. This targeted approach was conceived largely through the Food-for-Work, Rural Works, and Vulnerable Group Development programs. The main objectives of the Food-for-Work program are to improve the performance of the agriculture sector through construction and maintenance of physical infrastructure for production and marketing, to reduce physical damage and loss of human life from floods and cyclones by creating protective structures, and to generate productive seasonal employment for the very poor. The purpose of the Rural Works program is to build rural infrastructure such as roads, rural markets, and food storage facilities. Vulnerable Group Development aims to improve both income and employment of destitute women who are not able to take advantage of programs such as Food-for-Work. These programs represented the government's direct antipoverty schemes.

The Food-for-Work and Vulnerable Group Development programs are self-targeting and thus attract only those who are poor and depend on manual labor for daily wages (O. Chowdhury 1983; Mitra and Associates 1991). Although the programs seemed effective and provided basic infrastructure, the development of sustainable income generation and employment for the poor has been limited because of their temporary and seasonal nature (table 2.1). Food-for-Work created rural infrastructure that should have had secondary effects on income and employment. In fact, the benefits accrued largely to landed households that had the productive means to use these facilities. The induced effects on income and employment were negligible, because the roads that were built with these transfers were often washed away by floods or became useless because of poor maintenance. Asaduzzaman and Huddleston (1983) argue that although it is not possible to measure the quantity and quality of the work done under the program, there was considerable potential for malpractice and substandard work. Moreover, the implementation period of Food-for-Work projects conflicted with

TABLE 2.1

**Features of the Food-for-Work and Vulnerable Group Development
Programs in Bangladesh**

| Program feature | Food-for-Work | | Vulnerable Group Development |
| | Program 1 | Program 2 | |
| --- | --- | --- | --- |
| Sources of funds | United States Agency for International Development, government of Bangladesh | World Food Programme, other donors | World Food Programme, Canada, European Union, Australia, Germany, Belgium, Bangladesh |
| Commodity distributed | Wheat | Wheat | Wheat |
| Program size (1991/92) | | | |
| Amount of grain (tons) | 192,000 | 445,000 | 202,000 |
| Value of grain (U.S. dollars) | 33,000,000 | 78,000,000 | 39,000,000 |
| Number of beneficiaries | 600,000 individuals | 3,400,000 individuals | 50,000 families |
| Target group | Unskilled laborers | Unskilled laborers | Destitute women |
| Regional focus | National, 44 districts | National, 66 or more districts | Distressed regions |
| Season | January–May | Predominantly December–April | Year-round |
| Activities | Roads (80%) | Embankments and canals (40%), roads (30%), forestry (8%), fisheries (7%), other (15%) | Integrated poultry program, pilot credit scheme, self-employment through cottage industries, functional literacy, health, nutrition, and agricultural extension training |
| Leakage (percent) | 30–35 | 30–35 | 14 |
| Cost per taka income transfer (takas) | 1.8–2.4 | 1.8–2.4 | 1.5 |
| Year started | 1975 | 1975 | 1975 |
| Administered by | CARE | World Food Programme, government of Bangladesh | World Food Programme |

*Source:* Ahmed and others 1995.

crop production activities, causing labor shortages (Management Systems International 1987; Zohir 1990; Mitra and Associates 1991). Leakages were also high (30–35 percent in Food-for-Work and 14 percent in Vulnerable Group Development; Hossain and Akash 1993; Ahmed and others 1995). The cost for transferring 1 taka (Tk) to beneficiaries is about Tk 2 for Food-for-Work and Tk 1.5 for Vulnerable Group Development, suggesting that Vulnerable Group Development is better targeted and more cost-effective than Food-for-Work.

With help from donors, various nongovernmental organizations (NGOs), including BRAC, introduced noncredit targeted measures to help the poor in the aftermath of the 1971 war for independence and following natural disasters. The purpose of these programs was to reduce poverty by providing needed goods and services to the poor. NGOs soon realized, however, that poverty had to be confronted on a sustained basis and that human capital services such as adult literacy, skills training, and primary health care were inadequate to sustain poverty reduction among the rural poor (BIDS 1990; Holtsberg 1990). In addition to promoting the human development of the poor, programs needed to promote the productive capacity of the poor through physical means, such as acquiring physical capital with credit.

## The Group Approach to Targeted Credit

The poor have little or no access to institutional credit because they lack physical collateral and familiarity with institutional procedures. To help the poor, targeted credit programs must find ways to reach out to households that do not know how to obtain access to institutional credit.

All of the microcredit programs under study have separate programs for men and women, in accordance with the sociocultural norms of Bangladesh (table 2.2). Membership is strictly limited to people who own less than half an acre of land, are not members of the same household as another program member, have similar economic resources, and live in the same village. Experience shows that the spatial and social cohesiveness developed among individuals of the same gender, residing in the same village, and having similar economic backgrounds are important factors in the smooth functioning of these groups.

The five-member group is the central unit of Grameen Bank. BRAC uses village organizations that comprise 50–60 people from the target population. These village organizations are the central pillar of BRAC. But because the village organizations are difficult to manage, at least for credit delivery and repayment, BRAC introduced solidarity groups of five to seven people within the village organizations to monitor group performance. The village organizations, not the solidarity groups, are

TABLE 2.2
**Features of Three Microcredit Programs in Bangladesh**

| Program feature | Grameen Bank |
| --- | --- |
| Membership criteria | Maximum landholding of half an acre of land.Only one member allowed per household. |
| Group features | Five members form a group.<br>Five to eight groups constitute a center.<br>Separate groups for men and women.<br>Separate centers for men and women.<br>Weekly meetings of groups. |
| Savings mobilization | Tk 1 per week.<br>5 percent of each loan (nonrefundable) goes to group fund<br>0.5 percent of each loan used for group insurance. Option to buy shares worth Tk 100 per member. |
| Credit delivery mechanism | No collateral but group liability.<br>50-week installment of loan.<br>Interest at the end of loan cycle.<br>20 percent interest rate for general loan, 8 percent for housing loan.<br>Maximum loan Tk 10,000. |
| Social development | Training duration 15–30 days.<br>Review of code of conduct at center meetings see table 2.3).<br>Minimal skills-based training. |

*Source:* Khandker and Khalily 1996; Khandker, Khalily, and Khan 1995; Khandker, Khan, and Khalily 1995.

the principal functionaries, however. RD-12 follows a structure very similar to that of BRAC. Women join the Mahila (women's) Bittaheen (landless) Sambaya (cooperative) Society (MBSS); men join the Bittaheen Samabaya Society (BSS). These societies, consisting of 50–60 members, are federated into thana bittaheen central cooperative societies. RD-12 has found that the small group approach works better than the large group approach in monitoring group performance in loan utilization and repayment.

| BRAC | RD-12 |
|---|---|
| Maximum landholding of half an acre of land; at least one household member must work for wages. | Maximum landholding of half an acre of land; at least one household member must work for wages. |
| One household member may earn daily wages. | More than one member allowed per household. |
| Since 1992 one member allowed per household. | |
| 30–40 members form village organizations. | 15–35 members form primary cooperatives. |
| Village organizations are divided into solidarity groups of 5–7 members. | Primary cooperatives are divided into solidarity groups of 4–5 members. |
| Separate groups for men and women. | Separate cooperatives for men and women. |
| Each men's group has a counterpart women's group. | Separate groups for men and women. |
| Weekly meetings of solidarity groups. | Weekly meetings of cooperatives. |
| Tk 2 per week. | Tk 2 per week. |
| 4 percent of each loan (nonrefundable) goes to group fund. | 5 percent of each loan goes to group fund. |
| 1 percent of each loan used for group insurance. | Mandatory purchase of cooperative share of Tk 10 per member per year. |
| No collateral but group liability. | No collateral but primary cooperative liability. |
| 50-week installment of loan. | 50-week installment of loan. |
| Interest at the end of loan cycle. | Interest at the end of loan cycle. |
| 20 percent interest rate for production loans. | 16 percent interest rate for production loans. |
| Maximum loan Tk 10,000. | Maximum loan Tk 10,000. |
| Training duration 3–6 months. | Training duration 3–6 months. |
| Review of code of conduct at village organization meetings (see table 2.3). | Review of code of conduct at primary cooperative meetings (see table 2.3). |
| Substantial skills-based training. | Substantial skills-based training. |

In all three programs groups hold weekly meetings in the presence of a group organizer to review the group's performance and deposit their weekly savings of Tk 1–Tk 2. They also learn, practice, and discuss the rules of the program and other group activities (table 2.3). Weekly loan installments are also repaid at these meetings. Each group elects a leader, who is responsible for the discipline of group members. All members have the chance to lead their groups. The leader of the group initiates loan proposals at the monthly center or village organization meeting. A

TABLE 2.3
## Codes of Conduct for Members of Microcredit Programs

| Grameen Bank's 16 decisions | BRAC's 17 promises | RD-12's 21 oaths |
|---|---|---|
| 1. The four principles of the Grameen Bank—discipline, unity, courage, and hard work—we will follow and advance in all walks of our lives. | 1. We will not engage in malpractice or injustice. | 1. We will remain united. |
| 2. We will bring prosperity to our families. | 2. We will work hard and bring prosperity to our family. | 2. We will be sincere and sympathetic toward all. |
| 3. We will not live in dilapidated houses. We will repair our houses and work toward constructing new houses. | 3. We will send our children to school. | 3. We will follow the principles of the cooperatives. |
| 4. We will grow vegetables all year round. We will eat plenty of them and sell the surplus. | 4. We will adopt family planning and keep our family size small. | 4. We will strive for development through work and sincerity. |
| 5. During the plantation seasons, we will plant as many seedlings as possible. | 5. We will try to be clean and keep our house tidy. | 5. We will educate ourselves and send our children to school. |
| 6. We will plan to keep our families small. We will minimize our expenditures. We will look after our health. | 6. We will always drink pure water. | 6. We will adopt family planning methods. |
| 7. We will educate our children and ensure that we can pay for their education. | 7. We will not keep our food uncovered and will wash our hands and face before we take our meal. | 7. We will drink boiled water and use hygienic toilets. |
| 8. We will always keep our children and the environment clean. | 8. We will construct latrines and will not leave our stool where it doesn't belong. | 8. We will fight against polygamy and the abuse of women. |
| 9. We will build and use pit-latrines. | 9. We will cultivate vegetables and trees in and around our house. | 9. We will save a part of our income and deposit it with the society. |
| | 10. We will try to help each other under all circumstances. | 10. We will take loans from the society and strive to increase our incomes. |
| | 11. We will fight against polygamy and injustices to our wives and all women. | 11. We will not ask for aid from anybody. |
| | | 12. We will not run after relief. |

10. We will drink tubewell water. If it is not available, we will boil water or treat it with alum.

11. We will not take any dowry in our sons' wedding, neither will we give any dowry in our daughters' wedding. We will keep the center free from the curse of dowry. We will not practice child marriage.

12. We will not inflict injustice on anyone, nor will we allow anyone to do so.

13. For higher incomes we will collectively undertake bigger investments.

14. We will always be ready to help each other. If anyone is having difficulty, we will help him.

15. If we learn of any breach in discipline in any center, we will help to restore discipline.

16. We will introduce physical exercise in our centers. We will take part in all social activities collectively.

12. We will be loyal to the organization and abide by its rules and regulations

13. We will not sign anything without having a good understanding of what it means (we will look carefully before we act).

14. We will attend weekly meetings regularly and on time.

15. We will always abide by the decisions of the weekly group meetings.

16. We will regularly deposit our weekly savings.

17. If we receive a loan we will repay it.

13. We will not be lazy.

14. We will not remain illiterate.

15. We will not sign any paper without reading it.

16. We will not give or take any dowry.

17. We will not have very large families.

18. We will not break the rules and discipline of the cooperative societies.

19. We will not delay repayments of loan installments.

20. We will not listen to bad advice from mischievous persons.

21. We will not allow our organizations to be damaged in any way.

*Source:* Khandker, Khalily, and Khan 1995; Khandker, Khan, and Khalily 1995; Khandker and Khalily 1996.

community leader is elected to manage the centers, village organizations, or cooperative societies and is responsible for reviewing loan applications, monitoring loans, and performing other noneconomic services.

All targeted credit programs emphasize noneconomic issues, such as marriage, dowry, kitchen gardening, and children's education. Each program has its own agenda for social development, which it pursues through these groups. All programs provide human and social development inputs, including skills development, and other types of training, such as health, nutrition, and family planning, in order to improve the productive capacities of the poor. The extent of training varies from program to program; training is an essential precondition for access to credit for BRAC and to some extent for RD-12 members, but it is not a requirement for Grameen Bank, which believes that initially only training in bank procedures is necessary for a member to have access to credit. Grameen does encourage members to practice and follow various rules and regulations governing group behavior and members' social conditions to promote group performance and discipline.

Emphasis on women's membership is another dimension of the group–based social development model. It is very difficult to reach women individually in rural Bangladesh because of the *purdah* system, which secludes women in order to uphold standards of modesty and morality. Women may find it easier to counter seclusion as a group than as individuals. Although group solidarity is effective with men as well, it is particularly effective with women in Bangladesh, who find it more convenient to attend weekly group meetings, adhere to the rules and regulations of group solidarity and prosperity, and make small transactions with the programs. While other programs bypassed women because they were perceived as high credit risks (because of childbearing and associated health hazards), the targeted credit programs promote women's participation. This emphasis partly reflects the programs' emphasis on equity and long-term social and economic development and partly reflects the realization that loan recovery rates are higher for women than for men.

All three programs practice group–based credit delivery, which has yielded better loan recovery rates than the individual-based credit model in Bangladesh. This superior performance of group–based credit partly reflects peer pressure from group monitoring (Stiglitz 1990) where microcredit programs have been able to create social capital through group formation and training (Besley and Coate 1995). Lending to individuals with group liability and monitoring helps reduce the loan default costs resulting from behavioral risk.[1] Group lending enables programs to reduce the costs of obtaining information about borrowers and types of projects. It relies on peer pressure to monitor and enforce contracts, provides an incentive for borrowers to repay, and helps avoid adverse selection of borrowers.

Microcredit institutions also introduce a number of instruments to reduce the risk of loan default attributable to production risk. Savings mobilization, for example, is treated as an integral part of financial intermediation. Irrespective of their borrowing status, members are asked to save Tk 1–Tk 2 every week. Each program also asks all borrowers to contribute about 5 percent of their loan principal to a group fund. Borrowers are also required to contribute a certain portion of interest payments or principal to an insurance fund that protects both borrowers and lenders in the case of unwillful defaults (caused by health and natural causes). This aspect is critical for lowering the risk of loan default in poor agroclimatic areas without an insurance market.

Grameen has not been active in mobilizing savings from nonmembers.[2] This policy partly reflects the fact that Grameen Bank does not lend to nonmembers and allows only its member to purchase Tk 100 shares. Members' shares accounted for 90 percent of Grameen's paid-up capital in 1993, up from 55 percent in 1987. Grameen Bank also has easy access to foreign donor funds.

Unlike Grameen Bank, RD-12 and BRAC are not banks and are not allowed to mobilize savings from nonmembers. In addition to mandatory weekly and other savings, RD-12 requires members to buy a Tk 10 share in the society each year from their cooperative to save in share deposits. BRAC does not have this feature, although it has other schemes for mobilizing savings from members.

Successful financial intermediation also requires transparency in transactions. Many rural credit institutions developed by governments have failed partly because of corruption and embezzlement (Braverman and Guasch 1989). Such issues are carefully dealt with in the institutional framework of the targeted credit programs. The small groups meet monthly in a community-level organizational meeting, where each transaction is made openly in the presence of all members. All transactions are made only with the consensus of all members. Both group and community leaders are accountable to group members. If a leader does not behave properly, he or she can be replaced by a new leader. Both community and group leaders jointly monitor loan use daily. Loan use is also monitored at the outset by program staff. Any irregularity is reported at the community meeting, and a solution is sought jointly by members. Group-based financial intermediation mitigates problems of entrenchment of vested interests and deters individuals from taking actions that are not in the interest of the group (Fuglesang and Chandler 1988). Finally, peer monitoring of group–based financial intermediation works at both the group level and at the center or village organization level, thereby eliminating the possibility of collusion among members.

The success of a poverty alleviation program depends on how effectively it targets the poor. Targeting must be self-selective in the sense that only households willing to bear the cost of program participation choose to participate in the program. The Food-for-Work and Rural Works programs employ effective self-targeting methods in that only those who depend on wage labor find it remunerative to participate (Ravallion 1991; Datt and Ravallion 1995). The Food-for-Work program also provides wheat, which is consumed largely by poor people in Bangladesh (Ahmed and Hossain 1990; Ahmed and others 1995).

Is it possible to develop a self-targeting mechanism within financial institutions? Unlike the targeted wage employment approach, the targeted credit approach does not depend on manual labor, which is easy to monitor.[3] A microcredit program targeted to the poor faces two problems: the moral hazard of lending and identification of the poor. In order to be financially viable, a financial institution must carve out a clientele group that is creditworthy and has an incentive to repay loans. Targeting this type of clientele is difficult in a rural setting characterized by asymmetric information and imperfect incentives, which produce the moral hazard problem of lending.

Financial institutions try to select clients who are willing to repay loans on time and will abide by the rules and regulations established by the institution. Borrowers may fail to abide by these rules, either because they lack the incentive or the ability to do so. Incentive problems arise if there are no mechanisms forcing borrowers to repay the loan. This problem is particularly acute in many developing countries, where governments often write off institutional loans for political reasons. Borrowers may lack the ability to repay loans based on the income they earn from their financed projects or because of sudden shocks caused by unforeseen factors. Identifying the reason for default or sorting out whether loan nonpayment reflects an incentive or ability problem is difficult for lenders who suffer from problems of asymmetric information.

Microcredit programs have adopted innovative ways of tackling these problems. Like traditional moneylenders, microcredit programs deal informally with borrowers, so they know much about their clients. Informal lenders target clientele from their neighborhoods or select borrowers based on patron-client relationships (through employment or other transactions); they therefore have near-perfect information on their activities. Informal moneylenders are also able to closely monitor their clients. In contrast, commercial banks or other financial institutions lend on the basis of asset ownership to avoid adverse selection of borrowers. In order to reduce transactions costs and default risks, formal lenders target a clientele that is able to provide collateral of two to three times the amount of the loan itself. This protocol is based on the assumption that credit risk and transactions costs relative to transaction size are inversely related to individual asset ownership and that loan principal and interest are recoverable from collateral if the borrower defaults. However, experience suggests that asset-based identification of potential borrowers is not effective in reaching the clientele group that is willing to repay or has an incentive to repay loans in the absence of strict enforcement procedures. Successful targeting also requires that a program can monitor its clients.

All three targeted credit programs use a group–based approach to enforce their targeting criteria. group–based lending requires potential borrowers to self-select into groups whose members live in the same community and are thus in a position to enforce the eligibility criterion of owning less than half an acre of land. As Besley and Coate (1995) argue, group–based lending is a necessary but not a sufficient condition for better repayment or better functioning of a group. For effective functioning of groups, the group method has to create social collateral that imposes certain disciplinary actions on group members. A group–based method may fail to enforce eligibility criteria, for example, if the entire group colludes in doing so. To prevent this problem, all microcredit programs use a larger community-based organization to ensure that the group meets the eligibility criterion. Meeting the eligibility criterion is only a necessary condition for meeting the self-targeting requirement. Since borrowers need to be able to repay the loan, effective targeting also means that the loan contract must be enforceable. Microcredit programs use this community-based organization as social capital to enforce the loan contract.[4]

Unlike other lending systems, group-plus-community-based financial intermediation demands borrowers' active and direct participation in the lending process. Thus group members have a stronger incentive to enforce the ethics of group behavior and loan contracts. Of course, there are other ways to enforce loan contracts, such as pressure from a village leader or clan leader. Such an approach works in the case of individual-based lending, such as that done by Indonesia's Badan Kredit Kecamatan or Bank Rakyat Indonesia. But this external method may not be effective in reaching the poor because social institutions are not always a reliable tool for identifying poor people.

Can the self-selection process be used to attract the able poor who are able to use loans productively? After all, Grameen-type loans are not charity and must be repaid with interest. The self-selection process must thus ensure that only the able poor participate in these programs. The group–based approach introduces some implicit costs that members have to bear. For example, weekly group meetings, the small size of loans, group formation, training, and monitoring other group members' activities involve costs that could be high if the opportunity cost of an individual's time is high. Participation in a targeted credit program is demand-driven in the sense that those who are willing to bear these costs participate. Program participation depends on whether an individual has the ability to productively use the credit to generate returns large enough to meet interest costs and repay the loan. Because program participation is self-selective, targeting is effective in reaching only those who are willing to bear the risk of generating income from self-employment.

Is explicit targeting by landownership necessary when there is a self-selection process at work? Given the design of the targeted credit programs of Grameen Bank, BRAC, and RD-12, a requirement that members hold no more than half an acre of land may be necessary to reduce the cost of membership. If every household participates and many later discover that microcredit programs are not worth participating in, a large number of households that find the cost of membership high will drop out. Moreover, because group-based lending depends on group coercion, group functioning is bound to collapse if the group is composed of people with unequal power. Thus targeting people with roughly equal power is critical for effective functioning of the groups. If landholding is a proxy for power in a land-based setting, then targeting by landholding may be necessary to effectively reach the poor.[5]

But the self-selection process does not guarantee the effective functioning of group-based targeted credit programs. Participation in a program can increase income generation and improve other outcomes. Unless program participation helps sustain income generation that meets the costs of borrowing and those of program participation, groups will fail to act together.[6] Borrowers' continued participation in a program depends in part on whether microcredit institutions provide noncredit services, such as skills training, to make borrowers more productive.

## Provision of Noncredit Services by Microcredit Programs

A blend of credit and noncredit services is the hallmark of microcredit institutions, with the mix varying from institution to institution. Grameen Bank relies heavily on credit, while BRAC has an elaborate noncredit component. Program designs evolve over time and are conditioned by the philosophy of the program.

BRAC began with the idea that economic dependency on exploitative forces was the source of poverty in rural areas. It thus began to mobilize the poor and instruct them through consciousness-raising training about these exploitative forces. In this process the poor also tried to learn how to access public resources distributed by the government. Literacy and health programs were also provided. BRAC soon found that its training was inadequate to improve the conditions of the poor who did not own productive means, such as land or capital. It found that credit is needed to make the poor productive through self-employment. In order to receive credit from BRAC, however, the poor must go through rigorous training for at least six months.

Grameen Bank differs in its approach. It believes that the poor need training only on how to bank with an institution such as Grameen Bank. Since they are familiar with an informal activity, such as processing, transportation, or poultry raising, they can begin a productive activity immediately once they have access to credit. Hence Grameen Bank provides credit soon after its members are familiar with bank formalities. During this training period, group members are instructed in other areas, such as kitchen gardening, health care, nutrition, productivity, and housing. Grameen Bank distributes seeds and seedlings to members, supplies low-cost housing materials to borrowers, and encourages members to open nursery schools at centers for preschool children (so that preschool children are taken care of while mothers attend Grameen Bank meetings). Training in social and health issues is also part of regular programs.

BRAC and RD-12 offer similar training in social and health issues. BRAC also has developed a functional education program for its many illiterate members and a nonformal primary education (NFPE) program directed at school-age children who are out of school or have never attended school primarily for economic reasons. The objective of the NFPE is to help these children achieve basic literacy, numeracy, and social awareness. Older children complete this course in one and a half years and then become eligible to enroll in class six of formal middle school. Younger children complete this course in three years and follow the same path. BRAC employs the teachers of the NFPE school and provides books and learning materials; parents of BRAC members help run the school. Because of the success of the NFPE program, BRAC has helped a World Bank–funded general education project incorporate this idea nationwide. BRAC has developed similar innovative primary health care programs.

What makes BRAC and RD-12 distinct from Grameen Bank is their skills development training programs. Grameen Bank believes that skills development is not necessary for the poor to become productively self-employed; only the provision of credit is necessary. In contrast, BRAC assumes that while credit-only programs help the poor to become self-employed and generate cash income, the poor would benefit even more if they could use more modern methods and skills. This has led BRAC to invest staff time and other resources in developing training materials that improve productivity in key economic sectors, including poultry, livestock, sericulture, fisheries, and agriculture (irrigation and use of high-yielding seed varieties). BRAC's efforts have helped break the sectoral bottlenecks for improved productivity and have increased the income and employment of members. They have also helped spread technology to other members of the community.

Similar sector-specific training programs have been launched by RD-12. RD-12 follows the BRAC approach in providing skills training in key economic sectors. Members of primary cooperative societies are trained to undertake profitable and productive income-generating activities and to use credit and other external resources available for socio-economic development. The objective of skills-based training is to provide members with practical skills training directly related to their current or proposed income-generating activities. Training is provided in livestock and poultry raising, fisheries, processing, and repair and servicing of agricultural tools and equipment.

Translating the know-how already available in the research field into practice for poorly educated and illiterate households is a challenging task that requires staff commitment, leadership, and a decentralized institution that supports these noncredit services. Delivering these services and packaging the skills development and productivity-raising inputs are costly.

## Institutional Framework of Microcredit Programs

Mobilizing members in small groups and training them to foster group solidarity requires a flexible and nonhierarchical organization. A decentralized management structure that emphasizes constant monitoring and evaluation of staff and group performance is the key to the successful innovation of such an organization. The leadership also has to be committed, dynamic, and instrumental. Staff must have problem-solving skills and high ethical standards.

A decentralized organizational structure is a key within microcredit institutions. It starts with branches at the grassroots level, where staff are in close contact with borrowers. Branch staff are trained on how to mobilize, train, and prepare groups for carrying out effective financial intermediation with and for the poor. Field staff are also trained on how to provide social intermediation inputs to participating members. Field or group organizers are supervised by branch managers. Several branches form an area office, which helps branches manage and select loan portfolios. Several area offices form a regional office, which acts as a head office for many decisions. At the top the head office develops management style, disseminates grassroots findings, promotes effective training, and raises funds for on-lending and institutional development.

The organization is run by a management unit headed by the managing or executive director and overseen by a board of directors consisting of representatives of the target groups, as well as government officials and representatives of the private sector.

Professional management is another component of institutional development. The management structure must be responsive to the demands of its clients—clients who may not possess skills for effective communication. The management structure must be able to adapt its management style through field experience and learning. It should be based on an innovative approach to training, featuring a structured learning process that is continually fine-tuned by trial and error. Extensive staff training programs are the hallmark of all three of the targeted credit programs reviewed here. Grameen Bank has an extensive training and executive development program that helps prepare and motivate its managers to plan, organize, and implement bank programs without extensive supervision from the head office. A similar training approach is followed by BRAC and to some extent by RD-12. Training of branch-level staff is predominantly a hands-on process, with time spent mostly in the rural branches, where employees have direct contact with borrowers. In addition to mastering various program rules, trainees are required to familiarize themselves with local conditions and prepare detailed case studies of borrowers. The training emphasizes empathy and cooperation with target groups. Unlike formal financial institutions, microcredit programs aim to bring financial intermediation to the doorsteps of the borrowers. This requires a level of morale and commitment from staff.

## Summary

During the 1970s various programs sought to reduce poverty in Bangladesh by intermittently providing the poor with needed goods and services. The failure of these programs to address the root of the problem brought home the need to confront poverty on a sustained basis. Policymakers and NGOs recognized that both the human capital and the productive capacity of the poor needed to be improved in order to reduce poverty.

To address these needs, targeted microcredit programs were introduced in Bangladesh in the 1980s. Grameen Bank, transformed into a specialized bank in 1983, focuses on providing credit to poor people, particularly poor rural women, so that they can become self-employed. BRAC and RD-12 focus on developing skills and raising consciousness among the rural poor, to whom they also provide credit.

Like other targeted antipoverty measures, such as food-for-work and other wage employment schemes, microcredit programs are self-targeting. Group-based lending is used to self-select potential borrowers and reduce the risk of default. Participants form small groups that meet weekly in the presence of a group organizer to review the group's performance and deposit their weekly savings. Proposals for loans are discussed at monthly meetings of the village organization or the cooperative society. In addition to providing credit, all of the programs emphasize noneconomic issues, such as educating children, and all emphasize membership by women.

Institutionally, microcredit programs demand a flexible, decentralized, and nonhierarchical organization structure. They also require leadership that is committed, dynamic, and instrumental in achieving the program's goals.

## Notes

1. Although group lending reduces loan default costs, it introduces other costs—such as the costs of group formation, training, and other social intermediation—that are inevitable for maintaining group discipline and educating uneducated members of the group. Given these costs it is not clear whether group lending or individual lending involves lower overall transactions costs.

2. As a result of lack of regulation and other factors, most microfinance institutions do not have access to market resources, such as loanable funds from commercial banks or funds from the central bank. See chapters 5 and 6 for more discussion.

3. Unlike the case with Grameen Bank, at least one member of the household must work in the wage market before BRAC and RD-12 will extend a loan. This condition may make targeting monitorable.

4. Self-targeting of the poor is only one aspect of the targeting feature of microcredit programs in Bangladesh. Program officials also play an important role in identifying the poor. For example, bank workers, branch managers, and program officers of Grameen Bank visit the homes of new borrowers to verify the extent of poverty, often by observing the status of the house itself.

5. Similar argument holds for programs, such as BRAC, that target wage-employed households with equal status.

6. Of course, groups may change, as less successful members leave the program and groups replace them with new members. The dynamics of these groups need to be studied.

# 3

## Socioeconomic Impacts of Microcredit Programs

The poor participate in microcredit programs in the expectation that borrowing will increase their income and sustain self-employment. Whether participation does in fact reduce poverty in terms of consumption and help increase income and employment on a sustained basis can be measured directly. The benefits of program participation can also be measured indirectly, by measuring changes in socioeconomic outcomes such as contraceptive use, fertility, and children's schooling. These changes come about partly through income and employment effects and partly through changes in attitudes and behavior that occur as a result of a program's noncredit services.

Changes in income and employment among program participants may affect the local village economy. If the economic changes do not take jobs away from those who are already employed, the program has a positive overall impact. If instead program participants simply take jobs away from others in the village, the net impact on the village economy could be zero or even negative. Two important factors that determine the overall impact of the program are the growth potential of activities financed by microcredit programs and the extent of credit market imperfections that are resolved with enhanced availability of credit.

This chapter measures the effects of microcredit programs on participants in terms of consumption, nutrition, employment, net worth, schooling, contraceptive use, and fertility. These effects are assessed in terms of the impact of the cumulative amount of borrowing from microcredit programs, which reflects both the impact of credit and the duration of program participation. The effects on both male and female borrowers as well as the impact on the local economy are also measured.

Assessing impact at the participant level requires adjustments to control for differences in unobservable household and village characteristics. That is, to measure the credit impacts of programs that are due to variations in individual-level participation, it is necessary to control for differences in village-level characteristics that attract a program to a particular village. The impact of program placement on village-level average income, employment, and poverty is estimated by fitting a village-level regression that measures the differential impacts of program placement at the village level while controlling for observable characteristics of the village.[1]

## Survey Design

The analysis is based on data from a multipurpose household survey conducted in Bangladesh during crop year 1991–92 (July 1991 to June 1992). The survey was undertaken jointly by the Bangladesh Institute of Development Studies (BIDS) and the World Bank. The survey's main focus was to provide data for an analysis of three major credit programs (Grameen Bank, BRAC, and RD-12). The survey covered both program villages of each of these programs and villages in which neither these programs nor any other program providing credit or other activities operated. The survey covered both program target households (those owning no more than half an acre of land) and nontarget households (those that did not meet this eligibility criteria) in both program and nonprogram villages. The quasi-experimental survey design used to eliminate endogeneity of program inputs is discussed in appendix D. Exclusion of rural households owning more than half an acre of land is exogenously determined by program design, so quasi-experimental survey instruments include both target and nontarget households in both program and nonprogram villages. A detailed description of the survey is included in appendix B.

## Who Participates in Microcredit Programs?

An individual's decision to participate in a group-based credit program can be based on the joint production and consumption behavior of a household that is constrained in the formal credit market, lacks sufficient savings to finance an income-earning activity, or cannot rely on informal credit because of its high cost. It may be efficient for such households to borrow from a group-based credit program, which charges less than informal lenders, in order to make more efficient use of available resources, mainly family labor. The evaluation of the effects of program participation on household resource allocation is based on this efficiency argument.

The survey data show the extent and length of program participation, as well as cumulative borrowing and other household and intrahousehold outcomes. Among the selected villages, 72 had one program (each program operated in 24 villages under study) and 15 had no programs. Each program village selected for the study had only one type of credit program available, so household members could not choose which program they wanted to join.[2]

## Participation among Target Households

Less than half (45 percent) of all eligible households participated in microcredit programs (figure 3.1). The participation rates were 44 percent in Grameen Bank villages, 52 percent in BRAC villages, and 33 percent in RD-12 villages.

Women represented 76 percent of program participants in Grameen Bank villages, 73 percent in BRAC villages, 44 percent in RD-12 villages, and 67 percent in all program villages. The dropout rate among participating households was 9 percent in Grameen Bank villages, 8 percent in BRAC villages, and less than 1 percent in RD-12 villages. Net program participation among target households was 40 percent for Grameen Bank, 48 percent for BRAC, and 33 percent for RD-12.

The average length of program participation for current members was 3.7 years for all programs, 4.3 years for Grameen Bank, 3.8 years for BRAC, and 2.8 years for RD-12 (figure 3.2). Thus Grameen Bank members on average had more program exposure than members of other programs. Among participants who dropped out, the average length of program participation was 3.4 years, and it was higher for Grameen Bank and BRAC (3.5 years) than for RD-12 (2 years).

FIGURE 3.1
**Program Participation among Target Households**

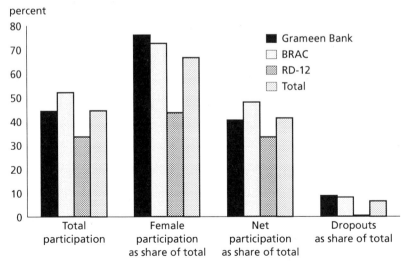

Source: BIDS–World Bank 1991/92 survey.

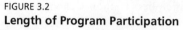

FIGURE 3.2
**Length of Program Participation**

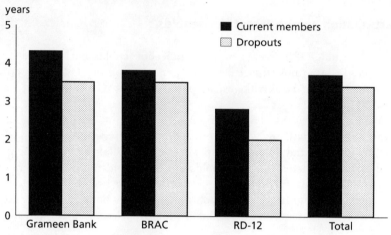

*Source:* BIDS–World Bank 1991/92 survey.

## Enforcement of Eligibility Criteria

Participating households must meet the eligibility criterion (namely, owning no more than half an acre of land). Households surveyed were asked about the extent of their landholding before they joined a program. The eligibility criterion was met by 79 percent of households in Grameen Bank villages, 83 percent in BRAC villages, and 85 percent in RD-12 villages. These findings suggest that these microcredit programs enforce their eligibility criteria tightly.

Among participants who met the eligibility criterion, a larger proportion came from landless households (owning no operational holdings) than from landed households (owning no more than half an acre of land). Landless households represented 55 percent of Grameen participants, 65 percent of BRAC participants, and 58 percent of RD-12 participants (figure 3.3). This suggests that BRAC is better at targeting the ultrapoor than Grameen Bank or RD-12.

## Defining Program Participation

Less than half of target households in program villages participated in microcredit programs, even where the programs had been available for more than three years. Program participation among target households is not exogenously determined by microcredit programs but depends on a number of factors, including household and community background

FIGURE 3.3

**Distribution of Agricultural Landholding among Program Participants**

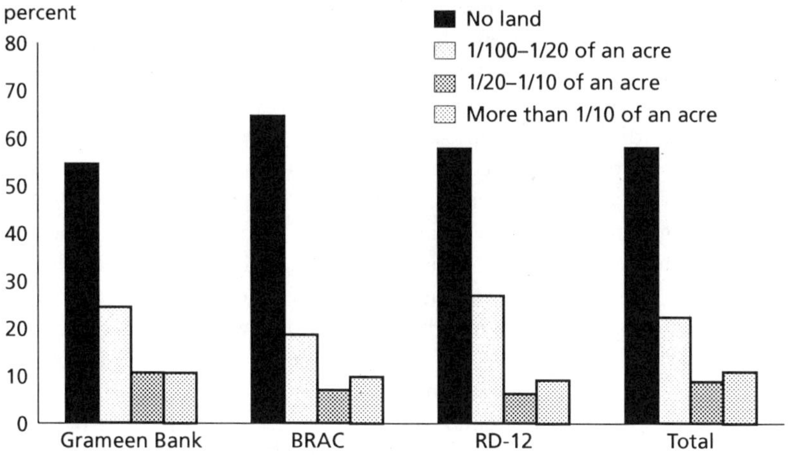

percent

Legend:
- ■ No land
- ☐ 1/100–1/20 of an acre
- ▨ 1/20–1/10 of an acre
- ▤ More than 1/10 of an acre

X-axis: Grameen Bank, BRAC, RD-12, Total
Y-axis: 0, 10, 20, 30, 40, 50, 60, 70, 80

*Source:* BIDS–World Bank 1991/92 survey.

variables. While community factors determine a program's placement and other opportunities for a household to join a program, household factors, such as education and landholding, determine a household's perceived ability to participate in a program.

To assess the impact of microcredit programs, some measure of program participation is needed. One measure would be simply whether or not a household participated in a microcredit program. Using a participation dummy (1 if a household participates, 0 if it does not) would allow the average returns to participation to be measured. From a policy perspective, however, a more interesting measure would be the marginal return to borrowing. This measure was estimated using the cumulative amount of borrowing over the five-year period before the survey was conducted.[3] Program participation so defined is a nonlinear variable, that is, 0 for nonborrowers (the 5 percent of participating households that did not borrow and nonparticipating households) and positive for borrowers. The objective is to assess the impact of borrowing on household- and individual-level outcomes of interest, including per capita weekly expenditure (food and nonfood), household net worth, women's nonland assets, labor supply of men and women, boys' and girls' school enrollment rate, contraceptive use, recent fertility (number of children born in the preceding five years), and nutritional status of children.

The program impact assessment was compared for each program and a series of tests was used to determine how impacts varied across programs. The impacts were expected to vary because loan sizes and program durations varied and because each program provides a different mix of credit and other services.

Tests were also performed to determine whether the impact of borrowing varied by gender. For various reasons female credit effects may differ from male credit effects. One reason this may be so is that perceived credit market imperfections may differ for male and female borrowers. Another reason is that men and women have different preferences, which are reflected through their borrowing. A third reason is that microcredit is not fungible across genders within a household (that is, the credit from microcredit programs given to women is not transferable to men and vice versa).

Assessing the impact of credit involves one basic problem: unless households are shown to be credit-constrained (meaning that households are constrained by a lack of liquidity and do not have access to credit to resolve their liquidity problems), it may be difficult to show the impact of credit on behavioral outcomes such as income and employment (Feder and others 1988). That is, if money is fungible, it is difficult to assess the impact of borrowing from a particular source, such as microcredit programs. Rather than formally test whether borrowers of group-based credit programs of Grameen Bank, BRAC, and RD-12 are credit-constrained, this study assumed that program participants were credit-constrained by program design. This assumption seems valid for several reasons. First, in the case of group-based lending to the landless, the time path of credit allocated to members is part of the dynamic optimization problem of a group, and the level of credit provided to each individual in the group is tailored to fund a new self-employment project of a certain size. Second, the cost of credit includes not only the interest rate but also the timing of repayment and the penalties associated with defaults. Third, group-based credit is packaged with both responsibilities (meeting attendance, forced saving, shared default risk) and benefits (training, insurance, and consciousness-raising), which are likely to make the cost of credit endogenously determined by household characteristics. Finally, the close monitoring aspects of group-based lending make group credit nonfungible. If there were no monitoring of the use of borrowed funds and no group responsibility and decisionmaking in the lending program, individuals would likely want to borrow much more than they actually do in order to capture the premiums associated with the soft terms of the loans. Indeed, as chapter 4 shows, more than 60 percent of households perceived themselves to be credit-constrained when all the restrictions associated with group-based credit or loan ceilings were relaxed. For these reasons, all participating households were presumed to be in the same credit demand regime.

## Factors Affecting Participation

Who participates in microcredit programs? Analysis of the characteristics of program participants was carried out by fitting a probit regression equation in which the decision to join a credit program (1 for those who participate, 0 otherwise) was regressed against a number of household variables, including age, sex, and education of the household head; landholding; village prices of major commodities; wages of different types of labor; village infrastructure, such as availability of paved roads; and the presence of microcredit programs, formal bank branches, and other programs.

Controlling for observable household- and village-level characteristics, program participation was at least 23 percent higher among households headed by women than among households headed by men. Controlling for other background characteristics of a household, landholding was associated with increased program participation among target households: the poorest of the poor in terms of landholding did not join microcredit programs (see chapter 7).

The prices of major commodities also influenced program participation, as did the wages for male, female, and child labor. Commodity prices can have both income and substitution effects on program participation. Their impact is thus unpredictable and can be positive or negative. Wages of adult labor represent opportunities for employment and unambiguously lowered the program participation rate. In contrast, higher child wages increased program participation, indicating that microcredit-induced self-employment is a complement to child labor and that self-employed activity financed by a microcredit program may facilitate child employment. Villages that did not have active labor markets for women had higher program participation rates. Irrigation density and roads were associated with higher program participation, while rural electrification was associated with lower participation. Overall, program participation was at least 14 percent higher in Grameen Bank villages and 65 percent higher in BRAC villages than in RD-12 villages.

## Controlling for Endogeneity

Even if the group-based credit obtained by a household is rationed by microcredit programs and groups, the credit amount cannot be taken as exogenous in explaining differences in behavioral outcomes. This is because the cumulative amount of borrowing measures both program participation and the decision to borrow and continue to participate in a microcredit program. It is likely that cumulative borrowing is determined by household characteristics, including characteristics of groups and microcredit programs. Unless such endogenous borrowing is controlled for, any assessment of the impact of borrowing is likely to be seriously biased.

As discussed in appendix C, inconsistency in credit impact assessments can arise in several ways. One potential source of bias is the possibility that program impacts vary because of unmeasured differences in the ability of individuals or households that cannot be controlled. The other source of bias is village heterogeneity. Unmeasured differences in villages that are not controlled in estimation cause program impacts to vary. For example, microcredit programs do not randomly place programs without regard to poverty in an area; unmeasured village characteristics may affect program placement. If their influence is not controlled, program impacts at either the village or the household level may measure the impact of these unobserved village characteristics.

Similarly, when credit impacts are differentiated by gender of borrowers, unobserved individual and household ability may also cause credit impacts to vary. For example, although membership is free, borrowing from a microcredit program such as Grameen Bank is costly not only in terms of the borrowing cost but also in terms of the opportunity cost of time spent on group-based activities. Women in rural Bangladesh bear additional membership costs: requiring female members to interact with people from outside their families, such as program organizers and other group members, challenges the practice of purdah, a system that secludes and protects women. Only households that can bear the full costs of membership, including the social stigma associated with female participation, will join microcredit programs.

It seems, therefore, that unobserved household attributes affect both participation in a microcredit program and household behavioral outcomes, such as labor supply to cash income-earning activities. Similarly, unobserved village attributes may affect credit impacts by influencing a household's decision to allow a woman to join a program. For example, programs may be placed in villages in which families are less traditional in their views toward women's role in society, including their reproductive roles. Ignoring such selection bias at the gender level would incorrectly ascribe to credit the differential impact of program borrowing by gender on outcomes such as labor supply, consumption, and contraceptive behavior.

The traditional way of resolving credit endogeneity is making instruments available that influence the amount of borrowing but not the behavioral outcomes affected by credit. As discussed in appendix C, no readily available uncontroversial instruments exist that control bias for both individual/household and village heterogeneity. The best way to control for such bias would be to compare outcomes between program participants and nonparticipants in a natural experiment in which program participation or exclusion is randomly assigned. Natural experiments in social science are unethical, however, and are difficult to conduct.

A quasi-experimental survey design was therefore used to collect data with which to verify whether program participation, as measured by the cumulative amount of borrowing, enhances household welfare. The survey design was quasi-experimental in that it used the programs' own restrictions that exogenously determine who participates in a credit program. Given the eligibility criterion of the programs, not all households are free to choose to participate in a program. Moreover, those that are eligible to participate are not automatically entitled to receive program benefits; they must demonstrate willingness to bear the implicit cost of group formation, training, and adherence to group discipline. Program participation is thus quasi-exogenous in that it is exogenously given by program eligibility criterion but depends as well on households self-selecting into programs.

Moreover, programs restrict group formation to one gender. If a woman wants to join Grameen Bank she cannot do so if there is no female group in her village. Program participation by gender is exogenous to individual households but conditional on village fixed effects that control for whether the village has a men's or women's group. Such exogenous restrictions satisfy the condition of identification of program impacts (see appendix C).

In this quasi-experimental survey design, neither program organizers nor researchers can control who among the eligible groups will participate in a program. Because both target households and the target gender are free to choose to participate in a program provided they are eligible and a program is available in their village, program participation is subject to unobserved individual and household characteristics. As identifying instruments are not available, survey instruments are used to control for such endogeneity of the amount of money borrowed by households from microcredit programs. (A formal discussion of endogeneity problems and the means used to resolve them appears in appendix D.)

## Estimating the Impact of Credit on Selected Household and Intrahousehold Outcomes

Men's and women's credit demand differ significantly, and women's (men's) borrowing is not affected by men's (women's) borrowing.[4] The household head's age and sex were important determinants of credit demand for both women and men, but they had different effects on the demand for credit by each gender (table A3.1). Having a male head of household reduced the amount of credit received by women. A test of the hypothesis that the slope parameters in women's and men's credit demand are equal was strongly rejected, reflecting to a large extent the opposite and significant effects of sex and age of household head. The set of variables describing the availability of potential sources of interfamily transfers was not a significant determinant of credit demand for either gender.[5]

What is the impact of male and female borrowing on household behavior, such as consumption and other outcomes of interest? The fixed-effects estimation technique was used to estimate the impact of cumulative borrowing by gender on a number of policy outcomes, such as consumption and employment. The impact of borrowing could be positive or negative, depending on the relative strengths of income and substitution effects. Substitution effects arise because of the changes in the opportunity cost of an individual's time when he or she borrows from a microcredit program, given that the household's preborrowing position does not change due to borrowing. Income effects measure changes in outcomes due to credit-induced income changes after the preborrowing situation is allowed to change.

Borrowing can exert both a positive income effect and an often negative substitution effect. For example, women's credit would be expected to increase the demand for boys' and girls' schooling if both goods are normal (a good is normal if demand for it increases as income rises). But credit increases women's opportunity cost and the cost of girls' time at school (because girls' time and their mothers' time may be substitutes in home production activities), thereby reducing girls' school enrollment rates. The net effect of the income and substitution effects is indeterminate a priori.[6] Similar arguments apply to other outcomes when the effect of conditional demand for credit is evaluated.

## Per Capita Expenditure

The most important effect of borrowing from a microcredit program is its impact on per capita expenditure.[7] As the regression results show, the effect of borrowing was positive for each category of credit from each program (table A3.2).[8] Not all credit parameters were statistically significant, however. Of the three men's credit parameters, only that for RD-12 was statistically significant. All three women's credit parameters were statistically significant at the 5 percent level. The men's credit parameters were not jointly significant, while the women's credit parameters were (table A3.3). A 10 percent increase in women's borrowing increased household per capita weekly expenditure by 0.43 percent for Grameen Bank, 0.39 percent for BRAC, and 0.40 percent for RD-12 (see table A3.2). The response elasticity of credit in per capita consumption was thus about the same for female borrowers in all three programs.

For all three microfinance programs, the impact on consumption of borrowing by women was about twice as great as it was for borrowing by men. One possible explanation for this difference is that women's absence from the labor market represents a greater production inefficiency than men's absence. The difference may also imply a higher consumption preference for women than for men for the same increase in income induced by borrowing from a microcredit program.

## Net Worth

Because borrowers are poor, increases in consumption as a result of borrowing from a microcredit program constitute an immediate welfare gain. But the impact could be short-lived unless enhanced income from borrowing supports asset accumulation. Moreover, because loan repayment in microcredit programs in Bangladesh is on a weekly basis, critics argue that repayment by poor borrowers sometimes takes place not from income receipts of microcredit-financed activities but from sales of household assets. It is, therefore, necessary to examine whether borrowing in fact enhances household net worth (the value of current assets less the value of loans outstanding).

Borrowing did indeed increase the household net worth of borrowers in all three programs, with the impact much stronger for men than for women (see table A3.2). A 10 percent increase in borrowing from BRAC increased household net worth 0.09 percent for female borrowing and 0.20 percent for male borrowing. A 10 percent increase in male borrowing from RD-12 increased household net worth 0.22 percent; female borrowing from RD-12 had no effect on household net worth. The increase in household net worth due to borrowing from Grameen Bank was about same for female (0.14 percent) and male (0.15 percent) borrowing.

## Women

Do women benefit from program participation? Women's gains can be examined from the perspective of their own consumption. Because individual-level data on food and nonfood consumption for adult members of households were not available, the impact of borrowing must be assessed using data on leisure or labor supply. Men and women specialize in certain types of production in rural Bangladesh, based on perceived constraints. When these constraints are changed as a result of improved access to borrowing, the time-use pattern is likely to change and in a different way for men and women.

An interesting indicator to compare is thus the labor supply, or time spent on income-earning activities, of men and women. Microcredit programs facilitate self-employment, mostly in rural nonfarm activities that can be undertaken at home without high transactions costs.

Targeted programs mostly benefit women, who can be self-employed at home for cash income generation. One would thus expect a sharp increase in time allocated to income generation by female program participants between the ages of 14 and 50. Of course, the amount of time devoted to income generation depends on the opportunity cost of leisure and the income effect on leisure, the relative effects of which may vary between men and women borrowers. Interestingly, women's borrowing from any program increased their labor supply, with positive impacts of borrowing that were individually significant at the 10 percent level and also jointly significant. As both labor supply and the amount of borrowing are entered in log form, the credit parameters are the elasticities of (latent) hours of market labor supply with respect to credit. The response elasticity of borrowing in labor supply of women was highest for Grameen Bank (0.10), followed by RD-12 (0.08) and BRAC (0.07; see table A3.2).

In contrast, both men's and women's borrowing reduced men's labor supply. Both own- and cross-effects were statistically jointly significant for both men's and women's credit. Since it seems unlikely that men are substituting home time for time spent in the labor market, the only plausible conclusion that can be drawn from these negative effects is that they reflect income effects. If the market value of men's time is unchanged by women's or men's borrowing, men's labor supply should fall if men's leisure is a normal good. This is plausible, given that men have access to the labor market before joining the program, so that program credit provides additional income that is proportional to the difference between program-induced income and available income from the next best alternative source. This explanation is consistent with the result that a 10 percent increase in women's borrowing reduced men's labor supply by as much as 2.3 percent while it increased women's labor supply by 1.04 percent. In contrast, a 10 percent increase in male credit was associated with a 1.6 percent decline in male labor supply and had no effect on female labor supply.

However, women gain from borrowing (at the cost of their leisure) by increasing their nonland assets. The effect of borrowing on women's nonland assets was positive and statistically significant for all three programs, and program results were jointly statistically significant (see table A3.2 and table A3.3). The impact of men's borrowing on women's nonland assets holding was not statistically significant. The response elasticity of women's borrowing in nonland assets was highest for RD-12 (0.22), followed by Grameen Bank (0.20) and BRAC (0.12). When expressed in marginal changes, this implies that at the mean of women's program loans (Tk 5,499) and nonland assets (Tk 7,399), every Tk 100 of increased credit to women from BRAC, RD-12, and Grameen

Bank increases their nonland assets by Tk 15, Tk 29, and Tk 27, respectively.

## Children's Schooling

Microcredit had a significant impact on children's schooling, especially for boys. The increase in boys' schooling was statistically significant for three credit variables (female credit from RD-12, female and male credit from Grameen Bank). For girls' schooling a statistically significant increase was shown for one only (female credit from Grameen Bank). Tests of the joint significance of the six credit variables studied found little evidence of joint significance for girls but much stronger evidence for boys (see table A3.3). The test statistics for women's credit were significant at the 1 percent level. The largest and most precisely estimated credit effects on both boys' and girls' schooling were the effects of female credit obtained from Grameen Bank. At the mean, a 1 percent increase in Grameen Bank credit provided to women increased the probability of school enrollment by 1.9 percent for girls and 2.4 percent for boys. In contrast, at the mean a 1 percent increase in male credit from Grameen Bank increased boys' school enrollment 2.8 percent, with no impact on girls' schooling. A 1 percent increase in credit to women from RD-12 had the largest impact on boys' school enrollment (3.1 percent) and no significant impact on girls' schooling.

Thus for both Grameen Bank and RD-12, female credit seems to benefit boys more than girls in terms of school enrollment.[9] The relatively smaller effect of women's credit on their daughters' schooling seems to reflect the close substitution of women's and girls' time in both household nonmarket production and self-employment activity financed by microcredit programs. Boys' time is likely to be a poor substitute for women's and girls' time, and hence boys are less likely to be drawn into self-employment activity or into household nonmarket production as a result of credit provided to women.

## Children's Nutrition

Women's credit had a large and statistically significant impact on two of three measures of the nutritional well-being of both male and female children (table A3.4).[10] Credit provided to men had no statistically significant impact except for girls' body mass index—where a 10 percent increase in male credit increased girls' body mass index about 3 percent. A 10 percent increase in credit provided to women increased the arm circumference of girls by 6 percent. Female credit also had significant positive effects on the height-for-age of both boys and girls, with response elasticities of 1.42 for boys and 1.16 for girls.

## Fertility and Contraception

Men's credit parameters for contraceptive use and fertility were jointly significant at the 5 percent level (see table A3.3), but only men's credit from Grameen Bank had a statistically significant effect in increasing contraceptive use among 14- to 50-year-old women in participating households (see table A3.2). Women's credit parameters were jointly and individually significant at the 10 percent level. Contrary to expectations, women's credit from any of the three programs reduced the use of contraceptives among participants. The effect was greatest for RD-12, followed by Grameen Bank and BRAC. The correlation coefficient for women's participation was positive and fairly large, implying that the women who join these microcredit programs have already been using contraceptives more than observationally equivalent women.[11]

The fertility effects of microcredit programs were consistent with the contraceptive use effects. Fertility increased with women's participation in BRAC and RD-12, although the effect was statistically significant only for BRAC. The set of both men's and women's credit parameters were jointly significant. Men's credit effects, however, were negative for Grameen Bank and RD-12. Male participation thus seemingly reduced fertility, while female participation increased it. The null hypothesis that women's and men's credit effects on fertility are the same was thus strongly rejected. These findings suggest that men as well as women should be targeted by family planning programs.

## Seasonality of Consumption and Labor

The weather-induced seasonality of the crop cycle is a major source of seasonality of labor use and income flows in Bangladesh. Households relying on agriculture are likely to reduce the effects of the seasonality of agriculture by diversifying into rural nonfarm activities. Group-based credit that generates income and employment flows that do not covary with income and employment from agriculture can help smooth consumption and labor supply. Indeed, an important motivation for credit program participation is the need to smooth the seasonal pattern of consumption and male labor supply.

Tables A3.5a and A3.5b shows the impacts of microcredit borrowing on the seasonality of consumption and labor supply. Notice that we did not distinguish among the three credit programs, as earlier work (Pitt and Khandker 1997) found no significance difference in the effects of borrowing from Grameen Bank, BRAC, and RD-12 on these two outcomes. Households that experienced larger than average seasonal variation in consumption flows were most likely to use microcredit, suggesting that these programs are successfully targeting potential borrowers. For both men and women the largest increases in household consumption took place during the lean (Aus) season (see table A3.5a). It is the extent of lean-season poverty that makes the households self-select into these programs. Women's credit had positive impacts on their labor supply, with very little seasonal variation (see table A3.5b). Given women's small share of market time in their total time, seasonality is less likely to affect their time allocation. In contrast, men's credit had a negative impact on their labor supply in the peak (Aman) season and women's credit had similar negative effects on men's labor supply except in the lean season. This is because, as the demand for men's labor was high during the peak season, men and women both borrowed more from the credit programs, reducing the market labor supply.

## Village-Level Program Impacts

Microcredit programs may affect nonparticipating households in program villages. By increasing self-employment, for example, microcredit could reduce the supply of wage laborers, possibly increasing the wage rate. A series of adjustments for nonparticipating households could be generated in terms of both labor supply and induced income changes.

Programs may also alter village attitudes and hence influence behavioral outcomes of nonparticipating households through demonstration, or spillover, effects. To capture the full impact of microcredit, village-level effects must be measured in addition to individual-level effects. The externalities of microcredit could be positive or negative, so the full impact of these programs could be larger or smaller than the direct effect of borrowing on participants.

One way to examine the full program effect is to compare aggregate village-level outcomes in program and nonprogram villages after controlling for village heterogeneity that induces programs to select a particular village. Weighted village-level average outcomes based on the village population distribution were calculated for both program and nonprogram villages (table A3.6). These outcomes are farm, nonfarm, and total production; farm, nonfarm, and total income; farm, nonfarm, and total employment; the rural male wage (an average of farm and nonfarm male wages); total school enrollment rates; and recent fertility (whether a woman between 14 and 50 gave birth in the previous five years). Substantial differences between program and nonprogram villages exist for some outcomes. For example, the value of annual production of program villages was more than twice that of nonprogram villages. The source of such large differences in production is primarily higher nonfarm production in program villages. Differences in income between program and nonprogram villages were also due largely to differences in nonfarm income. A third measure, the number of hours worked, was also higher in program villages than in nonprogram villages.

Insignificant differences in village-level socioeconomic indicators such as contraceptive use, fertility, and school enrollment rate are observable. The school enrollment rate, for example, was 50 percent in program villages and 49 percent in nonprogram villages. The number of births by women between 14 and 50 over the previous five years was 1.14 in program villages and 1.10 in nonprogram villages. The contraceptive use rate was 49 percent in program villages and 47 percent in nonprogram villages (not reported in table A3.6).

Comparison between program and nonprogram villages is meaningful if program placement is exogenous. If programs are not randomly placed, preprogram and postprogram comparisons are more appropriate. Because panel data were not available, however, the fixed-effects method used to control for village heterogeneity could not be used to document the overall impact of program placement on average household welfare in a village. Moreover, the fixed-effects method is not suitable for estimating impact if it uses dummy variables. A simple program placement dummy variable does not capture the causal impact of programs, as placement is endogenous in the sense that programs deliberately select poorer villages for operation.

No suitable instrument is available to control for such program endogeneity while allowing the full impact of program placement to be assessed. Village-level regressions are nevertheless presented, with the following caveats. The estimated coefficients may overestimate or underestimate the true program placement effects. From the earlier analysis on borrowing effects (see appendix D), it is clear that the extent of bias is more serious in the case of underestimation than overestimation. The nonfixed-effects method used to estimate the impact of program placement (both direct and indirect effects) on socioeconomic outcomes such as contraceptive use, fertility, and school enrollment thus yields estimates that would reflect only lower-bound estimates of the true effects. Program placement has an upward bias in the case of variables such as labor supply if a nonfixed-effects method is used. No bias was reported for consumption and household net worth. Village heterogeneity in the estimated program impact is likely to be higher for socioeconomic outcomes than for outcomes such as employment and consumption.

The outcomes shown in table A3.6 are weighted averages of household-level outcomes for all households (both target and nontarget) in the village. Program placement dummies measure whether the village had a program. Only 10 percent of sample villages had a branch of a commercial or agricultural development bank, while 32 percent had a Grameen Bank program, 28 percent had a BRAC branch, and 29 percent had a RD-12 program.[12]

## Production

Traditional banks and all three microcredit programs had significant impacts on total production at the village level. The dependent variable in the equation is the natural logarithm of average household production. The coefficients measure how household production increases when a program is present. The increase in average household production in program villages was 56 percent for Grameen Bank, 57 percent for BRAC, and 48 percent for RD-12. Production in villages with formal banks was 62 percent higher than in villages with no formal banks. These increases were due primarily to increases in rural nonfarm production, which rose 89 percent in Grameen villages, 83 percent in BRAC villages, 74 percent in RD-12 villages, and 92 percent in villages with formal banks.

## Average Household Income

All programs except RD-12 raised average household income from different sources. The increase in household income in program villages was 29 percent for Grameen Bank, 33 percent for BRAC, and 45 percent for traditional banks. Although the impact on aggregate income was not statistically significant for RD-12, it managed to increase farm income by 62 percent without a corresponding growth in rural nonfarm income.[13] In contrast, the main source of increases in aggregate household income for Grameen Bank and BRAC villages was rural nonfarm activities. Unlike RD-12, both Grameen Bank and BRAC reduced farm wage income and increased rural nonfarm income. Increases in self-employed nonfarm income for Grameen Bank (242 percent) and in wage nonfarm income for BRAC (228 percent) contributed most to increases in household income. Farm income (most significantly, wage income) was the source of the increase in total income for formal banks.

## Employment

Grameen Bank and commercial/agricultural development banks increased employment in villages, while BRAC and RD-12 reduced it. Interestingly, total employment increased in Grameen Bank villages because of large increases in self-employment in nonfarm activities. In villages with formal banks, increases in employment reflected increases in wage employment in nonfarm activities. In BRAC villages the reduction in employment largely reflected the reduction in farm employment. In RD-12 villages overall employment fell because the decline in farm employment exceeded the gains in self-employment in both farm and nonfarm activities. Such an overall reduction is possible if the positive income effect offsets the negative substitution effect in the demand for leisure.

## Wages

Formal banks and RD-12 increased wage farm income for the poor, while Grameen Bank and BRAC reduced it. But unlike traditional banks and RD-12, Grameen Bank helped increase nonfarm self-employed income; BRAC contributed to nonfarm wage income. Despite declines in wage income, increases in self-employment income were sufficient to raise overall household income in program villages. Total employment increased in villages with Grameen Bank or traditional banks but declined in BRAC and RD-12 villages. These increases, especially in Grameen Bank villages, resulted from large increases in self-employment, especially in the nonfarm sector, which offset the reduction in wage employment. Given that wage income falls with a reduction in wage employment, program placement could reduce the rural wage rate. It is possible, however, to show that a reduction in wage employment can lead to an increase in the wage rate, given supply and demand for labor.

Among the three microcredit programs only Grameen Bank had a positive and significant impact on rural wages (see table A3.6). After controlling for observable village attributes, including the extent of target households, wages rose about 21 percent (calculated from the coefficient in the wage regression, which is 4.929). Given that Grameen Bank operates in poorer villages (65 percent of households in Grameen villages and just 52 percent in nonprogram villages are target households), the wage increase is a clear sign that Grameen Bank contributed to the growth of the village economy. The rise in wages in Grameen villages may also indicate the absence of reverse causality of program placement impacts on village-level outcomes.

## School Enrollment and Fertility Rates

Only BRAC had an impact on village-level school enrollment rates. BRAC increased overall enrollment by 6 percent and enrollment of girls by 8 percent. This finding may appear inconsistent with the direct impacts reported in table A3.2, which shows that male and female borrowing from BRAC had no significant impact on children's school enrollment rate. The village-level findings may indicate the presence of large externalities to BRAC borrowing.

None of the programs had an impact on village-level contraceptive use, but Grameen Bank and the commercial banks had a negative impact on recent fertility: fertility among 14- to 50-year old women was 13 percent lower in Grameen Bank villages and 17 percent lower in villages with formal bank branches. Although participant-level impacts show that fertility increased as a result of female borrowing and fell as a result of male borrowing from Grameen Bank (see table A3.2), the net impact of Grameen Bank program placement was negative because the effect of male credit dominated the effect of female credit.

## Does Microcredit Reduce Poverty?

Can microcredit programs alleviate poverty? All three microcredit programs had significant positive effects on household per capita expenditure (table A3.2). The estimated impact coefficient of credit from Grameen Bank was 0.043 for women and 0.018 for men. That is, a 10 percent increase in borrowing increases expenditure by participating households by 0.4 percent when women borrow and by 0.2 percent when men borrow. Mean per capita expenditure in the survey households was Tk 4,004 a year. Average cumulative borrowing for all three programs was Tk 5,499 for women and Tk 3,692 for men. Assuming an average family size of six, the average annual household expenditure was Tk 24,024. Given an estimated marginal increase in household consumption of 18 percent for women's borrowing and 11 percent for men's borrowing, how long would it take an average borrower to lift his or her family out of poverty?

The extent of poverty can be defined in terms of consumption. In a country such as Bangladesh, poverty can be calculated based on nutritional requirements. According to the Food and Agriculture Organization, daily consumption of 2,112 calories is required to remain above the poverty line. The cost of meeting this requirement can be calculated by pricing various food items and adding a 30 percent allowance to cover the cost of nonfood items (Hossain and Sen 1992). As price differences were observed between villages, the poverty-line level of consumption varied from village to village. Village cost of living indices were used to establish Tk 5,270 per person per year as the cutoff for moderate poverty. Any household in which per person consumption was less than 80 percent of Tk 5,270 (Tk 3,330) was defined as living in extreme poverty (see Khandker and Chowdhury 1996).

## At the Household Level

Given required per person annual expenditures of Tk 5,270 and actual per person expenditures for participating households of Tk 4,004, how long would it take an average member of a participating household to rise out of moderate poverty? What level of cumulative borrowing would be necessary to allow him or her to do so? Assuming that the marginal increase in consumption as a result of borrowing is 18 percent for women and 11 percent for men, the additional borrowing required to achieve annual per capita consumption of Tk 5,270 is Tk 7,033 for women and Tk 11,509 for men. The time required to obtain this much credit will depend on how rapidly a borrower can absorb debt and how rapidly a program is willing to extend credit.

Comparing this poverty profile of program participants before and after program participation reveals the extent to which poverty was reduced. The net gains in consumption due to borrowing are calculated by multiplying the estimated coefficients of credit impact on consumption by the amount of cumulative borrowing.[14] These gains reflect consumption that would not have occurred had these households not joined a microcredit program. In order to estimate the impact on poverty reduction, the gains in consumption are subtracted from the current consumption level to obtain the preparticipation consumption level.

The head-count index of poverty is the percentage of households with per person consumption below the poverty line. The head-count index does not measure the depth of poverty (that is, how far the poor are from the poverty line). It is nevertheless the most common measure used to indicate the extent of poverty in a given population (see Foster, Greer, and Thorbecke 1984; Ravallion 1994).

The calculation of the two measures of poverty—moderate and extreme—are based on per person expenditure for participants before and after program participation (table 3.1). About 83 percent of Grameen Bank participants were moderately poor and 33 percent were extremely poor before joining Grameen Bank. After participating in Grameen Bank only 62 percent were moderately poor and only 10 percent were extremely poor. Thus about 21 percent of Grameen Bank borrowers managed to lift their families out of poverty within 4.2 years of membership. This means that 5 percent of Grameen Bank household rose above poverty each year by borrowing from Grameen Bank. Similarly, 3 percent of BRAC households and 6 percent of RD-12 households rose from poverty each year. Poverty reduction was thus highest for RD-12, followed by Grameen Bank and BRAC, although interprogram differences were not statistically significant.

Gains were smallest for RD-12 members who had participated in the program for more than 5 years. However, borrowers who recently joined a microcredit program were poorer than their predecessors, and the gains in poverty reduction were higher among Grameen and BRAC participants with at least 5 years of program experience than among those who recently joined either program. This result suggests that program participation impacts on poverty reduction are likely to be sustainable with microcredit programs. Net worth increased for all programs regardless of participation duration. However, only for Grameen Bank did it increase monotonically as participation duration increased.

## At the Village Level

What effect did microcredit programs have on village-level poverty? The incidence of moderate poverty among target households was 64 percent in Grameen Bank villages, 68 percent in BRAC villages, 67 percent in RD-12 villages, and 69 percent in nonprogram villages. Overall, 63 percent of rural households were moderately poor and 12 percent were extremely poor. In contrast, among target households 66 percent were moderately poor and 14 percent were extremely poor. A study in 1988–89 found a higher incidence of both moderate poverty (71 percent) and extreme poverty (28 percent) among target households (Hossain and Sen 1992). These figures imply that program interventions may have helped reduce aggregate poverty. Since program placement bias was not important for consumption impact estimates when a nonfixed-effects method was used, program placement impact on village-level poverty reduction was estimated by fitting a linear regression for the village-level poverty profile.[15] The variable to be explained measures the percentage of households in a village that are below the moderate and extreme poverty lines based on the consumption requirements. The explanatory variables are whether the village has a Grameen Bank, BRAC, or RD-12 program; whether the village has a paved road; whether it has a branch of a commercial or agricultural development bank; whether it is electrified; the village's distance from thana headquarters; whether the village has a development program; and the proportion of households owning less than half an acre of land.

All three microcredit programs reduced both moderate and extreme poverty (table A3.7). Aggregate village-level moderate poverty was 14 percent lower in RD-12 villages, 12 percent lower in Grameen Bank villages, and 10 percent lower in BRAC villages. Village-level poverty reduction associated with program placement was slightly lower than participant-level poverty reduction. In Grameen Bank villages, for

TABLE 3.1
**Rates of Poverty and Net Worth Accumulation before and after
Program Participation**

| Poverty variable | 0–36 months | | 36–60 months | |
|---|---|---|---|---|
| | Before program | After program | Before program | After program |
| *Grameen Bank* | | | | |
| Moderate poverty (percent) | 89.5 | 80.7 | 86.5 | 62.4 |
| Extreme poverty (percent) | 45.6 | 22.8 | 38.4 | 10.5 |
| Household net worth (taka) | 47,156 | 48,518 | 50,863 | 53,367 |
| Per capita yearly consumption (taka) | 3,688 | 4,393 | 4,043 | 5,074 |
| Household borrowing (taka) | 7,829 | | 14,391 | |
| *BRAC* | | | | |
| Moderate poverty (percent) | 81.8 | 67.0 | 85.5 | 76.3 |
| Extreme poverty (percent) | 38.6 | 13.6 | 31.6 | 13.2 |
| Household net worth (taka) | 64,440 | 65,736 | 67,991 | 69,580 |
| Per capita yearly consumption (taka) | 4,534 | 5,296 | 4,183 | 4,870 |
| Household borrowing (taka) | 3,457 | | 4,236 | |
| *RD-12* | | | | |
| Moderate poverty (percent) | 85.2 | 71.3 | 79.3 | 60.0 |
| Extreme poverty (percent) | 27.7 | 10.9 | 28.7 | 7.3 |
| Household net worth (taka) | 41,270 | 41,770 | 44,843 | 45,493 |
| Per capita yearly consumption (taka) | 4,253 | 4,858 | 4,140 | 4,827 |
| Household borrowing (taka) | 4,383 | | 5,698 | |

*Source:* Calculated from estimates presented in table A3.3 assuming that the same marginal return applies for different durations.

example, moderate poverty fell by 21 percent among program participants and by 12 percent for the villages. The direct impact may be higher than the total impact because program placement may be redistributing village income. The net contribution toward reducing rural poverty was positive, however.

| | 60+ months | | Aggregate | |
|---|---|---|---|---|
| | Before program | After program | Before program | After program |
| | 75.8 | 51.7 | 82.9 | 61.6 |
| | 20.8 | 4.2 | 32.9 | 10.3 |
| | 68,980 | 72,844 | 57,189 | 60,014 |
| | 4,623 | 5,672 | 4,202 | 5,180 |
| | | 22,207 | | 16,234 |
| | 78.3 | 69.2 | 81.3 | 70.4 |
| | 32.5 | 14.2 | 34.2 | 13.7 |
| | 63,870 | 66,387 | 65,121 | 67,040 |
| | 4,286 | 4,984 | 4,335 | 5,050 |
| | | 6,712 | | 5,117 |
| | 71.4 | 59.2 | 80.0 | 63.7 |
| | 32.7 | 18.2 | 29.0 | 10.3 |
| | 32,482 | 34,111 | 41,633 | 42,380 |
| | 4,757 | 5,400 | 4,279 | 4,931 |
| | | 14,294 | | 6,545 |

## At the National Level

Poverty in Bangladesh is largely a matter of not having enough to eat. Microcredit programs attack poverty at its source by increasing the household consumption expenditure of participants. Borrowing from a program is estimated to reduce moderate poverty among participants by as much as 20 percent and extreme poverty by as much as 22 percent. This means that as much as 5 percent of program participating households should be able to lift their families out of poverty every year by borrowing from a microcredit program.

What does this 5 percent annual poverty reduction for program participants mean at the national level? About half of the poor people in Bangladesh are eligible to participate in microcredit programs. Of those eligible about 45 percent participate. This means that microcredit programs effectively benefit only 20 percent of the population, and about 1 percent of the population (5 percent of 45 percent of 50 percent) can lift itself from poverty each year through such programs. Of course, this figure is based on the assumption that the number of poor is fixed. In fact, the number of poor people in Bangladesh is likely to be growing rapidly given annual population growth of 1.8 percent a year. If the number of poor people grows by more than 1 percent a year, the total number of poor people in the country will increase, despite the reductions in poverty brought about by microcredit.

Microcredit programs also seem to attack poverty on the social front. They empower women and thereby increase their role in household resource allocation. This effect directly increases the welfare of children. As the study results show, the beneficial impacts of microcredit programs differ substantially by gender of program participants. Women's credit has the largest impact on per capita consumption and nutritional status of children. Microcredit programs have substantial impacts on children's schooling, which in turn enhances the human capital status of a country. Microcredit programs also seem to attack poverty from a population growth perspective. Men's group-based credit yields substantial benefits, especially on the schooling of children, contraceptive use, and fertility. The findings on contraceptive use and fertility have a bearing on the practice followed in most developing countries of targeting family planning programs to women and not men, suggesting that men should be targeted equally in order to obtain maximum impact.

## Summary

Analysis of the results of a survey of 1,798 households in Bangladesh reveals that about 45 percent of eligible households participated in microcredit programs and that about two-thirds of participants were women. Households headed by women were more likely to participate in a program than were households headed by men, and poorer households were less likely to participate than less poor households.

Participation in a microcredit program had a positive effect on per capita expenditure, although the effect was not always statistically significant for borrowing by men. In contrast, all of the measures of impact of borrowing by women were significant, and the impact on consumption was about twice as great as it was for men. Borrowing also increased household net worth, with a greater effect for men than for women.

Microcredit also affected socioeconomic variables, including children's schooling, children's nutrition, fertility, and contraception use. Microcredit had a significant and positive impact on schooling, especially for boys. Borrowing by women (but not by men) improved the nutritional status of both male and female children. Borrowing by men appeared to reduce fertility, while participation by women appeared to increase fertility.

The village-level effects of microcredit were also studied. All three programs had significant impacts on production, increasing average household output in villages by about 50 percent. Grameen Bank and BRAC also had positive impacts on average household income. Only Grameen Bank had a positive and significant impact on rural wages, increasing wages at the village level by about 21 percent.

Consumption of about 5 percent of program participants increased to the point that their households rose above the poverty line. This figure suggests that microcredit could reduce poverty in Bangladesh by about 1 percent a year.

## Notes

1. Unobserved village characteristics that influence program placement cannot be controlled for because the village-level regression used cross-sectional data. However, program placement bias is controlled for in the household- and individual-level regression by using fixed-effects method. See appendix D for details.

2. A few people belonged to credit programs in other villages.

3. The amounts borrowed before 1991/92 (the year of the survey) were deflated by the consumer price index of each year, with 1991/92 the base year.

4. The findings of this section are drawn from Pitt and Khandker (1996, 1997) and Pitt and others (1995, 1998).

5. Although the interest rate is a relevant variable for explaining variations in the demand for credit, it was not included as a regressor because the interest rate charged by microcredit programs did not vary in a given year. The informal lending rate could not be included because it varies by village, and the village-level fixed effects capture the influence of all village-level variables, including the informal interest rate observed at the village level.

6. Women's access to the services of microcredit programs may also increase their empowerment within the household and hence the consumption of certain goods, such as children's education. Therefore, in addition to income and substitution effects, empowerment effect could also partially determine the outcomes.

7. Per capita income could be another important household welfare indicator. However, income is highly subject to measurement bias.

8. Table A3.2 excludes estimates of a number of variables that were included in the regression: age and education of the individuals, number of relatives that own land and are a potential source of transfers, age, sex and education of the household head, household's landholding, no adult male and female in household, and no spouse in household. Because of a very complicated maximum likelihood model estimated with more than 200 parameters (because of village dummies), we only estimated the credit impacts. Of course, interaction effects of credit with household characteristics could be added to allow program impacts to distributional impacts (including poverty). But, later in this section, we will provide estimated impacts of credit on poverty reduction based on the estimated impacts of credit on per capita consumption.

9. This finding is different from that predicted in a bargaining framework. For example, as Thomas (1993) shows for Brazil, boys' schooling depends on fathers' income, while girls' schooling depends only on mother's income. In Bangladesh, however, women seem to care more for boys than for girls, at least in schooling them.

10. Although the original household survey design called for anthropometric measures of individuals residing in nontarget households, the final survey included only those residing in target households. This precluded the use of the quasi-experimental survey design used to identify program impacts in Pitt and Khandker (1996). Since there were no differences across programs in terms of credit impacts, only the impacts of credit by gender of borrower are presented. The nutritional impacts are based on a smaller sample, and the estimation method used to estimate credit impact on three measures of nutrition (arm circumference, body mass index, and height-for-age) is also different (see Pitt and others 1998 for details).

11. Contraceptive use is a behavior for which village externalities may be important. Consequently, the total impact (participant-level impact plus village-level externality) may be positive.

12. Other explanatory variables in the village-level regressions include whether the village has a paved road, whether the village is electrified, the village distance from the thana headquarters, whether the village has any other development program, and the proportion of landless households in the village. These additional regressors control for the effects of observed village attributes in the estimates of microcredit program placement. The estimated coefficients of these regressors are not reported.

13. Although microcredit programs largely finance rural nonfarm activities, they generate induced effects on farm activities through backward and forward linkages. Moreover, as funds are fungible across activities, if not across individuals, microcredit programs may increase farm income.

14. Assuming diminishing marginal returns (where average returns are higher than marginal returns), this is an underestimate of the the net gains of borrowing. However, because in the analysis in this book the marginal returns to borrowing reflect returns to both amount of credit and duration of program participation, the assumption implies diminishing returns to both credit and duration of participation. Whether this is a valid assumption requires long-term impact analysis of both credit and duration, which is beyond the scope of this book.

15. This means that even if unobserved village heterogeneity is not controlled for, the program placement impacts on poverty are likely to be unbiased.

# 4

## Growth Potential of Activities Financed through Microcredit

Are the poverty alleviation impacts of microcredit programs sustainable? The answer depends largely on the growth potential of the activities financed by the programs. Because of a lack of agricultural sources of income, microfinance institutions finance mainly rural nonfarm activities in Bangladesh. If this rural nonfarm sector is to become a major source of income and employment for microcredit borrowers, the returns to capital and labor in the sector must be high.

Growth of the rural nonfarm sector was once thought to depend on the growth of industry: as the industrial sector grew, it was believed, reliance on the rural nonfarm sector would decline (Hymer and Resnick 1969). Recent findings from developing countries refute this proposition, however (Ahmed and Hossain 1990; Binswanger 1983; Chadha 1986; Hazell and Ramasamy 1991; Hazell and Roell 1983). These studies find important backward and forward linkages between the rural nonfarm sector and agriculture, indicating that income from the rural nonfarm sector increases as the agricultural sector grows. Growth in the rural nonfarm sector thus depends on growth in agriculture (Hazell and Haggblade 1991).[1]

In many countries without a strong modern sector, the rural nonfarm sector contributes to modernization of agriculture by providing employment and income for a large number of rural households involved in processing and other activities supporting agricultural growth. In Bangladesh, where agricultural growth has stagnated at 2 percent a year, the critical question is how far microfinanced rural nonfarm growth (which has grown by 4 percent a year) can lead agricultural and hence overall growth. This question is critical for an assessment of the long-term viability of microcredit programs and their beneficiaries.

Microcredit-led expansion in the rural nonfarm sector can increase agricultural income.[2] Can microcredit programs sustain these income and employment gains for a large proportion of the population in Bangladesh? More than 50 percent of rural households in Bangladesh are landless and have no productive employment options other than self-employment. Expansion of microfinance programs—both by increasing the number of villages that participate and by increasing participation within villages—would require higher income and employment potential of borrowers, as well as the emergence of micro-credit programs as full-fledged financial institutions.

Chapters 5 and 6 discuss the possibilities of microcredit programs becoming self-sustainable. This chapter examines the potential for the upward income mobility of microcredit borrowers, which depends large-ly on the growth potential of rural nonfarm activities. First, it identifies the factors influencing participation in the rural nonfarm sector, describes the distribution of activities within the sector, analyzes the sector's importance in terms of income and employment, and identifies the sources of productivity in the sector. Second, it examines the major sources of finance for rural nonfarm enterprises and describes the dif-ferent roles of formal and informal finance. Third, it studies the returns to capital of long-term program participants to determine the long-run effects of participation, and it identifies the main factors constraining expansion of the sector.

## The Nature of the Rural Nonfarm Sector

The rural nonfarm sector broadly includes all nonagricultural income-generating activities carried out in rural and semiurban areas. However, a few agricultural activities, such as fisheries, livestock, and poultry, when carried out with external financing on a larger scale, can be con-sidered as nonfarm activities. In most cases rural nonfarm activities are run with little or no fixed capital. Historically, growth in agriculture and related activities is a precondition for overall growth of the economy. But in a country like Bangladesh, where 80 percent of the population lives in rural areas and poverty is rampant, agriculture and its diversifi-cation alone cannot do the job. In particular, it is not possible for agri-culture to absorb a rapidly growing labor force that includes a signifi-cant portion of the landless poor. The rural nonfarm sector can play an important complementary role.

### Factors Influencing Rural Nonfarm Participation

About half of the households covered by the survey participated in the rural nonfarm sector at some time during the 1991–92 farming year. About 27 percent of households participated in the sector during all three seasons; 21 percent participated in the sector on a part-time basis.

What determines participation in this sector? Table A4.1 shows the probit estimates of this choice structure.[3] Participation is higher among male-headed households than among female-headed households. Landholding, which provides alternative employment opportunities, reduces the likelihood of participation. Higher prices for potatoes and sugar, which lead to higher farm income, encourage households to concentrate on farming rather than other activities. In contrast, higher beef prices and higher child wages increase rural nonfarm participation. Rural nonfarm participation is slightly higher in Grameen Bank villages than in BRAC, RD-12, or nonprogram villages. These results may indicate that BRAC and RD-12 provide additional capital to people already engaged in nonfarm activities rather than move people into these activities.

## The Distribution of Rural Nonfarm Activities

The rural nonfarm activities reported in the household survey were aggregated into five categories (figure 4.1).[4] About half of all households involved in the sector work in trading, the leading rural nonfarm activity. Only 19 percent of households are involved in manufacturing. The percentage of households involved in manufacturing is highest for Grameen Bank participants (23 percent), followed by RD-12 (20 percent) and BRAC participants (14 percent).

## The Rural Nonfarm Sector as a Source of Income and Employment

The rural nonfarm sector is an important source of income and employment for rural households, especially for the poor who lack enough land to support themselves. About two-thirds of Bangladesh's population is employed in agricultural activities (crop production and livestock), which accounts for only about 45 percent of household income (figure 4.2). Nonfarm activities employ about a third of the population but account for 55 percent of income.[5]

## Sources of Productivity in the Rural Nonfarm Sector

Why does the rural nonfarm sector contribute so much to income? Is productivity in the rural nonfarm sector capital-constrained? A Cobb-Douglas production function is used to identify the roles of various factors. Production is assumed to be subject to a liquidity constraint, so that the amount of credit obtained from institutional sources directly enters into the production function (Binswanger and Khandker 1995; Feder and others 1988). Borrowers are assumed always to prefer to borrow from institutional sources, given that institutional credit, including that of microfinance programs, is cheaper than informal credit, and informal credit is assumed to be an imperfect substitute for institutional credit. However, the amount of credit offered is likely to be rationed by suppliers when aggregate demand for institutional credit exceeds

FIGURE 4.1

**Distribution of Rural Nonfarm Activities, 1991–92**

percent

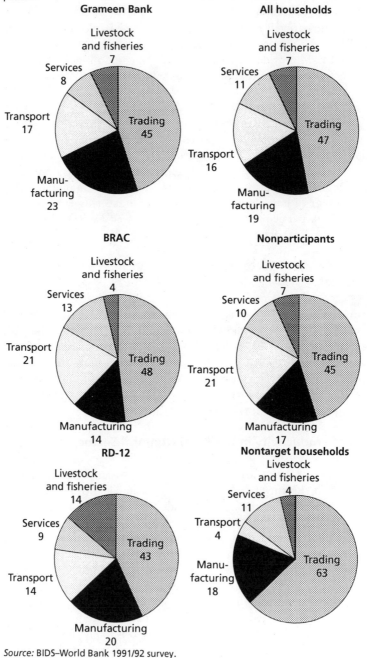

**Grameen Bank**

Livestock and fisheries 7
Services 8
Transport 17
Trading 45
Manu-facturing 23

**All households**

Livestock and fisheries 7
Services 11
Transport 16
Trading 47
Manu-facturing 19

**BRAC**

Livestock and fisheries 4
Services 13
Transport 21
Trading 48
Manufacturing 14

**Nonparticipants**

Livestock and fisheries 7
Services 10
Transport 21
Trading 45
Manufacturing 17

**RD-12**

Livestock and fisheries 14
Services 9
Transport 14
Trading 43
Manufacturing 20

**Nontarget households**

Livestock and fisheries 4
Services 11
Transport 4
Manu-facturing 18
Trading 63

*Source:* BIDS–World Bank 1991/92 survey.

66

FIGURE 4.2

**Distribution of Sources of Employment and Income in Bangladesh, 1991–92**

percent

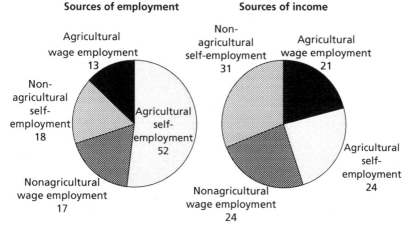

*Source:* BIDS–World Bank 1991/92 survey.

the supply. Given these assumptions, the availability of microcredit programs and formal banks in a village may indicate the extent of credit rationing from institutional sources for village-level production.[6]

Production function estimates are subject to simultaneity bias because of the jointness of inputs and output. Estimating a profit function rather than a production function would avert the problem, but doing so requires data on price variations of both output and inputs, which are not available. The Cobb-Douglas production function is restrictive in terms of the substitutability of inputs used in production. These limitations notwithstanding, estimates of the Cobb-Douglas production function for key activities and for the rural nonfarm sector as a whole are valuable. In addition to production inputs such as land, labor, and capital, variables such as the extent of landlessness and village characteristics were used to control for bias resulting from endogeneity of program placement. Both household and individual variables, such as age, sex, and education of the household head, were included in the production function to control for household heterogeneity. A separate aggregate rural nonfarm production function was estimated for target and nontarget households (table A4.2). Separate production functions could not be estimated for each major activity for nontarget households because of the lack of sufficient observations of the nontarget households.

The results of the Cobb-Douglas production function estimations show that the presence of one of the three microcredit programs increased productivity for the target households. For target households the average increase in production over nonprogram villages was 24 percent in Grameen Bank villages, 36 percent in BRAC villages, and 15 percent in RD-12 villages. On average the target group's annual production rose by Tk 35,522 in Grameen villages, Tk 53,283 in BRAC villages, and Tk 22,201 in RD-12 villages, with manufacturing accounting for the largest increase in productivity. BRAC also increased productivity for nontarget households, either through the induced demand of program participants or through demonstration effects.

Traditional banks increased overall rural nonfarm production by 28 percent for target households, and they increased production of services for nontarget households. These banks helped target households largely by increasing livestock and fisheries production (81 percent), trading (34 percent), and other services (34 percent).

Education had a positive impact on manufacturing, trading, and overall production for both target and nontarget households, but the

TABLE 4.1
**Sectoral Distribution of Loans, 1990–94**
(percent)

| Institution and year | Total amount disbursed (millions of taka) | Agriculture |
|---|---|---|
| *Grameen Bank* | | |
| 1990 | 2,245 | 4.4 |
| 1991 | 2,628 | 4.1 |
| 1992 | 5,189 | 26.8 |
| 1993 | 10,609 | 35.7 |
| 1994 | 13,892 | 35.0 |
| *BRAC* | | |
| 1990 | 393 | 8.8 |
| 1991 | 605 | 12.3 |
| 1992 | 731 | 11.3 |
| 1993 | 1,467 | 14.4 |
| 1994 | 2,042 | 16.2 |
| *RD-12* | | |
| 1990 | 66 | a |
| 1991 | 124 | a |
| 1992 | 308 | a |
| 1993 | 660 | a |
| 1994 | 608 | a |

*Note:* All sectoral figures represent percentages of total loans disbursed. Totals may not sum to 100 percent because of rounding error.
a. RD-12's agricultural loans are aggregated with "other activities."
*Source:* Grameen Bank, BRAC, and RD-12 annual reports, various years.

marginal return to education was low for both target (3 percent) and nontarget (5 percent) households.

## Financing the Rural Nonfarm Sector

Grameen Bank, BRAC, and RD-12 lent Tk 16,542 million in 1994, almost 70 percent of which supported rural nonfarm activities (table 4.1). Agriculture received an increasing share of loans from Grameen Bank and BRAC.[7] Agriculture which accounted for only 4 percent of Grameen Bank's lending in 1991, absorbed 35 percent of loans in 1994. For BRAC, agriculture's share of loans rose from 12 percent in 1991 to 16 percent in 1994. BRAC's agricultural lending supports mainly irrigation projects run by its members; Grameen Bank's agricultural lending supports a variety of agricultural activities, including crop production. It is not clear how much RD-12 supports agricultural

| Manufacturing and processing | Livestock, poultry, and fisheries | Trading | Other activities |
| --- | --- | --- | --- |
| 30.5 | 42.8 | 20.5 | 1.8 |
| 29.1 | 44.0 | 21.3 | 1.5 |
| 18.8 | 31.9 | 21.4 | 1.1 |
| 14.0 | 28.3 | 21.3 | 0.8 |
| 15.5 | 26.1 | 22.4 | 1.0 |
| 30.1 | 30.0 | 23.6 | 7.5 |
| 8.9 | 14.3 | 59.9 | 4.6 |
| 32.5 | 7.5 | 43.2 | 5.5 |
| 30.8 | 10.3 | 34.8 | 9.7 |
| 31.0 | 7.7 | 35.0 | 10.0 |
| 14.8 | 44.7 | 30.3 | 10.2 |
| 17.5 | 32.2 | 43.9 | 6.4 |
| 28.3 | 31.0 | 34.3 | 6.4 |
| 25.8 | 43.2 | 18.9 | 12.1 |
| 22.1 | 48.5 | 15.5 | 14.0 |

activities because agricultural loans are lumped together with other activities.

The rural nonfarm sector received the bulk of annual lending by all three programs. More than 90 percent of annual lending to the rural non-farm sector is for manufacturing, processing, livestock, poultry, fisheries, and trading. Livestock, poultry, and fisheries dominated Grameen Bank's nonfarm lending in 1994 (40 percent), followed by trading (34 percent), and manufacturing and processing (24 percent). The shares for manu-facturing and processing were smaller than in 1990. If manufacturing and processing represent high growth potential activities within the rural nonfarm sector, the distribution of Grameen's portfolio does not imply upward income mobility. In contrast, trading dominated nonfarm lending by BRAC in 1994 (42 percent), followed by manufacturing (37 percent) and livestock (9 percent). Manufacturing and processing represented a larger share of nonfarm loans in BRAC in 1994 than in previous years (except 1992). Not only that, their share of nonfarm loans was highest for BRAC among all three programs. For RD-12, livestock, poultry, and fish-eries dominated the loan portfolio in 1994 (49 percent), followed by man-ufacturing and processing (22 percent) and trading (15 percent).

How do microcredit programs compare with commercial banks, agri-cultural development banks, and informal lenders in terms of their financing of rural nonfarm activities? Because aggregate data are not available, the relative roles of different institutions are examined at the household level using the data collected in the 1991–92 survey of 1,798 households in 87 villages.

The rural nonfarm sector accounts for 48 percent of the loans advanced by formal financial institutions, 28 percent of the loans advanced by infor-mal lenders, and 60 percent of the loans advanced by microfinance insti-tutions (table 4.2). Informal lenders (family, friends, neighbors, input sup-pliers, moneylenders, and others) are more likely than other institutions to extend personal loans (which accounted for about half of the volume of informal loans).

The largest loans were extended by formal sources for nonagricultural purposes, such as the purchase of land, housing, transportation, or other inputs for nonfarm enterprises. Such loans made up 40 percent of all loans from formal institutions. Loans for these purposes made up 19 percent of the loan volume of microcredit institutions and informal lenders.

The primary purpose of loans from the three microcredit programs was to purchase nonagricultural equipment and capital. Loans for these purposes accounted for more than a third of the loan volume for each program.

Loans for the purchase of farm inputs constituted a much smaller proportion of loans from microfinance institutions than from other sources. While 23 percent of loans from formal institutions and 22 percent of loans from informal sources were extended for this purpose, only 7 percent of loans from microfinance institutions were used to finance farm inputs. Other NGOs and cooperatives provided more agricultural loans than the three microcredit programs, with loans for farm inputs accounting for 35 percent of the total loan volume.[8]

Overall, 36 percent of total loans were for nonagricultural equipment and capital. Loans for other nonagricultural purchases accounted for 19 percent of total loans, and loans for dairy cows accounted for 18 percent. Personal loans made up 15 percent of all loans, while agricultural loans made up 13 percent.

Participants in microcredit programs are much more likely than nonparticipants to borrow to finance rural nonfarm activities, with 61 percent of total loans allocated to that sector (table 4.3). Among individuals who were eligible but did not participate in any of the three

TABLE 4.2

**Size and Type of Loans by Formal, Microfinance, and Informal Lenders**
(taka)

| Type of lender | Agricultural[a] | Dairy cow | Nonagricultural equipment and capital | Other nonagricultural[b] | Personal[c] |
|---|---|---|---|---|---|
| Formal financial institutions[d] | 50,634 (22.8) | 5,190 (1.6) | 9,611 (8.2) | 64,114 (39.9) | 54,073 (27.3) |
| Microfinance institutions[e] | 3,350 (7.3) | 4,010 (24.5) | 3,387 (40.9) | 3,405 (19.2) | 3,138 (7.9) |
| Grameen Bank, BRAC, and RD-12 | 3,537 (6.8) | 4,021 (24.6) | 3,398 (41.5) | 3,411 (19.4) | 3,255 (7.7) |
| Other NGOs and cooperatives | 2,591 (35.3) | 3,268 (20.5) | 2,295 (9.1) | 3,100 (12.5) | 1,976 (22.4) |
| Informal lenders[f] | 2,483 (21.9) | 2,515 (0.4) | 3,800 (9.2) | 5,016 (18.7) | 3,482 (49.5) |
| All institutions | 3,444 (12.6) | 4,010 (17.7) | 3,843 (35.9) | 7,766 (18.5) | 5,341 (15.2) |

*Note:* Numbers in parentheses are percentages of total loans. Results are based on 2,985 observations. Totals may not sum to 100 percent because of rounding.
a. Includes the purchase or rental of deep or shallow tubewells for irrigation; the purchase of farm equipment, draft animals, or other farm inputs; and the purchase and mortgage acquisition of land.
b. Includes the purchase of a rickshaw, boat, fishing net, land, house, or other equipment for nonfarm enterprises.
c. Includes loans for activities such as consumption, house building or development, marital and other ceremonies, and consumer durables.
d. Includes the government, Krishi Bank, and commercial banks.
e. Include Grameen Bank, BRAC, RD-12, NGOs, and cooperatives.
f. Includes family, friends, neighbors, input suppliers, *mohajons* (moneylenders), landlords, employers, and others.
*Source:* BIDS–World Bank 1991/92 survey.

microcredit programs, rural nonfarm activities accounted for only 27 percent of borrowing. Among those who were ineligible to participate but borrowed from other sources, only 12 percent of borrowing was for rural nonfarm activities.

## Capital Intensity and Marginal Returns to Capital and Labor

For any production activity, it is important to measure output against inputs and the relative proportion of different types of inputs. This exercise determines the relative potential of a particular activity or a particular input for an activity, thereby establishing a basis for comparing different activities. The rural nonfarm activities discussed in this chapter were assessed using three well-defined criteria relating to inputs and output: marginal returns to capital, marginal returns to labor, and capital intensity. The output for these activities is the value of production, and the inputs are capital (fixed and working) and labor (own, family-member provided, and purchased or hired). As discussed in this section, the three measures have implications for the sources of funds for the activities involved, credit constraints of the entrepreneurs who use borrowed capi-

TABLE 4.3

**Size and Type of Loans by Program Participation Status**
(taka)

| Program participation status | Agricultural | Dairy cow | Nonagricultural equipment and capital | Other nonagricultural | Personal |
|---|---|---|---|---|---|
| Program participants | 3,498 (8.0) | 4,014 (20.8) | 3,395 (41.5) | 3,399 (19.6) | 3,281 (9.9) |
| Grameen Bank | 3,386 (5.2) | 4,130 (28.5) | 4,204 (43.6) | 3,917 (16.4) | 4,089 (6.1) |
| BRAC | 3,356 (11.6) | 4,028 (9.4) | 2,344 (42.7) | 2,998 (25.5) | 3,325 (10.7) |
| RD-12 | 4,047 (10.2) | 3,510 (16.1) | 2,590 (36.8) | 3,255 (20.6) | 2,748 (16.1) |
| Target group nonparticipants | 3,268 (24.8) | 3,315 (1.3) | 2,855 (8.7) | 4,988 (18.1) | 2,802 (47.1) |
| Nontarget group | 3,473 (52.2) | 4,036 (3.0) | 10,782 (6.0) | 57,454 (6.0) | 8,658 (32.6) |
| Total population (weighted) | 3,444 (12.6) | 4,010 (17.7) | 3,743 (35.9) | 7,766 (18.5) | 5,341 (15.2) |

*Note:* Numbers in parentheses are percentages of total loans. Totals may not sum to 100 percent because of rounding. Results are based on 2,985 observations. Loan types are defined in table 4.2.
*Source:* BIDS–World Bank 1991/92 survey.

tal for those activities, and overall market potential for the rural nonfarm sector.

## Marginal Returns to Labor and Capital

The marginal returns to labor and capital were calculated for both target and nontarget households (table 4.4).[9] The marginal return to labor for all activities was higher for nontarget (Tk 50 a day) than for target (Tk 37 a day) households. The figure for target households was close to the average daily wage of Tk 40 for nonagricultural labor. The productivity of labor in target households was highest for services (Tk 70 a day) and lowest for transport (Tk 7 a day). Interestingly, although trading was the dominant activity in the rural nonfarm sector, with 47 percent of rural households engaged in it (see figure 4.1), labor productivity (as measured by the marginal return to labor) in the sector had not fallen. The marginal return to capital for all activities was higher for target (48 percent) than for nontarget households (4 percent), possibly suggesting that target households are more capital-constrained than nontarget households. For target households the marginal return to capital was highest in manufacturing (62 percent), followed by trading (21 percent). Manufacturing seems to have provided a higher return to capital for target households than other rural nonfarm activities, providing the main source of rural nonfarm growth in Bangladesh.

## Capital Intensity of Rural Nonfarm Activities Financed by Microcredit

Capital intensity indicates the extent of capital involved in production per unit of labor and is measured by the capital-labor ratio—the sum of both fixed and working capital per day of labor. Capital intensity in rural Bangladesh was highest in trading, followed by services, manufacturing, livestock and fisheries, and transport (table 4.5).[10] Trading was found to be more capital intensive than other activities, largely because it requires working capital. Comparing the capital intensity with the estimates of marginal returns to capital reveals that returns to capital were highest in manufacturing for a given capital intensity of the production.

Capital intensity also varies by program participation status (table 4.6). Capital intensity was highest among nontarget households engaged in rural nonfarm activities, followed by Grameen Bank members, program nonparticipants, BRAC members, and RD-12 members. Among microcredit program members capital intensity was lowest for RD-12 participants and highest for Grameen Bank participants.

TABLE 4.4

**Estimated Marginal Returns to Labor and Capital for Selected Activities**

| Activity | Return to labor (taka per day) | Return to capital (percent) |
|---|---|---|
| *Manufacturing* | | |
| Target households only | 15.3 | 61.7 |
| Target and nontarget households | 17.5 | 66.9 |
| *Transport* | | |
| Target households only | 6.5 | 7.6[a] |
| Target and nontarget households | 6.4 | 7.7[a] |
| *Trading* | | |
| Target households only | 41.9 | 21.3 |
| Target and nontarget households | 27.5 | 12.4 |
| *Services* | | |
| Target households only | 69.6 | 28.1[a] |
| Target and nontarget households | 59.6 | 37.0 |
| *All activities* | | |
| Target households | 36.5 | 48.1 |
| Nontarget households | 49.8 | 4.4 |
| Target and nontarget households | 36.3 | 32.3 |

a. The *t*-statistics of labor and capital in the production function are not significant for these activities. For all other reported activities, *t*-statistics are significant at the 10 percent level or better. Livestock and fisheries were dropped because of an insignificant coefficient of capital and labor inputs in the production function.
*Source:* BIDS–World Bank 1991/92 survey.

## Do Microcredit Borrowers Generate Higher Returns to Capital and Labor over Time?

Are returns to capital higher for long-term program participants? Do rates of return to capital change with the length of participation? Are borrowers able to graduate from low-return activities to high-return activities? Do they enjoy higher returns from the same activities over time? Estimates of

TABLE 4.5

**Capital-Labor Ratios by Activity**

| Activity | Capital-labor ratio | Number of observations |
|---|---|---|
| Manufacturing | 31.7 | 449 |
| Transport | 7.3 | 415 |
| Trading | 96.9 | 1,142 |
| Livestock and fisheries | 15.5 | 218 |
| Other (mostly services) | 33.6 | 221 |
| Total | 55.3 | 2,445 |

*Source:* BIDS–World Bank 1991/92 survey.

TABLE 4.6
**Capital-Labor Ratios by Program Participation Status**

| Program participation status | Capital-labor ratio | Number of observations |
|---|---|---|
| Grameen Bank | 40.5 | 605 |
| BRAC | 36.8 | 373 |
| RD-12 | 26.0 | 547 |
| Nonparticipants | 40.2 | 661 |
| Nontarget households | 157.1 | 259 |
| Total | 55.3 | 2,445 |

Source: BIDS–World Bank 1991/92 survey.

marginal returns to capital and labor based on the Cobb-Douglas production function estimates reveal that except among Grameen Bank borrowers, the amount of capital increases with the length of program participation.[11] Long-term (five years or more) BRAC and Grameen Bank borrowers achieved higher returns to both capital and labor than RD-12 borrowers (table 4.7). This finding suggests that Grameen Bank and BRAC borrowers seem to benefit from program participation and borrowing over time. New borrowers of RD-12 had much higher returns on capital than their counterparts in other programs or longer-term borrowers of RD-12, possibly suggesting that new RD-12 borrowers were better off before joining the program than older RD-12 borrowers had been.

Do the accrued benefits from participation cover the cost of borrowing? That is, do households that borrow from microcredit programs to finance rural nonfarm activities generate enough returns to pay the cost of borrowing? Borrowers of all three microcredit programs seem to earn sufficient profits to cover their loans when the average cost of borrowing is less than 20 percent. If hidden costs are incorporated into the cost of credit, however, the effective cost of borrowing from microcredit programs is greater than 20 percent (as high as 30 percent, according to Hossain 1988). At this cost of capital many borrowers may not break even. If the interest rate is increased above 20 percent in order to make microcredit programs self-sustainable (as discussed in chapter 5), a large number of borrowers would not break even. To be able to borrow profitably at higher rates, microenterprises must be able to generate higher returns than they are currently earning. This may require a switch to more growth-oriented activities.

Another important issue is that the average size of capital increased over time for only RD-12 members (see table 4.7). For Grameen Bank and BRAC members the size of capital increased for the first 60 months but fell thereafter. Whether this reflects the lower returns earned by the borrowers or the dropout of more successful borrowers from the programs is not clear and deserves more analysis.

TABLE 4.7

**Marginal Returns to Capital and Labor for Nonfarm Activities by Length of Program Participation**

| Program and indicator | 0–36 months | 36–60 months | 60+ months | Aggregate |
|---|---|---|---|---|
| *Grameen Bank* | | | | |
| Returns to capital (percent) | 38.8 | 36.7 | 69.7 | 44.8 |
| Returns to labor (taka per day) | 34.1 | 38.5 | 39.5 | 38.1 |
| Size of capital (taka) | 17,222 | 21,402 | 12,708 | 17,760 |
| Number of observations | 118 | 264 | 222 | 604 |
| *BRAC* | | | | |
| Returns to capital (percent) | 57.7 | 22.0 | 55.8 | 44.9 |
| Returns to labor (taka per day) | 28.9 | 22.9 | 44.2 | 34.6 |
| Size of capital (taka) | 14,723 | 27,714 | 23,361 | 62,717 |
| Number of observations | 119 | 96 | 158 | 373 |
| *RD-12* | | | | |
| Returns to capital (percent) | 151.0 | 69.3 | 24.4 | 73.3 |
| Returns to labor (taka per day) | 45.2 | 38.8 | 32.8 | 40.3 |
| Size of capital (taka) | 7,088 | 13,466 | 20,976 | 12,518 |
| Number of observations | 178 | 296 | 69 | 543 |

*Source:* BIDS–World Bank 1991/92 survey.

## Extent of Capital and Credit Constraint among Borrowers

Nontarget households engaged in the rural nonfarm sector have higher capital-labor ratios and consequently higher output-labor ratios than do target program participants. In fact, the capital intensity of enterprises owned by program participants is less than 30 percent of that of nontarget households (see table 4.6). Does this suggest that program participants lack access to the funds required to switch to high-return activities or to improve returns on labor for existing activities?

Target households are severely capital-constrained, perhaps as a result of inefficient capital input markets. This constraint is clearly indicated by the very high marginal product of capital for target households, which is more than 10 times as high as that for nontarget households (see table 4.4). Household survey data were used to identify the extent of the credit constraint. The incidence of credit-constrained households was found to be highest among individuals who borrowed from government agencies and lowest among individuals who borrowed from relatives and friends (table 4.8). Among borrowers from banks the proportion of credit-constrained individuals was 63 percent for Grameen Bank, 67 percent for BRAC, 73 percent for RD-12, and 62 percent for commercial bank borrowers.

Microcredit programs, because of a shortage of funds or other reasons, are not always capable of supplying as much credit as their borrowers would like. This shortcoming may handicap rural industrialization and hence economic growth.

Households draw on various sources to finance their enterprises (table 4.9). For all groups the primary source for start-up capital was personal savings. For program participants borrowing from the programs represented the second most important source of funds.

## Market Niches for Microcredit Programs in the Rural Nonfarm Sector

If microcredit programs fail to provide the desired amount of credit to borrowers, they may not be able to retain market niches in the rural nonfarm sector and spur economic growth. Although formal and microcredit sources of financing are reaching two types of clients, they do not differ in terms of the types of activities they promote.[12] As shown earlier, both formal and microcredit institutions promote trading much more than other types of rural nonfarm activities: while about 45

TABLE 4.8
**Credit Constraints and Loan Amounts by Sources of Credit**

| Source of credit | Credit constraint (percent)[a] | Average cumulative loan amount per household (taka) | Number of observations |
|---|---|---|---|
| Grameen Bank | 63.2 | 4,211 | 817 |
| BRAC | 66.9 | 2,883 | 189 |
| RD-12 | 72.7 | 3,154 | 337 |
| Commercial banks | 62.2 | 23,156 | 9 |
| Government agencies | 93.2 | 2,512 | 11 |
| Relatives and friends | 29.7 | 4,726 | 86 |
| Other sources | 63.7 | 7,625 | 17 |
| All sources | 62.3 | 4,294 | 1,466 |

a. Percentage of borrowers whose optimum desired loan amount is higher than the actual amount received.
*Source:* BIDS–World Bank 1991/92 survey.

TABLE 4.9

**Sources of Start-Up Capital for Rural Nonfarm Activities by Program Participation Status**
(percentage of total)

| Source of start-up capital | Grameen Bank members | BRAC members | RD-12 members | Non-participants | Nontarget households |
|---|---|---|---|---|---|
| Personal savings | 49.8 | 58.7 | 58.8 | 66.5 | 82.0 |
| Relatives and friends | 4.2 | 3.2 | 6.0 | 13.1 | n.a. |
| Selling assets | 6.1 | 6.4 | 2.5 | 5.3 | 9.0 |
| Grameen Bank | 34.3 | n.a. | n.a. | n.a. | n.a. |
| BRAC | n.a. | 18.3 | n.a. | n.a. | n.a. |
| RD-12 | n.a. | n.a. | 23.1 | n.a. | n.a. |
| Commercial banks | n.a. | 0.8 | n.a. | 1.0 | 2.3 |
| Government agencies | n.a. | n.a. | 0.5 | n.a. | n.a. |
| Other sources | 5.6 | 12.7 | 9.1 | 14.1 | 6.7 |
| Number of observations | 213 | 126 | 199 | 206 | 89 |

n.a. Not applicable.
*Source:* BIDS–World Bank 1991/92 survey.

percent of microcredit program households are engaged in trading, 64 percent of nontarget households are involved in this category of rural nonfarm activities.

But despite its predominance in the rural nonfarm sector, trading has less growth potential than other activities. The activity with the most potential to promote rural growth is manufacturing and processing, which represents the second largest activity among

TABLE 4.10

**Marginal Returns to Capital and Capital-Labor Ratios by Primary Sources of Finance**

| Activity | Grameen Bank | | BRAC | |
|---|---|---|---|---|
| | Marginal return to capital | Capital-labor ratio | Marginal return to capital | Capital-labor ratio |
| Manufacturing | 0.5 | 15.5 | 0.4 | 28.0 |
| Transport | 0.2[a] | 3.1 | 0.0[a] | 30.8 |
| Trading | 0.2 | 101.0 | 0.3 | 36.9 |
| Livestock and fisheries | −0.3[a] | 18.1 | −5.4[a] | 3.5 |
| Services | 0.2 | 22.6 | 0.2 | 32.3 |
| All activities | 0.2 | 53.9 | 0.2 | 32.1 |
| Number of observations | 251 | | 69 | |

a. The *t*-statistics of capital in the production function of these activities are insignificant. For all other activities reported here, *t*-statistics are significant at the 10 percent level or better.
*Source:* BIDS–World Bank 1991/92 survey.

Grameen Bank and RD-12 program participants and the third largest activity among nontarget households involved in rural non-farm production.

Marginal returns to capital and capital intensity were calculated by primary sources of finance (table 4.10).[13] When all activities are taken into consideration, the marginal return to capital was highest for RD-12 (0.7), followed by commercial banks (0.5), Grameen Bank (0.2), and BRAC (0.2).[14] However, capital intensity (measured by the amount of capital per day of labor) was highest for commercial banks (119), followed by Grameen Bank (54), BRAC (32) and RD-12 (31).

In rural manufacturing, which is perhaps the principal source of rural industrialization and growth, the marginal return to capital is highest for commercial bank borrowers, followed by RD-12, Grameen, and BRAC borrowers. This finding suggests that RD-12 borrowers did better than other microcredit borrowers involved in manufacturing.[15] However, BRAC borrowers have the highest capital intensity in manufacturing, followed by Grameen Bank, commercial bank, and RD-12 borrowers.

## Market Size and Lack of Infrastructure as Constraints on Growth

Marginal rates of return to capital are high for most rural nonfarm activities (see table 4.4), suggesting that the market may not be a constraint on promoting sector growth. Of course, if every producer attempts to produce the same type of commodities, the market is likely to become saturated and the rate of return is bound to drop. Investment

| RD-12 | | Commercial banks | |
|---|---|---|---|
| Marginal return to capital | Capital-labor ratio | Marginal return to capital | Capital-labor ratio |
| 2.7 | 3.4 | 5.7 | 5.6 |
| 0.1[a] | 6.1 | n.a. | n.a. |
| 0.3 | 49.4 | 0.1 | 128.9 |
| 0.9[a] | 23.5 | n.a. | n.a. |
| 0.1 | 111.1 | n.a. | n.a. |
| 0.7 | 30.9 | 0.5 | 119.4 |
| 145 | | 13 | |

in infrastructure and other goods and services that facilitate the expansion of rural income and growth may increase demand for rural nonfarm goods. Such investment may prevent the returns to capital in rural nonfarm production from falling to the point that rural nonfarm production becomes unsustainable.

Two indicators of rural nonfarm growth are the size of the market and the quality of the infrastructure. Markets for rural nonfarm goods are likely to be stronger in areas with better infrastructure and high income growth, as revealed by the household survey. The survey areas can be classified as rural towns (growth centers) and purely rural areas.

The production function was fitted separately for households located in purely rural areas and households located in rural growth centers. Marginal returns to capital and labor were calculated along with the capital-labor ratios for both types of households (table 4.11). The marginal return to capital in aggregate rural nonfarm activities were higher in rural growth centers (0.5) than in purely rural areas (0.2); they were also higher for each major activity in rural growth centers. In manufacturing, for instance, marginal returns to capital were much higher in rural growth centers (1.1) than in purely rural areas (0.7). This finding shows the influence of growth centers in promoting rural industrialization and suggests that microcredit-led rural industrialization faces the problem of market saturation if it relies exclusively on local markets. Rural town markets must therefore be tapped in order to promote rural industrialization through microfinancing. Infrastructure investments—for example, in better transportation—are also necessary for sustaining rural nonfarm growth.

TABLE 4.11

**Marginal Returns to Capital and Labor and Capital-Labor Ratios for Purely Rural Areas and Rural Growth Centers**

| Activity | Purely rural areas | | | |
|---|---|---|---|---|
| | Marginal return to capital | Marginal return to labor | Capital-labor ratio | Number of observations |
| Manufacturing | 0.7 | 16.5 | 24.7 | 329 |
| Transport | −0.1[a] | 7.9 | 5.5 | 250 |
| Trading | 0.1[a] | 6.7 | 108.9 | 944 |
| Livestock and fisheries | −0.3[a] | 102.1[a] | 16.9 | 151 |
| Others | 0.1[a] | 59.9 | 32.6 | 141 |
| All activities | 0.2 | 29.1 | 60.8 | 1,730 |

a. The *t*-statistics of capital in the production function of these activities are insignificant. For all other activities reported here, *t*-statistics are significant at the 10 percent level or better.
*Source:* BIDS–World Bank 1991/92 survey.

## Summary

In a densely populated country such as Bangladesh, where agriculture offers few employment opportunities for the burgeoning labor force, expansion in rural nonfarm income and employment is necessary to promote broad-based economic growth. But Bangladesh's rural non-farm sector is dominated by rudimentary activities such as petty trading. Rural manufacturing and processing, the main source of rural industrialization and growth, accounts for only a small portion of rural nonfarm business. As the returns to capital are higher in manufacturing and processing than in trading, the dominance of trading in rural nonfarm production suggests a lack of skills among rural nonfarm producers.

Lack of access to affordable credit also appears to be a major constraint on rural nonfarm expansion. Poor producers are much more productive than richer nonfarm producers, where the capital intensity is much higher, suggesting inefficiency in the capital market.

Microcredit programs of Grameen Bank, BRAC, RD-12, and other organizations have clearly improved poor households' access to institutional credit. The rural nonfarm sector receives 60 percent of its financing from microcredit institutions. In contrast, formal financial institutions allocated only 48 percent and informal lenders only 28 percent of their funds to this sector. Better credit availability does not ensure growth in income and employment in the rural nonfarm sector, however. Skills development, market promotion, and other policies that enhance productivity must also be promoted, and the government should facilitate growth by investing in roads, electrification, and market expansion.

| Rural growth centers | | | |
| Marginal return to capital | Marginal return to labor | Capital-labor ratio | Number of observations |
| --- | --- | --- | --- |
| 1.1 | 53.6 | 39.8 | 120 |
| 0.2 | 5.7 | 10.2 | 165 |
| 0.2 | 63.7 | 75.5 | 298 |
| 1.0 | 7.9 | 13.1 | 67 |
| 0.2 | 36.6 | 34.8 | 80 |
| 0.5 | 37.4 | 47.1 | 730 |

## Notes

1. The causality between rural nonfarm growth and agricultural growth could, of course, run in either direction.

2. Evidence from India suggests that credit advanced to agriculture can also help the rural nonfarm sector grow (Binswanger and Khandker 1995).

3. Program placement of Grameen Bank, BRAC, RD-12, and commercial and agricultural development banks may not be random, in which case the estimates could be biased (see chapter 3).

4. Manufacturing includes processing of paddy and rice, handicrafts (cane and bamboo work, mat making, weaving, pottery, and so on), blacksmithing, and miscellaneous cottage or small industries. Transport includes earnings from van, rickshaw, boat, or other transport medium. Trading includes vending or hawking of rice, wheat, flour, vegetables, and fruit; grocery and stationery shops; clothing businesses; and other small, medium, and wholesale trading. Livestock and fisheries includes cattle and livestock trading, fishing, and fish-mongering. Services includes tailoring, meat slaughtering, barbering, repair work, pharmacies, contractorship, commissioning agencies, restaurants, motels and inns, and other services. Livestock and fisheries are traditionally considered part of agriculture but are classified as rural nonfarm activities when microcredit programs finance them as self-employed business activities. Farmers who own livestock and fisheries but do not borrow to finance them as part of their business activities are considered to be practicing agriculture and are excluded here.

5. The dominance of agriculture in employment is also supported by the 1991 labor force survey, which found that nonagricultural activities provide 31 percent of employment (18 percent as self-employment and 13 percent as wage employment), while agricultural activities account for the remaining 69 percent (56 percent as self-employment and 13 percent as wage employment).

6. As panel data were not available, cross-sectional data were used to analyze the program impact on productivity in the nonfarm sector. Because program placement in a village is not exogenously determined, estimates of the impact of program placement may be biased.

7. Grameen Bank's regular loans are for one year. In 1992 Grameen Bank introduced "seasonal loans," intended to be offered for a particular season (quarterly) to support members' agricultural activities on leased land.

8. Grameen Bank increased its agricultural lending in 1992. The low proportion of agricultural loans reflected in the 1991–92 household survey does not yet reflect this shift.

9. Because direct measurement of working capital is rather difficult, stocks of raw material and output were used as a proxy for working capital (Hossain 1984).

10. Trading involves mainly working capital. Because of the nature of nonfarm activities, the proportion of fixed capital in total capital (both fixed and working) is low for trading but high for manufacturing.

11. Assume that microcredit borrowers face the same production technology as target households engaged in rural nonfarm production. The Cobb-Douglas production estimates shown in table A4.2 were used to calculate the marginal

returns to capital and labor based on the average output-capital ratio and output-labor ratio for enterprises undertaken by borrowers of microcredit programs.

12. Formal banks are assumed to support mostly nontarget households (see chapter 6).

13. Individuals who used own savings as the primary source of finance are not shown in table 4.10 because they might differ from the included category of households in unobserved directions.

14. Two cautionary notes have to be made on table 4.10. First, because of a very small sample, the marginal return to capital and capital-labor ratio for commercial banks may have sample selection bias. Second, capital of RD-12 borrowers is underreported, which overestimates their return.

15. BRAC increased economywide returns most, however. Among all target households returns in manufacturing are highest in BRAC villages, followed by RD-12 and Grameen Bank villages. Relative to nonprogram villages, productivity in manufacturing among target households is 77 percent higher in BRAC villages, 41 percent higher in RD-12 villages, and 33 percent higher in Grameen Bank villages.

# 5

# Institutional and Financial Viability of Microcredit Programs

Microcredit programs have helped reduce rural poverty in Bangladesh.[1] But have they done so cost-effectively? This chapter looks at the cost of microcredit program interventions and examines the financial, economic, and institutional viability of these programs. These concepts are developed formally in appendix C.

## The Concept of Program Sustainability

Program sustainability refers to the financial, economic, and institutional viability of a program and its ability to promote economic viability among borrowers. A basic condition for sustainability is financial efficiency, that is, the ability to break even given the cost of lending. A sustainable program operates in such a way that the cost of making a loan—the cost of funds plus administrative and loan default costs—is equal to or less than the price (that is, the interest rate) it charges borrowers.

In many microcredit programs the cost of funds does not reflect market costs, because subsidized resources are used for on-lending and institutional development. Where subsidized funds are used, a program must be economically viable, in the sense that it breaks even at the opportunity cost of the subsidized funds.

## Behavioral Risk Factors in Loan Repayment

A program's sustainability depends on the resources that microcredit programs raise and control, on the repayment rate on loans, and on the programs' institutional development. Savings mobilization is an integral part of a sustainable financial institution, because it reduces dependence on external resources and the concomitant pressures from outside sources. Self-financing also improves financial discipline.

Repayment of loans depends partly on the loan recovery behavior of the borrowers, which is determined by behavioral, material, and external factors. Whether borrowers have the incentive to repay depends on individual attributes as well as socioeconomic factors. Asymmetric information is one determinant of loan repayment behavior that group-based microcredit programs try to overcome through group monitoring and social pressure to enforce loan contracts. Social or group pressure may be an overriding factor in enforcing loan contracts even if the local socioeconomic environment discourages repayment. One critical factor in the local environment is the government regulation that enforces loan contracts. In most developing countries, including Bangladesh, government enforcement of loan contracts is neither binding nor easily enforceable. Moreover, because of political reasons or social transfer policies, the government often writes off small loans or remits interest payments, which creates or promotes a culture of default.

## Material Risk Factors in Loan Repayment

Material risk factors also affect loan repayment behavior. An area's agroclimatic characteristics influence production conditions and hence the loan repayment capacity of borrowers. Better agroclimate means better income opportunities and a better repayment culture.

Concern over profitability dictates that formal financial institutions avoid lending in high-risk agroclimate areas. In contrast, microcredit institutions, which target the poor, may have to operate in risky agroclimate areas in order to reach their target population. The need to do so may reduce the financial viability of these institutions.

## Institutional Viability

Financial institutions must be institutionally viable. They must have effective procedures for ensuring administrative and management succession so that they are not dependent on the leadership of a particular person. A program's management and decisionmaking structure is one measure of its institutional viability. Institutional viability also depends on how staff and other institutional resources are allocated, how staff are remunerated, and how staff development and incentives contribute to productivity. A viable microfinance institution must allocate its resources to bring about internal cost efficiency.

An organization that delivers financial services to the poor must be client-based, and its delivery of financial services must be demand-driven. Members' demands for services are translated into program action through the program's group-based organization. An integral part of institutional viability is thus the viability of the groups formed.

Groups are the intermediaries between microcredit institutions and their members. An individual group member does not have an independent voice and can interact with programs only through his or her group. Microcredit programs interact with groups in order to reach target individuals and households. Through these interactions with group members, microcredit programs provide much more personalized services than traditional financial institutions. The sustainability of a microcredit institution depends on the viability of both groups and staff. The dynamics of groups and the management structure of the organization must be understood to determine whether a microcredit program is institutionally sustainable. This means examining the management structure, the structure of the incentive system, and the employee turnover rate.

The viability of groups ensures individuals' continued access to a microcredit program's services and thus affects the viability of borrowers and of the delivery mechanism itself: if groups are not sustainable, the group-based microcredit program cannot be sustained. Group-based lending can be risky because group cohesion is sometimes difficult to forge. Group viability depends on the willingness of members to adhere to program rules and regulations. This in turn depends on the benefits and costs of group formation and on keeping the group intact. If the costs of remaining in a group exceed the benefits, members will drop out and groups will fall apart. Examining members' dropout rate is thus a good way to evaluate the sustainability of a group-based microcredit organization. Another indicator of viability is the loan repayment behavior of members, which in turn determines the continued access of members to program services.

## Sources of Data

Program sustainability is analyzed based on program-level aggregate data as well as data collected from branch-level operations. The aggregate program-level data for Grameen Bank, BRAC, and RD-12 cover the period 1989–94. Analysis of program costs is also based on time series data for 1985–91 for a sample of 118 Grameen Bank and 126 BRAC branches and all 139 RD-12 branches. Branch-level data were complemented by thana-level data on rainfall, roads, electrification, schools, and some time-invariant characteristics, such as agroclimatic and locational factors. These branch- and program-level data were used to determine the cost of delivering financial services to the poor and the cost of developing an institution to deliver such services. Because not all data were comparable, economic analyses of the cost and revenue structures could not be performed for all three programs.

## Outreach

Microcredit programs are evaluated by their outreach not only in terms of their area coverage but also in terms of membership, the volume of lending, and the level of savings. A microcredit program's volume of lending and the level of members' savings indicate the depth of this outreach. Outreach can be increased by expanding membership within an existing branch network or by extending the branch network. Increasing membership per branch is probably less expensive.

### Growth in the Number of Village-Level Organizations and Branches

The number of village-level organizations operated by the three microcredit institutions grew rapidly in the early 1990s, increasing from fewer than 40,000 in 1989 to more than 100,000 in 1994 (table 5.1). The number of villages served also rose significantly. In 1994 Grameen served 34,913 villages, BRAC served 13,224 villages, and RD-2 served 14,577 villages.

All three programs have vertical hierarchical structures, in which village organizations are conglomerations of groups of five to eight members. These village-level organizations are federated under branches of Grameen Bank and BRAC or under thana-level offices such as the thana bittaheen central cooperative societies (TBCCSs) of RD-12. The branches of Grameen Bank and BRAC are controlled by an area office, which is under the control of a regional or zonal office, which in turn is under the supervision of the head office. In contrast, the TBCCSs of RD-12 are supervised by the head office in Dhaka. Grameen Bank calls its village-level organizations "centers," BRAC calls them "village organizations,"

TABLE 5.1

**Villages Covered and Number of Village-Based Organizations of Grameen Bank, BRAC, and RD-12, 1989–94**

| Year | Number of villages covered | | | Number of village-based organizations | | |
|---|---|---|---|---|---|---|
| | Grameen Bank | BRAC | RD-12 | Grameen Bank | BRAC | RD-12 |
| 1989 | 15,073 | 3,307 | 4,720 | 26,976 | 6,434 | 6,294 |
| 1990 | 19,536 | 4,238 | 6,499 | 34,206 | 8,263 | 8,124 |
| 1991 | 25,248 | 5,337 | 9,610 | 42,751 | 11,391 | 11,107 |
| 1992 | 30,619 | 6,878 | 12,201 | 51,367 | 13,967 | 14,355 |
| 1993 | 33,667 | 10,379 | 13,348 | 57,649 | 20,141 | 16,305 |
| 1994 | 34,913 | 13,224 | 14,577 | 59,921 | 24,859 | 16,565 |

*Source:* Khandker and Khalily 1996; Khandker, Khalily, and Khan 1995; Khandker, Khan, and Khalily 1995.

and RD-12 calls them "bittaheen [landless] societies." Grameen Bank had 26,976 centers in 1989 and 59,921 centers in 1994 (see table 5.1). BRAC had 6,434 village organizations in 1989 and 24,859 in 1994. RD-12 had 6,294 bittaheen societies in 1989 and 16,565 in 1994.

Branch-level program expansion was also rapid over the 1989–94 period (not reported in the table). Grameen Bank increased the number of branches from 641 in 1989 to 1,045 in 1994. BRAC expanded its branch network from 81 branches in 1989 to 195 branches in 1994. RD-12 increased its number of branches from 45 in 1989 to 119 in 1994.

## Growth in the Number of Members

Membership, the best indicator of a program's outreach, grew significantly between 1989 and 1994 at all three institutions, rising by about 24 percent a year at Grameen Bank and RD-12 and by 21 percent a year at BRAC (table 5.2). The percentage of women served rose as well: in 1994 women accounted for 94 percent of Grameen Bank's members, 88 percent of BRAC's members, and 70 percent of RD-12's members, a significant increase since 1989.

Unlike BRAC and RD-12, Grameen Bank is a specialized chartered bank, and its prime objective is lending. More than 90 percent of Grameen's members have thus been borrowers. BRAC and RD-12

TABLE 5.2

**Members and Borrowers of Grameen Bank, BRAC, and RD-12, 1989–94**

| Year | Number of members (thousands) | | | Borrowers as percentage of members | | |
|------|---------------|------|--------|---------------|------|------|
| | Grameen Bank | BRAC | RD-12[a] | Grameen Bank | BRAC | RD-12 |
| 1989 | 662.3 (88.9) | 352.3 (61.2) | 154.2 (35.5) | 97.9 (88.7) | 52.5 (57.6) | 10.9 (40.0) |
| 1990 | 869.5 (91.0) | 460.8 (64.4) | 198.1 (37.7) | 98.1 (91.0) | 53.5 (55.1) | 24.0 (42.0) |
| 1991 | 1,066.4 (92.5) | 598.1 (67.9) | 267.5 (46.1) | 97.7 (92.4) | 69.3 (67.1) | 39.2 (46.0) |
| 1992 | 1,424.4 (93.7) | 649.3 (74.2) | 346.3 (59.1) | 97.3 (93.6) | 66.4 (65.5) | 43.6 (59.3) |
| 1993 | 1,814.9 (94.1) | 825.8 (82.2) | 427.7 (67.7) | 92.7 (94.2) | 64.2 (57.7) | 63.7 (73.3) |
| 1994 | 2,015.1 (93.9) | 1,036.3 (87.7) | 452.0 (69.7) | 92.4 (94.2) | 71.4 (71.6) | 69.9 (77.1) |

*Note:* Numbers in parentheses are percentages of women in each category.
a. Mobilized members.
*Source:* Khandker and Khalily 1996; Khandker, Khalily, and Khan 1995; Khandker, Khan, and Khalily 1995.

provide funds only after training in skills development and social intermediation. Thus a smaller proportion of their members are borrowers,
although the figure has also risen significantly over time.

Membership growth per administrative unit—which measures the
depth of a program's outreach—can be calculated from tables 5.1 and
5.2 and from branch information mentioned before. In 1994 membership per branch was 1,928 for Grameen Bank, 5,314 for BRAC, and
3,252 for RD-12, indicating that Grameen Bank followed a horizontal
program expansion while BRAC and RD-12 increased outreach within
branches.

## Growth in Loan Disbursement, Loans Outstanding, and Member Savings

Annual disbursements by all three institutions increased significantly
between 1990 and 1994, growing at an average annual rate of 47 percent
a year at Grameen Bank, 45 percent a year at BRAC, and 64 percent a
year at RD-12 (table 5.3). These growth rates are higher than the rate
of growth of membership, indicating an increase in average loan size.

All three programs mobilize savings (mostly involuntary) from members. For all three programs the ratio of savings to loans outstanding fell
over the 1990–94 period, reflecting the large increase in outstanding
loans. In 1994 member savings accounted for 25 percent of Grameen

TABLE 5.3
**Loan Disbursements, Loans Outstanding, and Member Savings at Grameen Bank, BRAC, and RD-12, 1990–94**

| Item | 1990 | 1991 | 1992 | 1993 | 1994 |
|------|------|------|------|------|------|
| Annual disbursement (millions of taka) | | | | | |
| Grameen Bank | 2,656.1 | 3,706.8 | 6,361.1 | 12,443.0 | 15,395.3 |
| BRAC | 393.4 | 604.6 | 733.4 | 1,730.5 | 2,210.0 |
| RD-12 | 65.6 | 124.3 | 307.8 | 659.8 | 706.5 |
| Loans outstanding (millions of taka) | | | | | |
| Grameen Bank | 2,117.4 | 2,551.2 | 4,423.9 | 8,763.6 | 11,053.7 |
| BRAC | 350.6 | 578.3 | 645.9 | 928.1 | 1,352.3 |
| RD-12 | 43.2 | 105.4 | 195.9 | 361.2 | 275.5 |
| Savings-loans outstanding ratio (percent) | | | | | |
| Grameen Bank | 30.3 | 32.7 | 27.1 | 22.3 | 25.4 |
| BRAC | 44.3 | 44.8 | 45.9 | 42.8 | 34.7 |
| RD-12 | 99.1 | 62.3 | 51.4 | 44.9 | 76.9 |

*Source:* Khandker and Khalily 1996; Khandker, Khalily, and Khan 1995; Khandker, Khan, and
Khalily 1995.

TABLE 5.4

**Funds Received by Grameen Bank and BRAC, 1986–94**

| | Grameen Bank | | BRAC | |
|---|---|---|---|---|
| Year | Total (millions of taka) | Share of foreign funds in total (percent) | Total (millions of taka) | Share of foreign funds in total (percent) |
| 1986 | 887.0 | 90.9 | 53.5 | 100 |
| 1987 | 905.6 | 97.9 | 80.9 | 100 |
| 1988 | 1,413.5 | 99.0 | 67.3 | 100 |
| 1989 | 2,097.3 | 90.8 | 138.7 | 100 |
| 1990 | 2,853.7 | 93.6 | 437.8 | 100 |
| 1991 | 3,227.6 | 94.6 | 741.1 | 100 |
| 1992 | 4,324.1 | 99.9 | 512.2 | 100 |
| 1993 | 8,356.3 | 58.1 | 442.3 | 100 |
| 1994 | 7,011.5 | 3.7 | 1,095.9 | 100 |

Source: Khandker and Khalily 1996; Khandker, Khalily, and Khan 1995; Khandker, Khan, and Khalily 1995.

Bank's loans outstanding, 35 percent of BRAC's loans outstanding, and 77 percent of RD-12's loans outstanding.

Donor and government funds were instrumental in funding the phenomenal growth and development of the three programs (table 5.4). Grameen Bank received more than Tk 7 billion in grants in 1994, while BRAC received Tk 1.1 billion in 1994. RD-12 received Can$53 million from the Canadian International Development Agency (CIDA), which represented more than 95 percent of its total funding for the six-year project starting in 1988; data are not reported in the table. Although donor funding remains high, dependence on donors has declined. Grameen Bank has been particularly successful in reducing foreign dependence. In 1992 more than 99 percent of Grameen's funding came from foreign donors; by 1994 the figure had fallen to just 4 percent. Most of Grameen Bank's funding now comes from local donors.

## Institutional Structure and Efficiency

Both Grameen Bank and BRAC have depended largely on the ideas, commitment, organizational capabilities, and leadership of a single person (Muhammad Yunus at Grameen and F. H. Abed at BRAC). The successful replication of their ideas and the expansion of microcredit programs' branches across Bangladesh owes much to the decentralized administrative structure of these organizations and their professionalization of management. RD-12 is based on the bureaucratic cooperative structure of the Bangladesh Rural Development Board (BRDB). But the RD-2 project has introduced some form of both incentives and accountability for field-level staff.

## Institutional Hierarchy

Initially, both Grameen Bank and BRAC were composed of a head office and a few branches guided by the head office. As the organizations grew, decentralization became critical for ensuring efficient decisionmaking at all operational levels. Zonal or regional offices were established when the number of branches increased, and the leadership gradually delegated more decisionmaking authority to these intermediate administrative units. Grameen Bank and BRAC thus did not decentralize deliberately; they did so naturally as they grew. Field-level managers have authority to plan, organize, and implement the organization's policies and services at various levels, with little supervision from the head office or the zonal or regional offices. This devolution of many decisionmaking roles to the regional or zonal offices and the flexibility in branch operations allow the head office and the central leadership to focus on broader issues of policy and institutional development. Unlike many governmental and nongovernmental organizations that follow hierarchic and mechanistic organizational structures, both Grameen Bank and BRAC have few mechanistic procedures, and only a few intermediate levels exist between senior management and field-level management.

At the top of the management structures of Grameen Bank and BRAC, a board of directors, including the managing or executive director (Dr. Yunus and Mr. Abed, respectively), is responsible for planning, designing, implementing, monitoring, and evaluating activities. Members of Grameen Bank hold shares and contribute to equity, and representatives of shareholding Grameen members sit on its board. About 2 million members have bought shares valued at Tk 100 each, representing more than 90 percent of Grameen Bank's equity. The members' representatives are chosen through an elective process at the village centers. Currently, 9 of the 13 board members are shareholder representatives. BRAC's ultimate authority rests with a general body composed of nine members, seven of whom are elected to the governing body, which appoints the executive director. RD-12 has a two-way interaction between the project director and his small head office staff and the rural development officer in charge of the TBCCSs office.

In all three programs most of the central decisionmaking functions rely on field-level data, which are collected, analyzed, and disseminated by the monitoring and evaluation unit located in the head office. Monitoring and evaluation are critical to these organizations' operations, providing continuous feedback from field-level operations. The head office monitors the performance of branches and TBCCSs in terms of loan disbursement, savings mobilization, loan recovery, and so on from periodic information reported by zonal or regional offices. The comprehensive reporting forms the basis of the built-in learning process observed in these microfinance institutions. This information is also monitored daily by branch managers, who prepare statements for the head office.

## Staff Training, Incentives, and Performance

Professional management is a second important component of institutional viability. At both Grameen Bank and BRAC the management style has evolved in an effort to provide a range of financial and nonfinancial services to the rural poor. Management training combines learning, innovation, and flexibility at all levels (Fuglesang and Chandler 1988; Lovell 1992). Built-in adaptability has been refined through field-level experiences and is developed by the programs' in-house training and resource centers. The approach to training is innovative, featuring a structured learning process that is continuously fine-tuned by trial and error. Management training is developed and implemented in such a way that branch managers are able to plan, organize, and implement bank programs without extensive supervision from the head office. The importance attached to training is evident in the size of the training budget, which in 1992 accounted for 4.3 percent of Grameen's total expenditures and 3.7 percent of BRAC's total expenditures.

At BRAC, entry-level personnel are program organizers. They must be university graduates and are selected only after a careful screening process that includes written and oral examinations. Most of BRAC's managers started out as program organizers. Grameen Bank recruits two types of people at the entry level: bank workers and trainee branch managers. Bank workers must have higher secondary school certificates; trainee branch managers must be university graduates. RD-12 recruits university graduates to work as rural development officers at the thana level.

All three programs strongly emphasize the training of new recruits. Most officers receive introductory training at the head office and spend a probationary year in the field. Training for new staff is mainly hands-on, with most of the year spent at branch offices. Trainees work directly with villagers, leading and participating in discussions at regular group meetings. In addition to learning about the program and its procedures, they are required to familiarize themselves with local conditions and prepare detailed case studies of borrowers. They are given open-ended guidelines and are expected to act independently and flexibly. Training is very rigorous, and many recruits find it difficult, with more than a third of Grameen Bank's new recruits and half of BRAC's new recruits dropping out of the program.

Grameen Bank employees are paid according to the wage scale of the Bangladesh Bank. BRAC has its own wage structure, which is very competitive with the private sector. RD-12 uses the government pay scale. BRAC pays more than Grameen Bank or RD-12, with an average annual salary for branch managers of 7.5 times national per capita income (table A5.1). At Grameen Bank and RD-12 the average manager earns about four times national per capita income.

Branch managers are promoted based on performance and seniority. Almost all managerial staff assigned to the head office and regional offices have years of experience at the branch level. Branch-level training and experience is thus crucial for guiding program policies and decisionmaking. Managers' backgrounds and performance play an important role in determining promotions.

## Staff Growth, Staff Retention, and Staff Productivity

Staff size fell slightly at Grameen Bank in the early 1990s, to just under 11,000 in 1994 (table 5.5). Over the same period BRAC and RD-12 more than doubled the size of their staffs. In 1994 about 75 percent of Grameen Bank's staff, 71 percent of BRAC's staff, and 82 percent of RD-12 staff were field-level staff (excluding branch managers) directly in contact with members on a day-to-day basis. The staff retention level is high and rising for both Grameen Bank and BRAC. RD-12 loses more staff, with an annual dropout rate of 8 percent.

TABLE 5.5

**Staff Size and Dropout Rates for Grameen Bank, BRAC, and RD-12, 1990–94**

| Year | Staff size | | | Annual staff dropout rate (percent) | | |
|---|---|---|---|---|---|---|
| | Grameen Bank | BRAC | RD-12 | Grameen Bank | BRAC | RD-12 |
| 1990 | 11,964 (80.9) | 1,667 (66.6) | 1,279 (66.6) | 9.0 | 6.7 | 0 |
| 1991 | 10,904 (76.3) | 1,977 (65.8) | 1,817 (74.9) | 8.5 | 11.0 | 0 |
| 1992 | 10,531 (75.2) | 2,653 (68.6) | 2,254 (79.7) | 7.9 | 5.6 | 0 |
| 1993 | 10,499 (74.5) | 3,067 (69.9) | 2,474 (81.4) | 2.7 | 4.1 | 2.5 |
| 1994 | 10,861 (75.3) | 3,464 (70.9) | 2,550 (81.9) | 1.9 | 4.0 | 7.9 |

Note: Numbers in parentheses are field-level staff as a percentage of total staff.
Source: Khandker and Khalily 1996; Khandker, Khalily, and Khan 1995; Khandker, Khan, and Khalily 1995.

TABLE 5.6
**Staff Productivity at Grameen Bank, BRAC, and RD-12, 1990–94**

| | Members per staff | | |
| --- | --- | --- | --- |
| Year | Grameen Bank | BRAC | RD-12 |
| 1990 | 73 | 276 | 155 |
| 1991 | 98 | 303 | 147 |
| 1992 | 135 | 245 | 154 |
| 1993 | 173 | 269 | 173 |
| 1994 | 186 | 299 | 177 |

Source: Khandker and Khalily 1996; Khandker, Khalily, and Khan 1995; Khandker, Khan, and Khalily 1995.

Staff productivity is measured by the number of mobilized members, annual disbursement, and member savings per staff member. Since 1990 BRAC has had the highest ratio of members per staff (table 5.6). This higher ratio partly reflects the fact that unlike Grameen Bank and RD-12, BRAC is a multipurpose organization that provides not only credit but also noncredit services, such as consciousness-raising and literacy programs. The number of members per staff fluctuated only slightly for BRAC and RD-12 between 1990 and 1994. The ratio at Grameen Bank more than doubled, rising from 73 in 1990 to 186 in 1994. In terms of loan disbursement and savings mobilization, Grameen Bank staff are more productive than their counterparts in BRAC and RD-12, mobilizing more savings and disbursing more funds per staff member than either of the other programs.

## Pay Structure

Employment in microfinance institutions is more than a job—it involves working with poor people and changing their lives through lending and other services. The staff of microfinance institutions are likely to be highly motivated social workers. Nevertheless, to maximize their productivity, proper incentives must be in place.

In all three programs salaries are based on both experience and education. The estimated rate of return to education (that is, the increase in salary for each additional year of education) is about 7 percent at Grameen Bank and 6 percent at BRAC and RD-12 (see table A5.1).[2] The estimated rate of return to one additional year of service is 3 percent at Grameen Bank, 6 percent at BRAC, and 7 percent at RD-12. BRAC thus rewards experience slightly more than Grameen Bank and RD-12, while Grameen Bank rewards education slightly more than other programs.

| Annual disbursement per staff (thousands of taka) | | | Member savings per staff (thousands of taka) | | |
|---|---|---|---|---|---|
| Grameen Bank | BRAC | RD-12 | Grameen Bank | BRAC | RD-12 |
| 222.0 | 236.0 | 51.3 | 53.7 | 93.3 | 33.5 |
| 339.9 | 306.8 | 68.4 | 76.6 | 130.9 | 36.1 |
| 604.0 | 277.9 | 136.6 | 113.8 | 111.8 | 44.7 |
| 1,185.2 | 564.2 | 266.7 | 186.2 | 129.5 | 65.5 |
| 1,417.5 | 638.0 | 277.1 | 258.5 | 135.5 | 83.1 |

Analysis of salaries of branch managers reveals a small number of women managers in all three programs—4 percent at Grameen Bank, 6 percent at BRAC, and 15 percent at RD-12. At Grameen Bank male managers are paid 4 percent more than their female counterparts with the same age, education, and experience.[3]

### Group Viability: Member Dropout Rates

Because the poor are illiterate and often lack any organization through which to channel resources (particularly public resources) to their advantage, they need to be organized before they can gain access to bank credit. In Bangladesh, where all microfinance institutions mobilize their clients into groups, the sustainability of the group determines the sustainability of the program.

Group viability depends on the willingness of group members to adhere to the program rules. Whether members abide by these rules depends on the benefits they accrue from being part of the group and how well groups are disciplined with the active support of the field-level staff. Members' benefits include gaining access to institutional credit at a much lower rate than the informal lending rate, to training and other organizational inputs that promote trade-specific and managerial skills, and to social intermediation inputs that encourage social and financial discipline. Group dynamics depend on the staff's commitment to enforcing the program through interaction with and close monitoring of the groups. Thus two main factors determine groups' viability: members' alternative sources of funding and income and staff effectiveness.

Overall the annual membership dropout rate from all three programs is low (table 5.7). The high dropout rate at BRAC for both men (38 percent) and women (8 percent) in 1992 is attributable to policy changes, not an exogenous deterioration in group behavior. In 1992 BRAC adopted a policy of allowing only one member per household. It

TABLE 5.7
**Annual Member Dropout Rates for Grameen Bank, BRAC, and RD-12, 1986–94**
(percent)

| Year | Grameen Bank | | |
| | Male | Female | Total |
| --- | --- | --- | --- |
| 1986 | 3.8 | 4.2 | 3.5 |
| 1987 | 4.1 | 3.8 | 3.9 |
| 1988 | 2.9 | 3.8 | 3.7 |
| 1989 | 2.3 | 3.5 | 3.3 |
| 1990 | 2.7 | 4.5 | 4.4 |
| 1991 | 3.3 | 5.0 | 4.9 |
| 1992 | 2.4 | 4.4 | 4.3 |
| 1993 | 1.4 | 2.3 | 2.2 |
| 1994 | 6.4 | 4.5 | 4.6 |

n.a. Not available.
*Source:* Khandker and Khalily 1996; Khandker, Khalily, and Khan 1995; Khandker, Khan, and Khalily 1995.

also expelled members who defaulted on loan repayment or failed to keep up with organizational disciplines.

The dropout rate is affected by the benefits and costs of remaining with a program. If the benefits of remaining in or joining a program are higher than the opportunity cost of doing so, the dropout rate will be low. What specific factors determine the dropout rate, and what is the mechanism by which they do so?

At Grameen Bank rural electrification increased the dropout rate (table A5.2). At BRAC investment in roads reduced the dropout rate. Rural electrification and roads facilitate alternative income-earning opportunities for the poor. The presence of such infrastructure may have encouraged Grameen members to drop out. It may also have provided opportunities for self-employment if microcredit programs provide credit and training to facilitate the transition to self-employment in the rural nonfarm sector. The presence of such infrastructure may have encouraged members to remain with BRAC, explaining the low dropout rate. The dropout rate also depends on staff's input in terms of training and organizational input. While staff input is measured by the predicted salary of branch managers, organizational input is measured by the organization's investment in members' training, assuming that effective financial incentives can reduce the dropout rate.

Branch age is an important factor determining dropout rates at Grameen Bank (see table A5.2). Initially the dropout rate of Grameen Bank members increased with branch age, but as branches matured, this rate fell. Salaries of branch managers also affect member dropout rates. A

| | BRAC | | | RD-12 | |
|---|---|---|---|---|---|
| Male | Female | Total | Male | Female | Total |
| 1.0 | 0.6 | 0.8 | n.a. | n.a. | n.a. |
| 1.1 | 0.6 | 0.8 | n.a. | n.a. | n.a. |
| 0.9 | 0.5 | 0.7 | n.a. | n.a. | n.a. |
| 2.3 | 1.0 | 1.5 | 0.6 | 0.9 | 0.7 |
| 2.2 | 1.4 | 1.6 | 1.3 | 2.5 | 1.8 |
| 5.2 | 4.7 | 4.8 | 1.5 | 3.8 | 2.6 |
| 37.6 | 8.3 | 15.8 | 1.5 | 4.8 | 3.4 |
| 19.7 | 7.3 | 9.5 | 1.8 | 5.2 | 4.1 |
| 32.9 | 2.6 | 6.3 | 2.0 | 7.3 | 5.7 |

10 percent increase in managers' salaries reduced dropout rates by 2 percent at Grameen Bank. Member training in employment and income generation increased dropout rates, while training in other skills reduced them. This suggests that the positive externality of training is not neutral. Primary school density increased BRAC's dropout rate, while secondary school density reduced Grameen Bank's rate.

## Financial Viability

This section is based largely on financial data for Grameen Bank and BRAC; aggregate financial data were not available for RD-12. A formal analysis of this topic appears in appendix C.

### Are Microfinance Institutions Profitable?

If a microcredit program is to maintain its capital holdings, it must generate sufficient revenue to meet its operating costs, including the costs of administering loans, mobilizing and training groups, mobilizing funds for on-lending, and covering bad debts. The break-even interest rate is defined as the rate at which the cost of operation (administrative, borrowing, and default cost) equals interest income per dollar from lending. If the break-even interest rate exceeds the average on-lending rate, the microcredit program is not financially viable and requires a financial subsidy. If the break-even interest rate is lower than the average on-lending rate, the program earns a profit.

TABLE 5.8

**Cost Structure of Lending and Break-Even Interest Rates at Grameen Bank and BRAC, 1990–94**

(per taka, annual disbursement)

| Item | Grameen Bank | | | | |
|---|---|---|---|---|---|
| | 1990 | 1991 | 1992 | 1993 | 1994 |
| Total expenses as share of annual disbursement | 0.15 | 0.15 | 0.12 | 0.11 | 0.13 |
| Default costs | 0.05 | 0.07 | 0.04 | 0.04 | 0.04 |
| Break-even interest rate | 0.21 | 0.23 | 0.17 | 0.15 | 0.17 |
| Average on-lending interest rate | 0.12 | 0.14 | 0.15 | 0.16 | 0.17 |

Source: Khandker and Khalily 1996; Khandker, Khalily, and Khan 1995; Khandker, Khan, and Khalily 1995.

Both Grameen Bank and BRAC have been charging 20 percent a year on loans since 1991. Grameen Bank also offers a 10-year housing loan at 8 percent a year, which lowers its average on-lending rate. The break-even interest rate for BRAC was higher than its average on-lending rate until 1994 (table 5.8). Grameen Bank appears to have attained similar financial efficiency in 1993 (although as is shown later, this apparent financial efficiency is misleading, since the borrowing cost of on-lending funds is highly subsidized by donors).

One traditional indicator of profitability is the financial margin or net interest margin, defined as interest revenue minus interest expenses divided by average assets. Estimates of financial margins for BRAC's Rural Credit Program (RCP) and BRAC as a whole reveal that although BRAC as a whole incurred losses during the study period, the RCP, which is a four-year graduate of the Rural

TABLE 5.9

**Financial Margins and Profits at Grameen Bank and BRAC, 1991–94**

(percentage of assets unless otherwise noted)

| Item | Grameen Bank | | | |
|---|---|---|---|---|
| | 1991 | 1992 | 1993 | 1994 |
| Interest revenue | 10.7 | 12.0 | 12.8 | 13.5 |
| Interest expenses | 2.7 | 3.3 | 4.0 | 5.6 |
| Operating expenses | 9.6 | 10.1 | 9.7 | 8.5 |
| Salaries | 6.1 | 6.6 | 6.1 | 4.1 |
| Training | 1.4 | 0.8 | 0.1 | 0.3 |
| Other costs | 2.1 | 2.6 | 3.1 | 4.0 |
| Financial margin | 8.0 | 8.7 | 8.8 | 7.9 |
| Reported profits (millions of taka) | 11.9 | −5.7 | 9.6 | 21.7 |

Note: Financial margin is interest revenue minus interest expenses.
Source: Khandker and Khalily 1996; Khandker, Khalily, and Khan 1995; Khandker, Khan, and Khalily 1995.

| | BRAC | | |
|---|---|---|---|
| 1991 | 1992 | 1993 | 1994 |
| 0.36 | 0.35 | 0.18 | 0.15 |
| 0.07 | 0.05 | 0.05 | 0.03 |
| 0.47 | 0.43 | 0.24 | 0.19 |
| 0.17 | 0.22 | 0.22 | 0.21 |

Development Program (RDP), earned profits (table 5.9). In 1994 some 45 percent of BRAC's credit programs were part of the RCP and hence profitable. About two-thirds of Grameen Bank's branches earned profits in 1994. The financial margin was 7.9 percent for Grameen Bank, 9.4 percent for BRAC's RCP, and 9.6 percent for BRAC as a whole in 1994. These figures are 3–4 percentage points higher than the financial margin of commercial and development banks in the formal sector (see chapter 6). But because both onlending and institutional development funds are highly subsidized, the higher financial margins do not indicate profitability of the microcredit programs; profits include grants and so do not reflect the underlying subsidy dependence of these programs. When grants are excluded from the calculation, Grameen Bank does not earn a profit (Khandker, Khalily, and Khan 1995).

| BRAC's Rural Credit Program only | | | | BRAC as a whole | | | |
|---|---|---|---|---|---|---|---|
| 1991 | 1992 | 1993 | 1994 | 1991 | 1992 | 1993 | 1994 |
| 13.9 | 14.8 | 11.8 | 10.4 | 7.7 | 8.7 | 8.5 | 10.3 |
| 1.8 | 2.2 | 1.6 | 1.0 | 1.6 | 1.7 | 1.5 | 0.7 |
| 8.0 | 7.7 | 7.9 | 9.8 | 24.8 | 22.9 | 29.5 | 11.2 |
| 4.6 | 4.8 | 4.9 | 5.4 | 8.8 | 8.3 | 11.7 | 6.6 |
| 0.2 | 0.3 | 0.3 | 0.1 | 5.6 | 6.4 | 5.8 | 0.1 |
| 3.3 | 2.6 | 2.8 | 4.4 | 10.4 | 8.3 | 12.0 | 4.6 |
| 12.1 | 12.6 | 10.3 | 9.4 | 6.1 | 7.0 | 7.0 | 9.6 |
| 17.9 | 41.9 | 32.0 | 51.1 | −116.7 | −71.9 | −75.3 | −53.7 |

## What Determines the Loan Recovery Rate?

The loan recovery rates of all three microcredit programs exceeded 90 percent (Khandker, Khalily, and Khan 1995; Khandker, Khan, and Khalily 1995; Khandker and Khalily 1996). Loan recovery rates were at least 7 percent higher for women than men in all three programs, indicating that women are not higher credit risks, as is sometimes assumed (Rashid and Townsend 1994). Why is the loan recovery rate of microcredit programs so high relative to formal financial institutions?[4] According to one school of thought, group-based lending introduces peer pressure and monitoring (Stiglitz 1990) and can create social pressure to enforce loan contracts (Besley and Coate 1995). An alternative theory proposes that the high morale of program workers, their accountability, the transparency of loan transactions, and the staff incentive structure are the sources of the high loan recovery rates (Jain 1996).

Loan recovery rates from 118 Grameen branches and 109 RD-12 TBCCSs were regressed against branch manager salaries and other variables (table A5.3). The results show that staff incentives, as measured by the predicted salary of the branch manager, are not an indicator of high loan recovery rates. Branch age and area infrastructure investments accounted for about 55 percent of the variation in loan recovery rates of Grameen branches and 38 percent of variations in RD-12 TBCCSs. At RD-12 recovery rates were higher for younger branches. Investment in staff at Grameen Bank was also associated with higher branch-level loan recovery.

For Grameen Bank and RD-12 the density of roads was associated with higher loan recovery rates. This partly reflects the impact of roads on the income gains of microenterprises supported by microfinance institutions. Better school infrastructure, especially secondary schools, was associated with higher loan recovery rates at RD-12 branches but not at Grameen Bank branches. Higher rainfall was associated with higher loan recovery rates for Grameen Bank but lower rates for RD-12. Deviations from average rainfall acted as a good agroclimate condition, raising loan recovery rates at RD-12 branches. Variations in these findings partly highlight the different types of activities financed by these two programs. The presence of traditional bank branches was associated with higher recovery rates at Grameen branches but lower rates for RD-12 branches. These findings clearly indicate that the loan recovery rate of microfinance institutions is not inflexibly determined by program design, such as group pressure, or by staff morale.

## Marginal Cost of Membership, Lending, and Savings

Even with the favorable financial margins shown in table 5.9, microcredit programs cannot break even. Part of the problem is the high cost of operation. Administrative costs represent about 50 percent of total operating costs. To attain financial viability, microcredit programs must achieve cost-efficiency. Although Grameen Bank and BRAC do not have strict commercial objectives, their branches have the commercial objective of minimizing costs. Branches receive funds from the head office at the market rate of on-lending funds and are supposed to earn profits. BRAC's objective is more specific: it allows branches to receive subsidies for up to four years, after which they become part of the RCP and must finance themselves.

To earn profits, branches should minimize the cost of financial intermediation. Given its mandate to reach as many poor people as possible within a designated area, a typical branch aims to increase membership, credit disbursement, and savings mobilization. The transactions costs of member mobilization are high, given the training and other social intermediation aspects involved. The transactions costs of lending fall as more lending is done. Increasing membership yields more weekly savings, at a rate of Tk 1–Tk 2 per member. Increasing lending also increases savings, since 5 percent of each loan must be deposited. Because of the lack of prudent supervision and regulation, programs such as BRAC and RD-12 cannot mobilize savings from nonmembers. This restricts mobilization of savings to program members. Profit maximization thus requires increasing lending per borrower and increasing the levels of savings, which in turn depends on the loan absorption capacity and income-generating ability of the poor. To increase the ability of the poor to generate income, microcredit programs enhance members' skills through training and other social development programs. Expansion of microcredit programs thus involves additional labor and capital costs.

To find out whether the microcredit programs are cost-effective, a translog cost function was estimated using branch-level data. The cost function relates the total cost of a branch to its membership, loan volume, and savings, as well as to the price of labor and capital and control variables, such as infrastructure.[5] The estimated marginal costs of membership, lending, and savings mobilization are presented in table A5.4. The marginal cost of membership is positive (Tk 138) at Grameen Bank but insignificant (zero) at BRAC and RD-12. The marginal cost of lending is positive for all three programs (Tk 1.6 per Tk 100 of disbursement at Grameen Bank, Tk 10.1 at BRAC, and Tk 6.9 at RD-12).[6] The marginal cost of savings is not statistically different from zero at any of the programs. This is not surprising, since savings are a fixed proportion of membership and lending and savings are almost never mobilized from nonmembers.

How do the costs of making a loan to a new member compare across the three institutions? Consider the cost of admitting a new member and lending him or her Tk 2,000. At BRAC and RD-12 the marginal cost of membership is insignificant (zero), so the marginal cost of the loan is simply the marginal cost of lending (10.1 percent for BRAC and 6.9 percent for RD-12). At Grameen Bank the marginal cost of admitting a new member is Tk 138, and the marginal cost of making a loan is 1.6 percent of the loan. Thus a Tk 2,000 loan to a new member costs Grameen Bank Tk 170 (Tk 138 + Tk 32), or 8.5 percent of the loan. The fact that the marginal cost of membership is positive and the marginal cost of lending is low means that larger loans are more cost-effective at Grameen. None of the three programs is operating at the level at which the marginal cost of the loan equals the marginal revenue (the on-lending rate).

Estimates show that it takes about five years for an average Grameen or BRAC branch to break even (Khandker and Khalily 1996; Khandker, Khalily, and Khan 1995). Both institutions cross-subsidize new branches with the profits of older branches, and both subsidize branch staff training costs and other institutional development costs using grants or soft loans. At an on-lending rate of 15 percent, branches of all three institutions are cost-effective when the marginal cost of lending (including the cost of membership mobilization) is 10 percent of lending. If the cost of the head office is more than 5 percent of lending and this cost is added to the branch-level cost of lending, branch income does not cover costs. Both grants and subsidized resources are needed to sustain operations until expansion of lending and membership in existing branches makes the programs self-sustainable.

Significant economies of scale exist in branch operations of Grameen Bank (0.58) and BRAC (0.56; see table A5.4). This suggests that programs would be more efficient by expanding their operations within existing branch networks.

## Economic Viability

Although branches operate on a commercial basis, operations at the head office level are highly subsidized. All three programs receive substantial foreign donor resources, either as grants or concessional funds, although Grameen Bank has increasingly drawn on market sources in recent years. The financial margin, the break-even interest rate, and profitability all underestimate the extent of subsidy these programs enjoy. The full amount should include not only the financial subsidy but also the economic subsidy, defined as the difference between the opportunity cost and the actual cost of funds.[7] In order to be fully self-sustainable, microfinance institutions must be economically viable, that is, free of economic subsidy.

Total subsidy consists of interest subsidy, income subsidy, and equity subsidy. Interest subsidy is the main component among the three.

TABLE 5.10
**Interest Rates and Subsidies for Grameen Bank and BRAC, 1990–94**

| Item | 1990 | 1991 | 1992 | 1993 | 1994 |
|---|---|---|---|---|---|
| *Interest rates (percent)* | | | | | |
| Market interest rate | 14.0 | 13.75 | 13.0 | 13.0 | 8.5 |
| Concessional rate on foreign loans | 2.0 | 2.0 | 2.0 | 2.0 | 2.0 |
| Concessional rate on central bank loans | 3.0 | 3.0 | 3.0 | 5.0 | 5.5 |
| *Subsidies (millions of taka)* | | | | | |
| Grameen Bank | | | | | |
| Foreign loans[a] | 1,638.8 | 1,703.1 | 1,790.7 | 1,922.5 | 1,967.8 |
| Central bank loans[a] | 188.6 | 178.2 | 86.5 | 1,750.0 | 3,250.0 |
| Foreign grants[a] | 693.4 | 1,363.8 | 2,366.1 | 2,572.8 | 3,067.7 |
| Income | 75.7 | 73.4 | 62.4 | 86.9 | 76.3 |
| Equity | 72.0 | 93.2 | 131.9 | 149.7 | 183.3 |
| BRAC | | | | | |
| Capital funds[b] | n.a. | 959.9 | 1,527.2 | 2,013.5 | 2,262.8 |
| Revolving funds[b] | n.a. | 14.3 | 11.3 | 7.7 | 3.9 |

n.a. Not available.
a. Foreign loans, central bank loans, and foreign grants constitute Grameen Bank's interest subsidy.
b. Capital funds and revolving funds constitute BRAC's interest subsidy.
*Source:* Khandker and Khalily 1996; Khandker, Khalily, and Khan 1995.

Grameen Bank's interest subsidy comes from foreign and central bank loans and from foreign grants (table 5.10). Interest subsidies from the loans reflect the difference between the market interest rate and the concessional rate. No interest is charged on grants, so interest subsidies from grants are the market interest rate times the amount of the grant. BRAC's interest subsidies come from capital funds and revolving funds, both of which are provided at a zero concessional rate.

Income subsidy is equal to income grants, which are donations. Equity subsidy is the income from equity held by program members, government, and commercial banks, which is subject to market interest rates only. BRAC receives neither income nor equity subsidies. Net subsidies to both Grameen Bank and BRAC have been large: in 1994 Grameen received a net subsidy of Tk 556 million and BRAC received a subsidy of Tk 246 million (table 5.11). Grameen's subsidies represented about 6 percent and BRAC's subsidies represented about 22 percent of loans outstanding in 1994.

How much does it cost society to support microfinance programs at the borrower level? Taking Grameen Bank as an example, if the total subsidy is divided by the number of borrowers, the cost to society of reaching a poor household in rural Bangladesh with financial services of a microfinance program is about Tk 440 ($11) a year. This seems to be a small cost given that each year about 5 percent of program participants lift their families out of poverty through borrowing from a microfinance program (see chapter 3). Microfinance also enhances investment in children's education, changes contraceptive and fertility behavior of borrowers, and promotes female employment to generate cash income.

## Interest Rate Policy and Subsidy Dependence

Reducing dependence on subsidies is desirable not only for a program's sustainability but also for poverty reduction. One way to reduce subsidy dependence is to increase cost-efficiency. Another option is to raise the on-lending rate. How large an increase in the on-lending rate is required to eliminate the subsidy dependence of these programs?

TABLE 5.11

### Extent of Subsidies and Subsidy Dependence by Grameen Bank and BRAC, 1990–94

| Variable | Grameen Bank | | | | |
|---|---|---|---|---|---|
| | 1990 | 1991 | 1992 | 1993 | 1994 |
| Interest subsidy (millions of taka) | 314.5 | 406.8 | 513.2 | 686.0 | 486.2 |
| Income subsidy (millions of taka) | 75.7 | 73.4 | 62.4 | 86.9 | 76.3 |
| Equity subsidy (millions of taka) | 10.1 | 12.8 | 17.1 | 19.5 | 15.6 |
| Gross subsidy (millions of taka) | 400.2 | 493.0 | 592.7 | 792.3 | 578.1 |
| Reported profits (millions of taka) | 10.2 | 11.9 | –5.7 | 9.6 | 21.7 |
| Net subsidy (millions of taka) | 390.0 | 481.1 | 598.4 | 782.8 | 556.4 |
| Income from loans (millions of taka) | 220.8 | 336.9 | 522.1 | 1,055.6 | 1,646.4 |
| Subsidy dependence index | 1.8 | 1.4 | 1.1 | 0.74 | 0.34 |
| Loan outstanding (millions of taka) | 1,855.3 | 2,334.3 | 3,487.6 | 6,593.8 | 9,908.6 |
| Subsidy per taka loan outstanding (percent) | 21.0 | 20.6 | 17.2 | 11.9 | 5.6 |
| Average lending rate (percent) | 11.9 | 14.4 | 15.0 | 16.0 | 16.6 |
| Required lending rate to eliminate subsidies (percent) | 33.0 | 35.1 | 32.2 | 27.9 | 22.3 |

*Source:* Khandker and Khalily 1996; Khandker, Khalily, and Khan 1995.

The subsidy dependence index measures the subsidy dependence of microcredit and other government-directed finance (Yaron 1992a). It is expressed as net subsidy (gross subsidy minus accounting profit) as a percentage of interest income received from on-lending. This financial ratio measures the percentage increase in the average on-lending interest rate required to eliminate all subsidies in a given year while keeping the return on equity equal to the nonconcessional borrowing cost. Between 1991 and 1994 the subsidy dependence index improved for Grameen Bank and BRAC (see table 5.11).

To eliminate all subsidies, Grameen Bank would have had to increase its on-lending rate from 16.6 percent to 22.3 percent in 1994; BRAC would have had to raise its on-lending rate from 20.8 to 42.5 percent. Can microcredit programs increase on-lending interest rates to eliminate all subsidies?

| BRAC | | | |
|---|---|---|---|
| 1991 | 1992 | 1993 | 1994 |
| 133.9 | 200.0 | 262.8 | 192.7 |
| 0 | 0 | 0 | 0 |
| 0 | 0 | 0 | 0 |
| 133.9 | 200.0 | 262.8 | 192.7 |
| −116.7 | −71.9 | −75.3 | −53.7 |
| 250.6 | 271.9 | 338.1 | 246.3 |
| 79.1 | 135.6 | 175.5 | 237.5 |
| 3.17 | 2.01 | 1.93 | 1.04 |
| 464.4 | 612.1 | 787.0 | 1,140.2 |
| 54.0 | 44.4 | 43.0 | 21.6 |
| 17.0 | 22.2 | 22.3 | 20.8 |
| 71.0 | 66.7 | 65.3 | 42.5 |

Unlike government-controlled financial institutions such as agricultural development banks, microcredit programs are allowed to set their own on-lending rates to offset the cost of lending. Grameen Bank and BRAC both currently charge 20 percent a year, significantly more than the 9–13 percent charged by commercial banks. The 20 percent is only the nominal rate of interest, however. Including extra fees raises the effective rate to as much as 30 percent (Hossain 1988).

Between 1983 and 1991 Grameen Bank charged 16 percent interest on regular one-year loans. The rate was raised to 20 percent in 1991 following a wage hike in the government sector that raised salaries of Grameen Bank staff. At the same time, the on-lending rate for housing loans (usually of 10-year maturity) was raised from 8 percent to 12 percent. Neither the demand for regular loans nor the demand for housing loans fell as a result of the increase in the on-lending rate, although the loan recovery rate fell by 1 percentage point (from 98.8 percent in 1990 to 97.8 percent in 1991). It is not clear, however, if the decline reflected the increase in the interest rate.

Interest rate policy should be evaluated in terms of the nominal and real lending rates. Data on the inflation rate, and on the nominal and real rates charged by Grameen reveal that Grameen's nominal lending rates did not reflect real lending rates during 1989–94 and that the variance in its real lending rates was much more pronounced than the variance in its nominal interest rates (table 5.12). Real lending rates ranged from 5.5 percent to 20.0 percent. If the real interest rate could reach 20.0 percent in 1993 without an apparent reduction in the demand for credit and negative impact on loan recovery rates, it follows that Grameen Bank could have raised its lending rate earlier, which could have reduced its subsidy dependence. Grameen Bank's housing loan rate could probably also have been raised, which could have contributed to attaining self-sustainability earlier. The lesson to be learned is that microcredit institutions cannot ignore the role of inflation rates in setting interest rates for loans, as well as the role of an appropriate interest rate policy in achieving financial sustainability.

## Poverty, Agroclimate Risk, and Subsidy Dependence

Although microcredit programs could reduce their subsidy dependence by raising interest rates, because of the nature of their clients they have to rely on subsidized resources to develop institutionally before they can compete for market resources.

Microfinance programs face high agroclimate risks. Agroclimate risk affects both farm and nonfarm production and thus affects the loan repayment behavior of borrowers and hence the performance of financial institutions (Binswanger and Rosenzweig 1986). In order to become

TABLE 5.12
**Nominal and Real Lending Rates Charged on Regular Loans by Grameen Bank, 1989–94**
(percent)

| Indicator | 1989 | 1990 | 1991 | 1992 | 1993 | 1994 |
|---|---|---|---|---|---|---|
| Nominal lending rate | 16.0 | 16.0 | 18.0 | 20.0 | 20.0 | 20.0 |
| Real lending rate | 5.5 | 7.3 | 10.1 | 15.1 | 20.0 | 15.9 |
| Real return on average annual loan portfolio | 2.0 | n.a. | n.a. | n.a. | 16.0 | 12.5 |
| Inflation in Bangladesh | 9.9 | 8.1 | 7.2 | 4.3 | 0.0 | 3.6 |

n.a. Not available.
Source: Yaron, Benjamin, and Piperk 1997.

financially and institutionally sustainable, microcredit programs would have to avoid risky areas of operation. But because these programs seek to reduce poverty—which is widespread in regions with unfavorable agroclimate conditions—they cannot reduce their risk by limiting lending to regions with better agroclimate, as commercial institutions do. Analysis of the impact of fixed agroclimatic, location-specific, and other environmental factors on program placement of Grameen Bank, BRAC, RD-12, commercial and agriculture banks, and government infrastructure investments reveals that while traditional banks and the government respond negatively to agroclimate risk—by avoiding flood-prone areas, for example—Grameen Bank does not consider such factors as important determinants of program placement (Khandker, Khalily, and Khan 1995), and RD-12 and BRAC respond only partially to such risk factors.

Another factor that increases the subsidy dependence of microcredit programs is landlessness. Microcredit programs in Bangladesh target landless households (households that own less than half an acre of land). As table 5.13 shows, landlessness was highest in BRAC villages (78 percent), followed by RD-12 (66 percent) and Grameen Bank (65 percent) villages and villages without any microcredit programs (52 percent). Extreme poverty was highest in RD-12 villages (17 percent), followed by BRAC (15 percent),

TABLE 5.13
**Landlessness and Poverty in Target Households, 1991/92**
(percent)

| Indicator | Grameen Bank villages | BRAC villages | RD-12 villages | All program villages | Non-program villages | All villages |
|---|---|---|---|---|---|---|
| Landlessness | 65.4 | 78.4 | 65.9 | 69.9 | 52.1 | 66.9 |
| Extreme poverty[a] | 12.9 | 14.6 | 17.2 | 14.9 | 9.7 | 14.3 |

a. Average household per capita consumption of less than Tk 3,330 a year.
Source: BIDS–World Bank 1991/92 survey.

Grameen Bank (13 percent), and nonprogram villages (10 percent).[8] This placement of programs in areas in which poverty is high justifies subsidized funding of microfinance institutions in the early years of their operation.

## Summary

Although the twin objectives of reducing poverty and earning profit may be in conflict, microcredit programs must try to attain financial self-sustainability at an earlier stage of operation. To facilitate self-sustainability, programs must have access to market resources to break even through expansion. For different reasons, however, microcredit programs' access to market resources is restricted in Bangladesh. When Grameen Bank issued bonds in 1995 to generate market resources at the market interest rate, it had difficulty mobilizing market resources. In that year all nationalized commercial banks had tremendous liquidity and were eager to buy Grameen bonds, but with the government's guarantee. The government had to step in, and Grameen Bank was rescued for its shortage of liquidity in that year. BRAC also reportedly failed in several attempts to borrow money from commercial banks. A mechanism needs to be developed to allow linkages between formal banks and microcredit programs without direct government involvement (World Bank 1996a, b).

Some rural credit programs have been subsidized in their early years but attained self-sustainability over time. For example, Indonesia's Badan Kredit Kecamatan (BKK) and Bank Rukyat Indonesia (BRI) were given funds as seed capital, with the understanding that they would become self-sustaining within the shortest possible period of time (Chavez and Gonzalez-Vega 1996). Of course, there are fundamental differences between the Indonesian and Bangladeshi institutions. Unlike the Indonesian banks, Bangladeshi microcredit programs have some inherent institutional weaknesses. BRAC, for example, is not a chartered bank and thus cannot mobilize savings from nonmembers. Grameen Bank is a bank, but it is a bank for the poor and finds it difficult to attract deposits from the nonpoor. Given their institutional weaknesses for attaining self-sustainability, both BRAC and Grameen Bank must raise interest rates consistent with inflation rates and find other ways to attain financial self-sustainability. If subsidy is unavoidable in order to attain the primary objective of poverty reduction, it has to be used in the most efficient manner possible.

## Notes

1. This chapter draws heavily on Khandker and Khalily (1996), Khandker, Khalily, and Khan (1995),and Khandker, Khan, and Khaliliy (1996). Some

estimates were recalculated based on revised data released by the three microcredit programs.

2. These estimates are based on a Mincerian log-wage function that was fitted to the 1991 salaries of 131 branch managers of Grameen Bank, 97 branch managers of BRAC, and 86 rural development officers of RD-12. The log of monthly wages was regressed against age, experience, education, and gender of the manager or officer.

3. At Grameen Bank a junior or a senior officer could be a branch manager. Lack of information about the status of branch managers made it impossible to control for seniority in the salary regression. Since most women branch managers at Grameen Bank are junior officers, there should be no wage difference between male and female branch managers.

4. See Chapter 6 for recovery rate of formal banks.

5. A translog specification is better than the widely used Cobb-Douglas function because it is less restrictive. The cost function estimates allow the marginal cost of membership, lending, and savings, as well as economies of scale in program operation, to be calculated. For details on the cost function estimates, see Khandker and Khalily 1996; Khandker, Khalily, and Khan 1995; and Khandker, Khan, and Khalily 1995.

6. The marginal cost estimate for RD-12 is an underestimate because it does not include the use of local government premises.

7. The definition of the opportunity cost of subsidized funds and grants received by Grameen Bank and BRAC from donors and government is highly contentious. The deposit rate of 36-month Bangladesh Bank securities is used here as the opportunity cost of these funds, since grants and concessional money from donors could be deposited in this type of fixed deposit for investment.

8. These figures underestimate the ex ante level of poverty in program villages because the programs reduced the ex post rate of poverty (see chapter 3).

# 6

# Microcredit Programs and Rural Financial Markets

Microcredit programs were developed in response to the failure of traditional financial institutions, such as agricultural development banks, to serve the credit needs of the poor and small rural producers. Comparison of their performance relative to that of traditional financial institutions reveals the relative sources of their strengths and weaknesses and will allow policymakers to assess the cost-effectiveness of alternative programs serving different client groups.

Imperfect information and imperfect enforcement make rural lending difficult. Because of poor program design, traditional financial institutions have failed to enforce loan contracts, and they have faced serious loan recovery problems. Consequently, many financial institutions that serve groups such as farmers are not financially viable and are, therefore, heavily subsidized by the government.

Informal lenders are able to enforce loan contracts, and their loan recovery rates are high. The interest rates they charge are high, however, inhibiting the growth of small rural producers and prompting government efforts to curb their role. Despite these efforts informal lenders remain prevalent in many countries, and informal interest rates remain high (Adams and Fitchett 1992; Ghate 1992; Hoff and Stiglitz 1990; Murshid and Rahman 1990).

Microcredit institutions have successfully incorporated some of the salient features of informal lending, such as close monitoring and supervision of borrowers, which has improved their loan recovery rates. They charge much lower interest rates than informal lenders and operate mostly with donor funds. Like formal financial institutions operating in the rural sector, microcredit programs are not self-sustainable. The sources of subsidy for microcredit and traditional financial institutions are, however, different.

This chapter attempts to identify the extent and source of subsidy of formal and microcredit institutions. It also investigates the effect of microcredit programs on rural financial markets. It looks at the effect of microfinance on both the volume and the rate of informal lending and formal lending in rural areas. It also examines the effect of institutional finance (formal and microfinance) on interhousehold resource transfers. Past research has shown that when a credit market is not well developed, inter-household transfers make up for the absence of an active credit market. For example, where income risk due to production risk can be mitigated by interfamily transactions, rural households engage in marital contracts (such as marrying off daughters to husbands outside the village) that help smooth consumption (Rosenzweig and Stark 1989). If microcredit or formal financial institutions have an impact on village credit markets, the incidence of interhousehold transfers would be expected to diminish.

Another important issue examined is whether microcredit programs or formal financial institutions, such as agricultural development banks, have had any impact on agricultural financing. Because of seasonality, agriculture is a high-risk activity, and so is financing for agriculture. Often the amount advanced to agriculture by formal financial institutions is smaller than the amount advanced to nonagricultural activities, even within the rural sector. Microcredit programs offer credit to members of functionally landless households who use the loans largely for rural nonfarm production (see chapter 4); agriculture financing makes up a very small portion of microcredit. Nevertheless, because funds are fungible across activities, if not across individuals, microfinance and formal finance may have increased the supply of institutional credit to agriculture. If the supply of credit has increased, which farmers have benefited most from which types of institutional finance? Past research has shown that large farmers are the principal beneficiaries of traditional financial institutions (Z. Ahmed 1989; Hossain 1988; Braverman and Guasch 1989). Microfinance institutions largely benefit marginal farmers and landless households (Hossain 1988; chapter 3 of this book). Thus a large group of small and medium-size farmers are likely to lack access to institutional credit.

Finally, the chapter identifies the lessons policymakers can learn from microfinance in terms of program design, coverage, and the financial viability of rural finance institutions. In particular, it shows that the approaches used to reach landless households could be used to design a program that would serve groups neglected by both formal and microfinance institutions.

## The Structure of Rural Finance: The Roles of Formal, Informal, and Microfinance Institutions

The rural credit market in Bangladesh is highly segmented. Formal lenders, such as commercial and agricultural development banks, are guided by the rules and regulations of the central bank. Informal lenders (professional moneylenders, input dealers, friends, and relatives) are virtually outside the control of the government. Between these two types of lenders are microcredit programs and institutions, such as Grameen Bank and BRAC; government cooperative structures; and NGOs, which are involved in financial transactions with minimum financial regulations from the government.

Households borrow for different purposes. According to the Rural Credit Survey of Bangladesh, about 36 percent of rural households borrowed in 1987 (Bangladesh Bureau of Statistics 1989). According to the more recent Bangladesh Institute of Development Studies–World Bank household survey, about 49 percent of rural households borrowed in 1991/92. Comparison of the sources of finance revealed by the two surveys shows a decline in the role of informal finance (figure 6.1). In 1987 informal lenders were the primary source of credit in rural areas, accounting for 64 percent of all loan transactions. Formal lenders accounted for 27 percent and microcredit institutions for 9 percent of all loan transactions. By 1991/92 microfinance had become the leading source of rural credit, accounting for 45 percent of all loans. Formal finance had also grown, and the importance of informal finance had declined.[1]

Despite this growth, institutional finance (both formal and microfinance) plays only a very limited role in the rural economy of Bangladesh. In terms of yearly loan disbursement, Bangladesh's financial sector accounted for only 1.8 percent of GDP in 1992/93. Formal credit accounted for 2.5 percent of agricultural GDP in 1989/90, 2.9 percent in 1992/93, and 3.5 percent in 1993/94, down from 6.7 percent in 1983/84 (table 6.1). The financial sector is growing even more slowly than either aggregate GDP or sectoral GDP in agriculture: between 1983/84 and 1993/94 the average annual growth in credit disbursed to agriculture was only 0.03 percent, while agricultural GDP grew by an average annual rate of 5.3 percent.

Formal credit plays an even smaller role in crop production than in noncrop and rural nonfarm production. Between 1983/84 and 1993/94 crop GDP accounted for more than 72 percent of agricultural GDP, while crop credit accounted for only about 51 percent of total formal credit. Over the same period crop credit accounted for 2.5 percent of crop GDP, while noncrop credit (including term agricultural credit) accounted for 6.6 percent of noncrop GDP. While crop credit declined 1.8 percent over this period, noncrop credit grew 2.2 percent. Rural production is largely self-financed. Noncrop production seems to be preferred over crop production by formal financial institutions because it is less risky.

Microfinance seems to have played a larger role than formal finance in agriculture in Bangladesh, and its role is growing. Total credit advanced to the rural sector from the major formal financial institutions declined from Tk 9,950 million in 1983/84 to only Tk 1,108 million in 1993/94. Total credit advanced by Grameen Bank, BRAC, and RD-12 in 1993/94 was Tk 16,500 million (Grameen Bank

TABLE 6.1

**Agricultural GDP and Formal Agricultural Credit in Bangladesh, 1983–94**
(tens of millions of taka at current prices)

| Year | GDP at market price Agriculture | Crop | Agricultural loans by type Crop | Term credit[a] | Other[b] | Total | Formal credit as percent of agricultural GDP |
|---|---|---|---|---|---|---|---|
| 1983/84 | 14,840.3 | 12,000.9 | 635.9 | 278.7 | 80.8 | 995.3 | 6.7 |
| 1984/85 | 16,997.0 | 13,503.1 | 564.8 | 421.1 | 145.9 | 1,131.7 | 6.7 |
| 1985/86 | 18,838.2 | 13,948.9 | 275.6 | 192.8 | 168.8 | 631.8 | 3.4 |
| 1986/87 | 21,976.1 | 16,497.5 | 312.5 | 129.8 | 148.0 | 590.3 | 2.7 |
| 1987/88 | 23,162.3 | 16,764.6 | 383.1 | 130.3 | 142.9 | 656.3 | 2.8 |
| 1988/89 | 24,539.2 | 17,646.7 | 340.0 | 186.7 | 171.0 | 697.7 | 2.8 |
| 1989/90 | 27,179.0 | 19,421.1 | 359.8 | 156.9 | 170.1 | 686.8 | 2.5 |
| 1990/91 | 30,059.6 | 21,782.3 | 302.5 | 139.7 | 153.4 | 595.6 | 2.0 |
| 1991/92 | 31,243.8 | 22,451.0 | 346.4 | 260.4 | 187.8 | 794.6 | 2.5 |
| 1992/93 | 28,884.2 | 18,466.0 | 388.5 | 247.2 | 197.2 | 832.9 | 2.9 |
| 1993/94 | 31,494.5 | 19,725.8 | 515.1 | 392.4 | 193.3 | 1,108.0 | 3.5 |

a. Includes agricultural term credit as well as financing for marketing, transportation, and agroindustries.
b. Includes loans for fisheries, tea production, and cold storage facilities for agricultural products.
*Source:* Bangladesh Bank.

alone disbursed about Tk 13,847 million), representing about 5.2 percent of agricultural GDP.

## Performance of Commercial and Agricultural Development Banks

Bangladesh's formal financial institutions comprise four nationalized commercial banks—Sonali Bank, Agrani Bank, Rupali Bank, and Janata Bank—and two major agricultural development banks—Bangladesh Krishi Bank (BKB) and Rajshahi Krishi Unnayan Bank (RAKUB).[2] Under government pressure to expand their network in rural areas, both the nationalized commercial banks and the agricultural development banks opened many branches without considering their financial viability. They also expanded credit to priority sectors, such as agriculture and industry, without paying sufficient attention to loan recovery and creditworthiness of borrowers, often risking loans at interest rates that were lower than their cost of funds or operations. These misdirected policies led to inefficient resource allocation and widespread loan delinquency (World Bank 1993, 1996a).

Because of its inefficiency, the banking sector failed to play an important role in promoting economic growth in Bangladesh. The poor performance of the country's financial system has reduced investment,

FIGURE 6.1
## Sources of Rural Loans, 1985 and 1991/92
(percent)

### Rural Credit Survey of Bangladesh, 1987

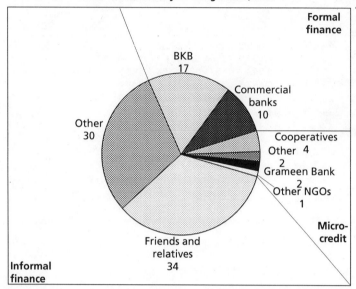

*Source:* Bangladesh Bureau of Statistics 1989.

### BIDS–World Bank 1991/92 survey

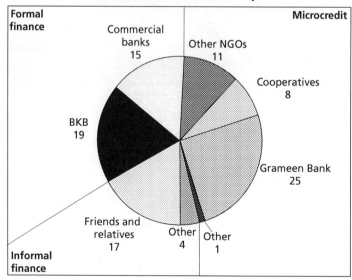

*Source:* BIDS–World Bank 1991/92 survey.

productivity, and growth of savings, diminishing the country's growth potential and reducing employment opportunities. In fact, Bangladesh's history of stagnant growth and investment may partly be due to stagnation and inefficiency in the financial sector (World Bank 1987).

A large number of bank branches operate in rural areas. As of June 30, 1993, there were 5,664 branches of formal financial institutions, of which about 70 percent were located in rural areas and more than 60 percent were run by nationalized commercial banks. Often the choice of branch location has been guided not by profitability but by government directives to improve the outreach of formal financial services. As a result many rural branches have been unprofitable. In 1994 more than 70 percent of BKB branches registered losses.

The major problem facing these institutions is their poor loan recovery rates, which fell from 48.5 percent in 1981/82 to 13.7 percent in 1990/91 (table 6.2). Since 1990/91 this rate has improved slightly. In 1994/95, 37 percent of funds due were recovered by nationalized commercial banks, and agricultural development banks recovered 65 percent of funds due (table 6.3). Despite this improvement, however, more than 75 percent of the agricultural loan portfolio of both agricultural development banks and nationalized commercial banks are in arrears for all loans combined, indicating that formal financial institutions must improve their loan recovery even further.

The low loan recovery rate is due partly to the loan write-off policy of the government and partly to institutional weakness. In 1991/92 alone the government wrote off Tk 3,509 million in loans. This policy destroys

TABLE 6.2
**Loan Recovery on Agricultural Loans by Formal Lenders, 1981–93**

| Year | Amount disbursed (millions of taka) | Amount due for recovery (millions of taka) | Amount recovered (millions of taka) | Recovery rate (percent) |
|---|---|---|---|---|
| 1981/82 | 423.8 | 648.3 | 314.3 | 48.5 |
| 1982/83 | 678.6 | 817.3 | 342.3 | 41.9 |
| 1983/84 | 1,005.3 | 1,238.2 | 517.6 | 41.8 |
| 1984/85 | 1,152.8 | 1,515.0 | 583.9 | 38.5 |
| 1985/86 | 631.7 | 2,375.2 | 607.2 | 25.6 |
| 1986/87 | 667.3 | 2,683.5 | 1,107.6 | 41.3 |
| 1987/88 | 656.3 | 2,528.2 | 595.8 | 23.6 |
| 1988/89 | 807.6 | 3,044.7 | 578.0 | 19.0 |
| 1989/90 | 686.8 | 3,986.3 | 701.9 | 17.6 |
| 1990/91 | 595.6 | 4,556.7 | 625.3 | 13.7 |
| 1991/92 | 794.6 | 4,170.2 | 662.1 | 15.9 |
| 1992/93 | 841.9 | 4,719.9 | 869.2 | 18.4 |
| 1993/94 | 1,093.5 | 5,138.6 | 957.8 | 18.6 |

*Source:* Bangladesh Bank.

TABLE 6.3

**Recovery Rates on Agricultural Loans by Formal Lenders, July 1, 1994, to June 30, 1995**

| Institution | Recovery of loans overdue from previous years | | |
| --- | --- | --- | --- |
| | Amount due (millions of taka) | Amount recovered (millions of taka) | Percentage of total |
| Commercial banks | 1,042 | 153 | 14.7 |
| Sonali | 595 | 59 | 9.9 |
| Janata | 240 | 43 | 17.9 |
| Agrani | 142 | 43 | 30.3 |
| Rupali | 65 | 8 | 12.3 |
| Agricultural development banks | 2,315 | 165 | 7.1 |
| BKB | 1,563 | 106 | 6.8 |
| RAKUB | 753 | 59 | 7.8 |
| Cooperatives | 831 | 10 | 1.2 |
| Bangladesh Rural Development Board | 652 | 8 | 1.2 |
| Bangladesh Samabaya Bank Limited | 179 | 1 | 0.6 |
| Total, 1994/95 | 4,188 | 327 | 7.8 |
| Total, 1993/94 | 3,921 | 371 | 9.5 |

*Source:* Bangladesh Bank.

the credit discipline of borrowers and reduces the viability of financial institutions. The lack of a regulatory and legal framework for enforcing loan contracts; an interest rate ceiling, which promotes rent-seeking; lack of an appropriate incentive structure for staff; lack of accountability and transparency in the administrative structure; lack of innovation in product design and marketing; and more reliance on external resources than internal resources (mobilized savings) for on-lending are also responsible for the low loan recovery rate (see World Bank 1996a).[3]

Against this dismal picture stand the high loan recovery rates of Grameen Bank, BRAC, and other microfinance institutions which recover more than 90 percent of their loans. Of course, loan recovery is only one indicator of performance. Other indicators, such as subsidy dependence, profitability, and staff productivity, are also critical factors that determine the financial and institutional viability of financial institutions.

## Comparing the Performance of Agricultural Development Banks and Microfinance Institutions

Comparison of the performance of agricultural development banks and microfinance institutions between 1990 and 1994 reveals several impor-

| Recovery of loans due in current year | | | Recovery of all loans | | |
|---|---|---|---|---|---|
| Amount due (millions of taka) | Amount recovered (millions of taka) | Percentage of total | Amount due (millions of taka) | Amount recovered (millions of taka) | Percentage of total |
| 360 | 134 | 37.2 | 1,402 | 287 | 20.5 |
| 149 | 61 | 40.9 | 744 | 120 | 16.1 |
| 103 | 40 | 38.8 | 343 | 83 | 24.2 |
| 94 | 30 | 31.9 | 236 | 73 | 30.9 |
| 14 | 3 | 21.4 | 79 | 11 | 13.9 |
| 943 | 609 | 64.6 | 3,258 | 774 | 23.8 |
| 642 | 488 | 76.0 | 2,205 | 594 | 26.9 |
| 300 | 120 | 40.0 | 1,053 | 179 | 17.0 |
| 83 | 27 | 32.5 | 914 | 37 | 4.0 |
| 82 | 27 | 32.9 | 734 | 35 | 4.8 |
| 1 | 0.3 | 30.0 | 180 | 1.3 | 0.7 |
| 1,386 | 770 | 55.6 | 5,574 | 1,097 | 19.7 |
| 1,221 | 608 | 49.8 | 5,142 | 979 | 19.0 |

tant differences. Agricultural development banks were more productive than microfinance institutions in terms of mobilizing deposits, especially in the earlier years (figure 6.2). This difference clearly reflects the limited target clientele of microfinance institutions. Microfinance institutions appear to disburse more loans per employee than agricultural development banks, but branch performance by microfinance institutions in terms of deposit mobilization and loan disbursement has not been as good as that of agricultural development banks. These results hold despite the fact that agricultural development banks have coverage across all types of rural households. Microfinance institutions cover only households that own less than half an acre of land, and their savings mobilization is limited largely to members. Even with these institutional limitations, deposit mobilization per employee and per branch increased at a higher rate at Grameen Bank than at the agricultural development banks.

In terms of net financial margin, agricultural development banks had negative and worsening margins since 1992, when the government implemented its major loan write-off policies. Performance by the microfinance institutions varied. Grameen Bank enjoyed a positive return every year except 1992, while BRAC suffered losses, albeit at a declining rate over time (table 6.4).

FIGURE 6.2
**Productivity of Agricultural Development Banks and Microfinance
Institutions, 1990–94**
millions of taka

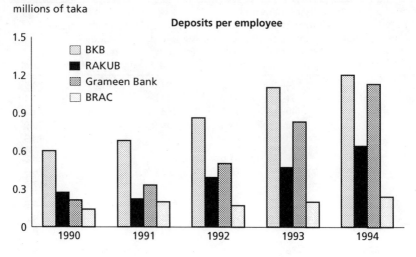

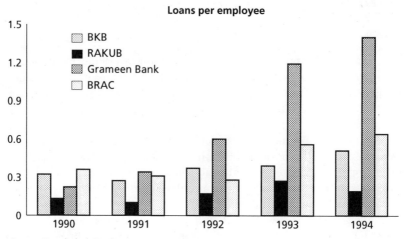

*Source:* Bangladesh Bank.

The problems of agricultural development banks start with their interest rates, which are set at 9–13 percent—much lower than the 20 percent
charged by Grameen Bank and BRAC. The interest margin (expressed as
a percentage of assets) is thus much higher for Grameen Bank and BRAC
than for BKB and RAKUB (see table 6.4). The interest margin is higher for
microfinance institutions than for agricultural development banks because
the microfinance institutions pay zero or concessional interest rates for on-

millions of taka

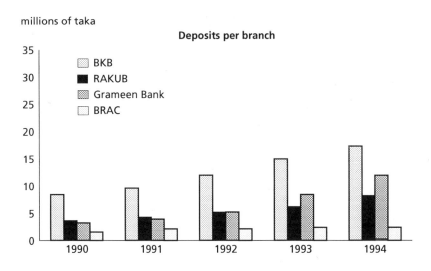

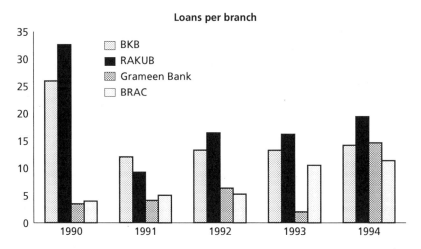

lending funds. Both agricultural development banks and microfinance institutions pay similar rates to depositors or members who save with them.

Microcredit programs incur much greater costs than agricultural development banks. In 1994 operating costs represented 5–7 percent of assets at BKB and RAKUB and 9–14 percent at Grameen Bank and BRAC. Staff costs constituted about 50 percent of operating costs at Grameen Bank and BRAC and 35 percent at BKB and RAKUB. At all institutions these

TABLE 6.4

**Performance of Major Financial Institutions, 1990–94**
(percentage of assets)

| Performance indicator | RAKUB | | | | | BRAC[a] | | | |
|---|---|---|---|---|---|---|---|---|---|
| | 1990 | 1991 | 1992 | 1993 | 1994 | 1991 | 1992 | 1993 | 1994 |
| Interest received | 9.1 | 10.1 | 8.7 | 4.6 | 4.3 | 7.7 | 8.7 | 8.5 | 10.3 |
| Interest paid | 5.0 | 4.5 | 5.0 | 4.7 | 3.9 | 1.6 | 1.7 | 1.5 | 0.7 |
| Interest margin | 4.1 | 5.6 | 3.7 | −0.2 | 0.4 | 6.1 | 7.0 | 7.0 | 9.6 |
| Other income | 0.1 | 0.0 | 0.0 | 0.1 | 0.2 | 2.3 | 2.7 | 2.9 | 1.8 |
| Gross financial margin | 4.2 | 5.6 | 3.7 | −0.1 | 0.6 | 8.3 | 9.6 | 9.9 | 11.4 |
| Operating costs | 2.2 | 4.7 | 8.1 | 2.3 | 5.4 | 18.1 | 17.0 | 25.5 | 13.5 |
| Staff costs | 2.2 | 1.7 | 1.8 | 2.1 | 2.0 | 8.8 | 8.3 | 11.7 | 6.5 |
| Other expenses | 0.0 | 3.1 | 6.3 | 0.3 | 3.4 | 9.3 | 8.8 | 13.8 | 7.0 |
| Net financial margin | 2.0 | 0.9 | −4.3 | −2.4 | −4.7 | −9.7 | −7.4 | −15.7 | −2.1 |
| Assets (millions of taka) | 9,631 | 12,459 | 12,425 | 12,816 | 14,050 | 1,031 | 1,562 | 2,071 | 2,353 |

a. 1990 Information for BRAC was not available.
*Source:* Bangladesh Krishi Bank, Rajshahi Krishi Unnayan Bank, Bangladesh Rural
Advancement Committee, and Grameen Bank.

costs represented a major source of inefficiency. Another major source of
inefficiency at agricultural development banks is their high default costs,
which accounted for more than 60 percent of operating costs. Rising loan
default costs have become a major source of financial unsustainability for
BKB and RAKUB. At BRAC other expenses per asset are high because the
program provides noncredit services such as literacy, health, and other
training programs. These noncredit costs represent as much as 50 percent
of other expenses. BRAC must find ways to reduce such noncredit costs
further to attain financial self-sustainability.

Agricultural development banks depend on government support to
sustain their operations, while Grameen Bank and BRAC depend on
donors. Subsidized funds are used by these institutions for on-lending and
institutional development. Pricing subsidized resources using the central
bank's long-term deposit rate yields a total subsidy of 11.3 percent of outstanding loans for BKB, 8.4 percent for RAKUB, 5.6 percent for Grameen
Bank, and 21.6 percent for BRAC in 1994 (table 6.5).[4] The subsidy dependence index—the ratio of net subsidy (total subsidy less profit) to interest income on loan portfolio (interest rate paid on loans times the amount
of loans outstanding)—is highest for RAKUB (1.5), followed by BKB
(1.3), BRAC (1.0), and Grameen Bank (0.3). These figures indicate that
to eliminate reliance on subsidies, Grameen Bank would have to increase
its average on-lending rate by 34 percent, BRAC by 104 percent, BKB by
130 percent, and RAKUB by 154 percent. Thus the subsidy-free average

| | BKB | | | | | Grameen Bank | | | |
|---|---|---|---|---|---|---|---|---|---|
| 1990 | 1991 | 1992 | 1993 | 1994 | 1990 | 1991 | 1992 | 1993 | 1994 |
| 10.1 | 9.0 | 8.7 | 9.4 | 7.1 | 9.8 | 10.7 | 12.0 | 12.8 | 13.5 |
| 6.7 | 6.6 | 6.9 | 6.5 | 6.0 | 3.0 | 2.7 | 3.3 | 4.0 | 5.6 |
| 3.5 | 2.4 | 1.8 | 2.9 | 1.1 | 6.8 | 8.0 | 8.7 | 8.8 | 7.9 |
| 0.3 | 0.2 | 0.2 | 0.2 | 0.4 | 2.3 | 1.8 | 1.2 | 1.1 | 0.7 |
| 3.7 | 2.6 | 2.0 | 3.1 | 1.5 | 9.1 | 9.8 | 9.9 | 9.8 | 8.6 |
| 2.4 | 2.6 | 6.7 | 5.4 | 7.4 | 8.8 | 9.6 | 10.0 | 9.7 | 8.5 |
| 2.4 | 2.2 | 2.4 | 2.6 | 2.7 | 5.0 | 6.1 | 6.6 | 6.1 | 4.1 |
| 0.0 | 0.4 | 4.3 | 2.7 | 4.7 | 3.8 | 3.5 | 3.4 | 3.6 | 4.3 |
| 1.3 | 0.0 | –4.7 | –2.2 | –5.9 | 0.3 | 0.3 | –0.1 | 0.1 | 0.2 |
| 26,404 | 28,641 | 30,851 | 32,696 | 32,844 | 3,437 | 4,502 | 5,863 | 9,580 | 14,211 |

on-lending rate would be 22 percent for Grameen Bank, 42 percent for BRAC, 24 percent for BKB, and 15 percent for RAKUB.

Raising interest rates and reducing administrative costs can reduce the subsidy dependence of these organizations. For agricultural development banks the key to reducing subsidy dependence is reducing loan default costs.

## What Has Been the Impact of Institutional Lending?

How has institutional lending affected household borrowing in rural villages in Bangladesh? In particular, have subsidized financial operations increased access to institutional credit, thereby reducing borrowing

TABLE 6.5

**Subsidy Dependence of Formal Finance and Microfinance Institutions, 1994**

| Measure | RAKUB | BRAC | BKB | Grameen Bank |
|---|---|---|---|---|
| Subsidy dependence index | 1.5 | 1.0 | 1.3 | 0.3 |
| Subsidy as percentage of loans outstanding | 8.4 | 21.6 | 11.3 | 5.6 |
| Average on-lending rate (percent) | 5.7 | 20.8 | 10.3 | 16.6 |

Source: Khandker and Khalily 1996; Khandker, Khalily, and Khan 1995; World Bank 1996a.

from informal lenders? What has happened to the rate of interest charged for loans in rural villages? How have interfamily transfers been affected by the institutional lenders? Finally, what has happened to agricultural financing?

## Household Borrowing

Among the 5,499 individuals from the 1,798 households surveyed, 17 percent took out loans. About 10 percent of loans came from formal sources, 31 percent came from informal sources, and 59 percent came from microcredit sources. Since November 1986, 44 percent of the cumulative amount borrowed came from microcredit programs, 34 percent came from formal sources, and 22 percent came from informal sources.

The decision to borrow and to borrow from a particular source is based on a set of variables reflecting both the demand for and supply of credit. Variables such as the age, education, and sex of the individual (above age 15), the household's landholding, the extent of landlessness in the village, whether the village is electrified, and whether the village has a paved road all determine the demand for credit. Whether the village has a formal bank branch or a microcredit program determines the supply of institutional credit. Estimates of the impact of availability of microcredit programs may be biased because program or bank branch placement may be endogenous. Program placement endogeneity was not observed for all outcomes, however. As panel data were not available, cross-sectional results are presented to assess whether provision of institutional credit affects demand for credit in rural areas.

The probability of an individual borrowing from any source is nonlinear (1 for those who borrow, 0 for those who do not borrow) and hence is estimated by a method called the probit (see Maddala 1988). The estimated coefficient measures the probability of borrowing for changes in any explanatory variable. To measure the marginal change in borrowing with respect to changes in an explanatory variable, the probit coefficients are multiplied by the density function of the standard normal. The amount of borrowing is zero for nonborrowers and the actual amount for borrowers. The amount of borrowing is estimated using a tobit method, which is better than an ordinary least squares regression. Both probit and tobit estimates are shown in table A6.1. In order to obtain marginal changes, the tobit coefficients presented in table A6.1 are multiplied by the probability of borrowing from a source (McDonald and Moffitt 1980). The probability of borrowing is 0.08 for formal sources, 0.32 for informal sources, and 0.71 for microcredit sources, as shown by the cumulative density function.

Men on average borrow at least 8 percent more than women, and they borrow more from formal and informal sources than from microcredit sources (see table A6.1). For a given landholding and education level, men borrow 62 percent more from formal sources than women and three times as much from informal sources. In contrast, women's cumulative borrowing from microcredit sources is more than four times as great as men's.

Borrowing increases with education and education increases an individual's borrowing from formal and informal sources more than from microfinance sources. The impact of education on the amount of borrowing is higher for formal (6 percent) than for informal (2 percent) sources. Education also reduces borrowing from microcredit sources (18 percent), suggesting that poorly educated individuals have better access to microcredit. Landholding is negatively related to the decision to borrow, implying that large landowners borrow less than small landowners. A 10 percent increase in landholding is associated with a 2 percent decline in borrowing. But once individuals decide to borrow, landholding increases individuals' borrowing from both formal and informal sources but reduces amount of borrowing from microcredit programs. Better roads increase the amount of borrowing from informal sources and reduce the amount of borrowing from institutional (formal and microcredit) sources.[5]

The presence of a branch of a traditional (commercial or agricultural development) bank reduces the amount of borrowing from informal sources but increases the amount of borrowing from formal and microcredit sources. This finding reinforces the argument that institutional credit is a substitute for informal credit and that subsidized operations of formal banks seem to have had a positive impact on rural finance (Binswanger and Khandker 1995). The increase in microcredit suggests that it complements formal credit.

The presence of a microcredit program increases borrowing from microcredit sources and reduces borrowing from informal sources. Borrowing from informal sources is 128 percent lower in Grameen Bank villages, 145 percent lower in BRAC villages, and 38 percent lower in RD-12 villages than in nonprogram villages. Microcredit, especially from Grameen Bank, also complements formal credit, implying that the reduction in the price of microcredit because of the availability of microcredit programs increases demand for both microcredit and formal credit. Microcredit programs may have generated a better loan repayment culture in the villages in which they operate, possibly encouraging formal banks to perceive these villages as better credit risks than villages without microcredit programs. Formal lenders may thus supply more credit in microcredit program villages than in villages without such programs.

## The Informal Borrowing Rate

Has provision of institutional credit helped reduce the informal lending rate? The 1991/92 survey found that households paid annual interest of 85 percent on borrowing from informal sources, 20 percent on loans from microcredit institutions, and 16 percent on borrowing from banks.[6] The informal lending rate varies by loan maturity length. According to village surveys, monthly rates were 14.0 percent for 0–3 month loans, 11.6 percent for 3–6 month loans, 10.9 percent for 6–12 month loans, and 10.6 percent for loans of more than 12 months.

Village-level regressions indicate that traditional banks have no significant impact on informal lending rates, except for informal loans of three months or less, for which rates are lower in their presence (table A6.2). The informal lending rate on loans of more than 12 months is lower only in Grameen villages and higher in BRAC villages for all other durations. However, individual-level regressions show that BRAC's presence indeed lowers the interest rates (see table A6.3). The negative effect of institutional credit on the informal lending rate may be an outcome of a positive externality. However, perverse (positive) effects of institutional credit on the informal lending rate are also possible because of a negative externality among informal lenders or because of a loss of scale economies with the advent of institutional credit (Hoff and Stiglitz 1997). The positive association between BRAC and informal lending may also reflect endogenous program placement.

## Interhousehold Transfers

Lack of access to financial institutions is overcome in traditional settings through interhousehold transfers. The demand for credit is influenced by the extent of these transfers. When financial intermediation by institutional sources deepens, interhousehold transfers can be expected to decline. The extent of substitutability between interhousehold transfers and institutional credit depends on borrowers' transactions costs as well as their access to financial institutions.

The household survey data were used to analyze the impact of bank and microcredit programs on interhousehold transfers. Of 1,798 households, 15 percent received transfers, 7 percent remitted transfers, and 21 percent received net transfers (some households that received transfers also remitted transfers). Household transfers were assumed to depend on household characteristics, such as the household head's age, education, and sex, and household-landholding, and on village characteristics, such as the availability of traditional banks, microcredit institutions, electrification, roads, and other types of infrastructure. Tobit estimates indicate that landholding increased the amount remitted by a household (table A6.4). Households headed by women had higher net transfers, as did households in which the household head had more education.

Better roads were associated with a lower level of interhousehold transfers. The presence of a commercial or agricultural development bank in a village and village electrification had no effect on interhousehold transfers. The presence of Grameen Bank or BRAC was associated with a lower level of interhousehold transfers. The amount of net transfers into households was about 46 percent lower in Grameen Bank villages and 26 percent lower in BRAC villages than in nonprogram villages. Microcredit programs play an active role in the rural economy by providing alternative sources of finance so that families can reduce their dependence on interhousehold transfers as a major source of finance.

## Agricultural Financing

On average, men borrowed more from formal and informal sources than from microcredit sources to finance agriculture (table A6.5). A higher level of education was associated with more borrowing for agriculture from formal sources and less borrowing for agriculture from microcredit institutions. Landholding was associated with increased borrowing for agriculture from all three sources, but its impact was greatest for informal sources (28 percent), followed by formal sources (21 percent) and microcredit sources (7 percent). The amount borrowed from formal sources for agriculture was lower in villages with paved roads. The presence of a commercial or agricultural development bank in a village was associated with decreased agricultural borrowing from informal and microcredit sources. A similar negative impact on agricultural borrowing was found for electrification. Borrowing for agriculture from informal sources was lower in villages with microcredit institutions.

The seasonality and covariate risk inherent in agricultural production discourages financial institutions from lending to the sector (Binswanger and Rosenzweig 1986). Diversifying the loan portfolio across areas and sectors may be an efficient way of reducing risk in agricultural lending. Nationalized commercial banks in Bangladesh have the ability to lend across sectors and areas (urban and rural). They are thus in a better position to reduce their total risk. In contrast, agricultural development banks lend only in rural areas, and extend more loans to rural areas than commercial banks do. In 1993/94 agricultural development banks lent Tk 7,423 million to agriculture, while commercial banks lent Tk 3,573 million.

Because crop production is much riskier than rural nonfarm production, however, both commercial and agricultural development

TABLE 6.6

**Average Loan Size and Distribution of Loans by Sector**

| Source | Agriculture | | Livestock | |
|---|---|---|---|---|
| | Average loan size (taka) | Percentage of total disbursed by source | Average loan size (taka) | Percentage of total disbursed by source |
| Formal finance | 9,423 | 19.2 | 8,006 | 1.2 |
| BKB/RAKUB | 10,716 | 20.0 | 9,044 | 2.0 |
| Commercial banks | 8,091 | 18.1 | 3,857 | 0.3 |
| Microcredit | 2,114 | 8.6 | 1,973 | 23.7 |
| Grameen Bank | 1,571 | 4.0 | 2,068 | 29.9 |
| Other NGOs | 2,550 | 16.2 | 2,678 | 13.0 |
| Cooperatives | 2,011 | 12.5 | 1,364 | 20.6 |
| Other | 11,340 | 16.9 | 0 | 0.0 |
| Informal finance | 3,796 | 24.0 | 5,064 | 0.7 |
| Friends and relatives | 3,851 | 27.1 | 5,064 | 0.9 |
| Other | 3,362 | 11.7 | 0 | 0.0 |

a. Mostly consumption loans.
*Source:* BIDS–World Bank 1991/92 survey.

banks allocate more of their loan portfolios to rural nonfarm than to crop production. Agriculture (mainly crop activity) accounted for about 20 percent of agricultural development bank loans, 18 percent of commercial bank loans, 9 percent of consumption loans, and 24 percent of informal loans (table 6.6). If livestock production is considered part of agriculture, agriculture accounted for 20 percent of formal bank loans and 32 percent of microcredit loans. Among microcredit institutions livestock production accounted for 24 percent of all loans, while agriculture financing accounted for 9 percent.[7] Rural nonfarm production accounted for 53 percent of formal finance and 60 percent of microcredit loans.

What is the record of informal lenders in financing agriculture? Informal lenders finance both consumption and production (see table 6.6). About half of informal lending financed consumption. Agriculture received only 24 percent of informal loans, while nonfarm activities (including livestock production) received 26 percent. Among informal lenders, friends and relatives—the largest source of informal credit in Bangladesh—provided more loans to agriculture (27 percent) than did moneylenders and other informal lenders (12 percent).

Do these figures indicate that credit is not required for crop production? Farmers owning less than 2.5 acres of land were likely to be more liquidity-constrained than large farmers. Production function analysis shows that the marginal product of capital was Tk 0.41 for marginal farmers (those owning less than half an acre of land), Tk 0.35 for small and medium-size farmers (those owning 0.5–2.5 acres of land), and Tk

| Nonagriculture | | Other[a] | |
| Average loan size (taka) | Percentage of total disbursed by source | Average loan size (taka) | Percentage of total disbursed by source |
| --- | --- | --- | --- |
| 115,425 | 52.5 | 111,562 | 27.1 |
| 175,186 | 77.0 | 5,669 | 0.9 |
| 47,127 | 22.3 | 175,098 | 59.3 |
| 1,728 | 59.7 | 1,620 | 7.9 |
| 2,033 | 61.2 | 1,711 | 4.8 |
| 1,797 | 61.9 | 2,034 | 8.9 |
| 997 | 49.9 | 1,339 | 17.0 |
| 3,504 | 78.3 | 3,239 | 4.8 |
| 4,754 | 25.0 | 4,568 | 50.3 |
| 4,579 | 24.6 | 4,121 | 47.4 |
| 5,506 | 26.9 | 6,782 | 61.4 |

0.07 for large farmers (those owning more than 2.5 acres of land). These figures clearly show that small and medium-size farmers are more credit-constrained than large farmers. In contrast, the marginal product of labor was Tk 18 for marginal farmers, Tk 27 for small and medium-size farmers, and Tk 53 for large farmers. Small and medium-size farmers thus face higher prices for capital but lower prices for labor than large farmers, indicating that farming is more capital-intensive for large farmers than for small and medium-size farmers.

Small and medium-size farmers received only 13 percent of loans disbursed by formal financial institutions, and marginal farmers received less than 5 percent (table 6.7). In contrast, marginal farmers received 72 percent of microcredit, 24 percent of microcredit went to small and medium-size farmers, and 4 percent went to large farmers. About 35 percent of informal loans went to small and medium-size farmers; large farmers received 27 percent of informal loans and marginal farmers received 38 percent. For small and medium-size farmers, friends and relatives provide the bulk of loans supporting agricultural activities.

Farmers' savings financed more than 80 percent of investment in pump irrigation; formal banks financed only 14 percent (AST-MOA 1991). More recent data confirm that self-finance is the principal source of investment in agriculture, with more than 65 percent of the owners of irrigation equipment financing their investment from savings. Only 28 percent of farmers used credit to finance these investments, from which a mere 18 percent used loans from banks (IIMI/BSERT 1995). A large percentage of purchases of irrigation

TABLE 6.7

**Average Loan Size and Distribution of Loans by Landholding**

| | 0–50 decimals | | 51–250 decimals | | 250+ decimals | |
|---|---|---|---|---|---|---|
| Source | Average loan size (taka) | Percentage of total disbursed by source | Average loan size (taka) | Percentage of total disbursed by source | Average loan size (taka) | Percentage of total disbursed by source |
| Formal finance | 5,442 | 4.6 | 11,445 | 12.9 | 90,647 | 82.5 |
| BKB/RAKUB | 5,564 | 5.5 | 12,871 | 14.2 | 132,859 | 80.3 |
| Commercial banks | 5,223 | 3.5 | 9,767 | 11.2 | 66,208 | 85.2 |
| Microcredit | 1,684 | 71.6 | 2,135 | 24.4 | 2,474 | 4.0 |
| Grameen Bank | 1,936 | 70.2 | 2,117 | 25.5 | 2,603 | 4.4 |
| Other NGOs | 1,871 | 72.2 | 2,494 | 25.9 | 1,834 | 1.9 |
| Cooperatives | 1,098 | 77.1 | 1,659 | 19.7 | 1,581 | 3.1 |
| Other | 2,557 | 49.5 | 11,340 | 16.9 | 7,526 | 33.6 |
| Informal finance | 2,470 | 37.9 | 6,863 | 34.8 | 11,742 | 27.3 |
| Friends and relatives | 2,282 | 36.7 | 7,398 | 39.7 | 8,977 | 23.6 |
| Other | 3,427 | 42.2 | 4,031 | 15.9 | 36,078 | 41.9 |

*Source:* BIDS–World Bank 1991/92 survey.

equipment was associated with the sale of land, livestock, and other assets or with land mortgaging. The incidence of mortgaging in the purchase of irrigation equipment was 80 percent among small farmers, 42 percent among medium-size farmers, and 51 percent among large farmers.

This equity-based investment pattern in agriculture is surprising in a country in which farmers are poor, and it means that farmers without equity or access to financial services are unable to invest in agriculture. It follows, therefore, that without savings and access to credit, most small and medium-size farmers operate at the subsistence level. The low growth rate (1–2 percent) of the crop sector may be a result of inadequate access to institutional credit by the majority of Bangladeshi farmers. Targeting this important group of rural households is thus an important policy directive for promoting growth in agriculture and reducing poverty.

## Meeting the Credit Needs of Small and Medium-Size Farmers

Small and medium-size farmers must have access to institutional credit, both to reduce poverty and to spur economic growth. Efforts to reduce poverty should be directed not only at reaching the poor but also at preventing the process by which small and medium-size farmers become landless. Improving access to credit by small and medium-size farmers should also promote agricultural and economic growth.

Meeting this group's need for credit may be problematic, however, because of the covariate risk in farm production, the relatively high transactions costs of making small loans, and the government's policy of writing off small loans for political reasons. Because transactions costs are largely fixed, banks prefer to make large loans. As a result large landowners are the main recipients of formal finance. Covariate risk affects all types of farmers equally, but the ability to bear this risk is perceived to be higher for large farmers. Thus formal financial institutions prefer to lend to large landholding households. The government's practice of writing off small loans actually hurts small and medium-size farmers, because it makes banks reluctant to extend loans to them.[8]

How can the microcredit experience be used to develop a viable financial system for agriculture that will address the needs of small and medium-size farmers? First, delivery of credit must be based on the concept of financial intermediation and not on the more limited objective of delivering credit using donor-supplied funds. Savings mobilization must be an integral part of lending to the farmers.

Second, delivery of financial services must be done on a cost recovery basis. Even if seed capital is required to develop such a system, financial sustainability must be made a top priority. Sound financial management policies must be adopted for mobilizing savings and approving loans.

Third, given the covariate risk of farm production, credit delivery should be innovative. Financial institutions must be ready to handle the seasonal demand pattern of agricultural households. To do so, they must diversify loan portfolios across geographic areas and economic sectors. Grameen Bank's introduction of seasonal loans and family loans shows how loans can be diversified between sectors and genders to reduce loan default risk.

Fourth, experiments must be conducted to determine whether group-based or individual-based lending is an appropriate credit delivery model for small and medium-size farmers. Grameen Bank's group-based lending concept was introduced for small and medium-size farmers in a pilot scheme administered by RAKUB in the Kurigram district, and the loan recovery rate exceeded 95 percent over the life of the project. That model has not been well tested across groups of different types of farmers and diversified crop cultures, however.

The seasonality of farm production should be taken into consideration in scheduling loan repayment. One way to resolve seasonalities in input and output markets is to lend and repay loans in kind, a practice used by Grameen's offshoot, Krishi Foundation. Although it is too early to assess this model, preliminary analysis shows that it reduces farmers' risk in both allocating inputs and marketing output, raising farm productivity (Rahman 1996).

Finally, interest rates must be set at a level that is self-sustainable and reflects both market conditions and the cost of operations. Interest rates should not be set below market rates, a practice that leads to credit rationing and rent-seeking behavior. Using market rates would also help financial institutions cover the full cost of lending. Although subsidized funds and grants may be needed to develop a financial system for small and medium-size farmers, permanent subsidization should not be permitted.

## The Government's Role in Rural Finance

Despite the government's active lending policies, formal institutions as a whole provide no more than 20 percent of rural credit, accounting for only about 4 percent of agricultural GDP. Experience in different countries suggests that government should be a facilitator rather than a provider of rural finance. The experience of microcredit programs in Bangladesh indicates that the government can effectively serve client needs in rural areas with minimum interference in the financial system. The government should establish a prudent regulatory and supervision scheme that ensures the functioning of a financial intermediary that allows individuals to participate in the decisionmaking process. An appropriate legal and regulatory framework must be designed so that microcredit programs and informal lenders can gain access to market resources. Politically motivated loan write-offs and interest remission should not be allowed, and banks should not be used to deliver direct transfers intended to alleviate poverty or respond to natural disasters. If public transfer is necessary, other delivery mechanisms should be used.

The government should allow financial institutions to charge a premium for the covariate risk involved in crop production. The government should also allow experimentation in developing an appropriate financial system for groups that are not served because of market failure. The government and donors may provide seed capital to cover the initial costs of developing such a system.

## Summary

In Bangladesh microcredit programs are supporting more landless households and women and financing more rural production than formal financial institutions. For example, in 1994/95 microcredit programs disbursed Tk 17,850 million, compared with Tk 14,800 million advanced by formal banks, including Bangladesh Krishi Bank. The landless poor and women received more than 80 percent of the loans disbursed by microfinance institutions.

Microcredit programs seem to reduce both the volume and the interest rate of informal lending, increase borrowing from institutional sources, and reduce the net flow of interhousehold transfers. Compared with microcredit programs, government-directed finance has played a limited role. The roles that formal financial institutions are playing in rural areas are unsustainable, however, without government assistance. Formal banks suffer from poor loan recovery rates (less than 30 percent), high administrative costs, and negative returns on assets. Microcredit programs are unable to function without donor assistance and they must find ways to reduce administrative costs and implement more cost-effective methods of financial intermediation with the poor.

The majority of rural households with limited access to institutional credit are small and medium-size farmers, who constitute more than 45 percent of rural households and cultivate more than 55 percent of cultivable land. Improving this group's access to institutional credit is critical to agricultural growth and poverty reduction in Bangladesh. With donor support microcredit programs have improved the access of landless farmers and women to institutional credit. Resources have not been made available to develop similar programs for small and medium-size farmers.

Seasonality and production risk explain why institutional lenders (both formal and microcredit) allocate fewer funds to agriculture than to nonagricultural sectors. But the experience of Grameen Bank, Grameen Krishi Foundation, and other organizations suggests that it is possible to develop financial projects for small and medium-size farmers. Appropriate design of financial products (both savings and credit) is necessary to improve access by small, medium-size, and other farmers to bank services.

Unless rural financial systems are shown to be financially viable, private banks and agencies will not move to the rural sector. The government could adopt a two-prong approach for rural finance. First, it could restructure the publicly owned agricultural banks (BKB and RAKUB), making self-sustainability a prerequisite for their continued functioning. Second, the government could encourage NGOs and other actors to reach small and medium-size farmers and other unserved groups to improve access to institutional financial services.

## Notes

1. The extent of informal lending may be underestimated because only loan transactions that exceeded Tk 500 were included in the BIDS–World Bank survey.

2. Another bank, Samabay (Cooperative) Bank, is also active in rural finance but its loan disbursement to agriculture is low.

3. In recent years formal financial institutions have been supporting some NGOs or running small-scale microfinance programs. Their loan recovery rates for microfinance are about 90 percent. Loan recovery rates for larger loans remain low, however.

4. Subsidy dependence figures for microcredit programs and agricultural development banks are not really comparable. The financial data used for Grameen Bank and BRAC were audited by international standards; the financial data for RAKUB and BKB were provided by bank staff and may not be reliable. RAKUB and BKB were criticized in a World Bank report (1996a) for not undertaking a proper evaluation of their financial positions. It is likely that profit was overstated and that the provision for loan losses was inadequate, in which case the subsidy dependence of these banks is likely to be understated.

5. This result is counterintuitive. Given the cross-sectional nature of the data analysis, the result should be interpreted with caution.

6. Friends and relatives often charge no interest on loans. If zero interest rates are included in the calculation of the informal lending rate, the rate is 47 percent instead of 85 percent.

7. In recent years Grameen Bank has increased lending to agriculture through the introduction of seasonal loans, which finance crop production. In 1993–94 agriculture accounted for about 35 percent of total loans from Grameen Bank.

8. Large farmers also prefer taking out small loans in order to take advantage of the government's loan write-off policies. Given the excess demand for institutional loans, small and medium-size farmers are largely rationed out.

# 7

## Cost-Effectiveness of Alternative
## Poverty Alleviation Programs

Microcredit programs are more cost-effective in delivering financial services than state-controlled agricultural development banks, as chapter 6 showed. But how do they compare with other antipoverty programs such as Food-for-Work in terms of delivering services to and generating benefits for the poor? Both targeted credit and targeted food programs are effective in reaching the poor because self-selection rules are built into the program design. The two types of programs differ, however, in that targeted credit programs provide support on a continuous basis, while targeted food programs operate only part of the year. The two types of programs also serve beneficiaries with different levels of skills.

Poverty may also be combated by investing in infrastructure. Unlike targeted food programs, which affect only consumption, or targeted credit programs, which tend to finance low-growth activities, investment in infrastructure may promote broad-based growth that will reduce poverty. This chapter compares the cost-effectiveness of microcredit, formal rural financial intermediation, targeted food interventions, and rural infrastructure development projects in Bangladesh in order to determine which poverty alleviation programs are most cost-effective and to identify which programs benefit which types of beneficiaries.

### Measuring Cost-Benefit Ratios

Measuring cost-benefit ratios requires assessing benefits and costs separately for alternative program interventions.[1] Identifying benefits both at the participant level and at the community level is difficult because of program placement and participation endogeneity. If programs were placed randomly, comparison of income, consumption, and other outcomes between program and control villages would measure the extent of program benefits at the village level. But program placement is not exogenous—village attributes influence placement. Program participation is also endogenous, so simple comparison of outcomes between participants and nonparticipants (either within the same village or between different villages) does not measure the causal impacts of program participation. Complicated estimation and data survey methods are required to circumvent these problems.

The benefits of all of the programs examined are measured in terms of their effect on consumption, an approach that has some limitations. Consumption is a short-term measure of program benefits that does not measure total benefits. Many antipoverty programs have long-run impacts, including impacts on human and physical capital accumulation. Including only consumption effects in cost-benefit ratios understates the potential of some antipoverty programs to increase growth and reduce poverty. Targeted food programs, for example, may increase growth through their effect on infrastructure. The social and private gains from creating jobs when jobs are scarce and the fact that the people employed in these programs and their families represent the most vulnerable group in the society are also not reflected in cost-benefit ratios that consider only consumption effects. Such programs may provide enormous benefits to society and to the households affected by reducing the costs of vulnerability (such as incapacitation or death of a family member due to hunger) of the poorest of the poor. These limitations notwithstanding, cost-benefit analysis in terms of consumption does shed light on the cost-effectiveness of alternative antipoverty programs.

## Cost-Benefit Analysis of Credit Instruments

From the viewpoint of a delivery system, the cost-effectiveness of a credit program can be measured in terms of the social costs incurred for each unit of financial services it provide its clients. The social cost of a subsidized credit program is measured by its negative economic profit, which is the net subsidy allocated to the program (accounting profit minus the cost of subsidized resources, including grants, at their opportunity or market costs).

The costs of different credit programs vary depending on the type of financial service delivered (table 7.1). The economic cost of an outstanding loan of Tk 1 is Tk 0.098 for RAKUB, Tk 0.146 for BKB, Tk 0.172 for Grameen Bank, and Tk 0.444 for BRAC.[2] Thus BRAC is the least cost-effective program, and formal banks appear to be more cost-effective than microcredit programs in terms of loans outstanding. In terms of loan disbursement, however, formal banks are less cost-effective than microcredit programs. To disburse a Tk 1 loan, Grameen Bank spends Tk 0.119, BRAC spends Tk 0.407, BKB spends Tk 0.768, and RAKUB spends 1.814. Grameen Bank also appears to be the most cost-effective at mobilizing savings. To mobilize Tk 1 of savings, Grameen spends Tk 0.135, BRAC spends Tk 0.984, BKB spends Tk 0.319, and RAKUB spends Tk 0.680.[3]

TABLE 7.1
**Costs of Delivering Services of Alternative Credit Programs, 1991/92**

| Item | Grameen Bank | BRAC | BKB | RAKUB |
|---|---|---|---|---|
| Net subsidy (millions of taka) | 598 | 272 | 2,943 | 896 |
| Loans outstanding (millions of taka) | 3,488 | 612 | 20,098 | 9,174 |
| Annual disbursement (millions of taka) | 5,034 | 669 | 3,830 | 494 |
| Total savings (millions of taka) | 4,410 | 276 | 9,217 | 1,318 |
| Economic cost per taka loan outstanding (taka) | 0.172 | 0.444 | 0.146 | 0.098 |
| Economic cost per taka loan disbursed (taka) | 0.119 | 0.407 | 0.768 | 1.814 |
| Economic cost per taka savings mobilized (taka) | 0.135 | 0.984 | 0.319 | 0.680 |

*Source:* Khandker and Khalily 1996; Khandker, Khalily, and Khan 1995; World Bank 1996a.

Cost-effectiveness is measured by the cost-benefit ratios of these programs, where benefits are measured in terms of the program's impact on the consumption of borrowers after controlling for all possible sources of bias, and costs are the social costs (net subsidy) associated with the programs (table 7.2). Cost-effectiveness measures how much it costs to deliver a given level of benefits (induced consumption) to a program participant. The marginal return to consumption per household for borrowing from Grameen Bank was estimated at 18 percent for borrowing by women and 11 percent for borrowing by men (see chapter 3). That is, for every TK 100 of borrowing from Grameen, an average household consumes an additional Tk 18 if women are the borrowers and Tk 11 if men are the borrowers. These figures underestimate actual consumption because 5 percent of all loans are deducted immediately as group savings. Real borrowing is thus 5 percent less than reported borrowing, which means that the actual impact is 5.3 percent (1/95) higher, as table 7.2 shows.

The social cost of lending is the net subsidy involved in program placement. If the average loan outstanding is the amount that borrowers keep for supporting their income-earning activities,[4] the total benefit from borrowing is the average loan outstanding times the marginal return to borrowing.[5] For Grameen Bank average loans outstanding in 1991/92 were Tk 3,488 million. These loans contributed to Tk 659 million by female borrowers and Tk 405 million worth of consumption by male borrowers. Cost-benefit ratios for Grameen and BRAC are calculated by dividing the social cost (net subsidy) by the total benefits in terms of consumption. For

TABLE 7.2
**Cost-Effectiveness of Alternative Credit Programs, 1991/92**
(millions of taka unless otherwise noted)

| Measure | Grameen Bank | BRAC | BKB | RAKUB |
|---|---|---|---|---|
| Social cost (net subsidy) | 598 | 272 | 2,943 | 896 |
| Average loan outstanding | 3,488 | 612 | 20,098 | 9,174 |
| Marginal return to borrowing (percent) | 18.9, 11.6 | 17.2, 12.5 | 3 | 3 |
| Total benefit[a] | 659, 405 | 77, 105 | 603 | 275 |
| Cost-benefit ratio[b] | 0.91, 1.48 | 3.53, 2.59 | 4.88 | 3.26 |

*Note:* The two values for marginal return, total benefit, and cost-benefit ratio for Grameen Bank and BRAC show figures for women and men borrowers, with figures for women borrowers appearing first.
a. Average loan outstanding times the marginal return to borrowing.
b. Total cost divided by total benefit.
*Source:* Estimated from Grameen Bank, BRAC, Bangladesh Krishi Bank, and Rajshahi Krishi Unnayan Bank data.

Grameen Bank the cost-benefit ratios are 0.91 for female borrowing and 1.48 for male borrowing. This means that society pays Tk 0.91 for every Tk 1 of consumption generated by borrowing by women and Tk 1.48 for every Tk 1 of consumption generated by borrowing by men from Grameen. The cost-benefit ratios for BRAC are 3.53 for female borrowing and 2.59 for male borrowing.[6]

Estimates of the marginal return to consumption for loans from agricultural development banks (BKB and RAKUB) are needed to compare the cost-effectiveness of such lending with the cost-effectiveness of microcredit. Like microloans, however, formal loans are endogenously determined by the same characteristics that affect a household's per capita consumption. Valid instruments must thus be used to estimate the marginal return to consumption. The instruments used are the extent of target households in the village interacted with household and individual characteristics, both of which appear in the borrowing equation but not in the per capita consumption equation. Because microcredit is available only to the poor, the extent of target households is a valid instrument for households that have access to both formal and microcredit loans. Interactions with household characteristics reveal how borrowing from formal sources responds to these characteristics when households meet the target criteria. A two-stage least squares regression was used to estimate the impact of formal borrowing on per capita consumption (regression results not reported here). The borrowing impact could not be estimated by gender because formal credit is extended largely to men. Using these estimates along with data on average household consumption and borrowing, the marginal return to consumption of formal finance was estimated at 3 percent a year (see table 7.2).

The estimated induced consumption benefits of borrowing from formal institutions was high (Tk 603 million for BKB and Tk 275 million for RAKUB). The social costs of such lending were also high (Tk 2,943 million for BKB and Tk 896 million for RAKUB).[7] Dividing the estimated social cost (net subsidy) by the estimated total benefit yields cost-benefit ratios of 4.88 for BKB and 3.26 for RAKUB. These cost-benefit ratios were higher than those for Grameen Bank and BRAC. Grameen Bank and BRAC are thus relatively more cost-effective at raising household consumption than other credit programs.

## Cost-Benefit Analysis of Targeted Food Interventions

Antipoverty wage employment programs have smoothed consumption in Bangladesh, India, and elsewhere (Alamgir 1983; Datt and Ravallion 1996; Hossain and Asaduzzaman 1983; World Bank 1990; Subbarao and others 1997). The two most prominent antipoverty programs in Bangladesh are Food-for-Work and Vulnerable Group Development. Both programs are intended only to smooth consumption rather than to promote economic growth.

Food-for-Work is a wage employment-generating program that targets the wage-employed poor who find it difficult to find employment during the lean season. The larger of the program's two components is run by the World Food Programme; the smaller component is run by CARE on behalf of the U.S. Agency for International Development (see table 2.1). In 1991/92 the program disbursed 637,000 metric tons of grain, worth $111 million (WGTFI 1994). Four million people were served by the program in 1991/92, at an operating cost of $180 million. The program employs poor people to build rural roads and other types of infrastructure, including canals and embankments. It is self-selecting in that only the very poor are willing to accept the low-level manual jobs the program offers. About 60 percent of program participants come from the poorest quartile of rural households (Ravallion 1991).

Vulnerable Group Development is a self-employment-generating program that uses food (mostly wheat) to promote productive self-employment for poor people not covered by Food-for-Work. The program is managed by the WFP and is largely donor-funded, with some support from the government of Bangladesh.[8] It has an annual operating cost of about $50 million. During 1992, 192,000 metric tons of wheat, worth $33.5 million, were disbursed to more than 450,000 households in 84 thanas. In addition, since 1988 a range of development services have been provided, including training in functional literacy and numeracy, health and nutrition, income-earning skills (primarily poultry rearing), group formation, legal awareness, savings, and access to credit.

Vulnerable Group Development operates in regions that are most at risk, and its principal beneficiaries are destitute women (A. Ahmed 1993). Screening is done by a committee consisting of local-level (union council) officials. Each beneficiary is entitled to a free monthly allotment of 31.25 kilograms of wheat for 24 consecutive months. Allotments are distributed at the union council office.

The benefits of the Food-for-Work and Vulnerable Group Development programs include the food allocated to program participants and the increase in consumption associated with the improvements in infrastructure created by the programs. The costs of the programs are indicated in program documents. Cost-benefit ratios based only on the food allocated are taken from published sources.

Estimates of the impact of infrastructure investment on consumption were estimated by measuring the impact of electricity and paved roads on average household consumption in a village, after controlling for other village attributes, including the extent of landlessness in the village. (The regression is similar to those reported in chapter 3.) The cost of developing infrastructure in a village was derived from World Bank documents on rural roads and market development projects in Bangladesh (World Bank 1996c).

Researchers from both inside and outside of Bangladesh have evaluated the cost-effectiveness of Food-for-Work and Vulnerable Group Development (see Ahmed and Hossain 1990, Quasem and Hossain 1985, Osmani and Chowdhury 1983, and WGTFI 1994; some of the earlier studies are reviewed by Ahmed and others 1995). According to these studies, Food-for-Work participants received as little as 38 percent of the project's delivered wheat; as much as 40 percent of program funds went toward administrative costs, and up to 36 percent was lost to leakages. Vulnerable Group Development performed far better than Food-for-Work, with less than half the level of leakage (8–14 percent compared with 30–35 percent ). High administrative costs and leakages increased the cost of delivering aid through Food-for-Work, which delivered Tk 1 worth of benefit at a cost of Tk 1.7–Tk 2.6. Vulnerable Group Development provided the same level of benefits at a cost of Tk 1.5–Tk 1.7 (table 7.3). Food-for-Work's high system losses are caused partly by the design of program delivery. Program participants must convince local leaders (who organize and monitor the tasks assigned to the participants) to pay them their full entitlement, and payment is usually on a daily basis. In contrast, Vulnerable Group Development disburses allotments once a month, and all beneficiaries receive their allotments on the same day, at the same location. This gives program beneficiaries the chance to take collective action if they feel they are being cheated.

TABLE 7.3
**Cost-Effectiveness of the Food-for-Work and Vulnerable Group Development Programs, 1991–92**

| Indicator | Vulnerable Group Development | Food-for-Work (CARE) | Food-for-Work (World Food Programme) |
|---|---|---|---|
| Cost (dollars per ton of grain) | 252 | 299 | 258 |
| Income transfer (dollars per ton of grain) | 164[a] (153[b]) | 114 | 151[a] (128[c]) |
| Cost-benefit ratio | 1.54[a] (1.65[b]) | 2.62 | 1.71[a] (2.02[c]) |

a. World Food Programme figures.
b. International Food and Policy Research Institute figures.
c. Bangladesh Institute of Development Studies/International Food and Policy Research Institute figures for 1982–83.
*Source:* WGTFI 1994.

Income transfers to Vulnerable Group Development beneficiaries represent about 22 percent of their total income, and calorie consumption is almost 15 percent higher among program participants (WGTFI 1994). Food-for-Work also helps its beneficiaries. Participating households earn 55 percent more in wages than nonparticipating households (Osmani and Chowdhury 1983). During 1991/92 Food-for-Work generated about 22 person-days of employment per participant, up from 17 person-days in 1982/83.

The development impact of Food-for-Work at the village level is mixed. Although projects are appropriately designed, the work done through the program is not uniformly sound. Only a third of all projects were completed in a satisfactory manner, according to one engineering survey (Nishat and Chowdhury 1983). Moreover, the gains from infrastructure development are higher for landed households than for landless households (Ahmed and Hossain 1990; Quasem and Hossain 1985). Nevertheless, when induced income changes stemming from direct income transfers are taken into account, benefits exceed costs by as much as 65 percent. The methodology used for this type of benefit-cost ratio is not rigorous, however, because the results are not corrected for either household or village heterogeneity. These estimates are thus not fully comparable with those reported for the credit programs.

## Cost-Benefit Analysis of Infrastructure Projects

More than half of the population of Bangladesh lives below the official poverty line. Reducing poverty requires broad-based economic growth that generates employment and income for a large number of poor households. Interventions involving microcredit programs that support rural nonfarm activities to generate income and employment for the poor may be inadequate because they finance activities with limited potential for growth. Moreover, the poverty reduction impact of micro-credit may be short-lived if a transition toward more growth-oriented activities cannot be attained.

Infrastructure development in rural areas is often considered a tool for promoting broad-based economic growth. A village with electrifica-tion, paved roads, and other infrastructure is able to generate higher income and employment for its entire population, thereby promoting growth and reducing poverty (Ahmed and Hossain 1990). With the help of the World Bank and other donors, the government of Bangladesh has been developing rural infrastructure (World Bank 1996c). This type of rural investment can be viewed as part of a broad-based economic growth strategy, the cost-effectiveness of which can be compared with that of alternative poverty reduction programs.

Rural infrastructure can generate immediate income and employ-ment for the wage-employed poor. It also induces future income and employment growth and is hence the source of economic growth and sustained employment. A study analyzing the historical development of rural infrastructure and its impact on agricultural growth and poverty reduction in India found that road infrastructure and rural electrifica-tion have had substantial effects on rural economic growth (Binswanger, Khandker, and Rosenzweig 1993).

Rural infrastructure has had significant effects on rural incomes in Bangladesh. In a study comparing 16 villages (7 developed villages and 9 undeveloped villages), Ahmed and Hossain (1990) estimated that house-hold income in villages with developed infrastructure was 32 percent higher than in undeveloped villages. This income gain is inflated because of the bias in program placement and must be adjusted by the proportion of developed villages in Bangladesh, which is about 40 percent according to the 1991/92 Bangladesh Institute of Development Studies–World Bank household survey. The expected income gain from development for an average Bangladeshi village is thus about 13 percent (0.40 x 0.32).

The consumption impact of infrastructure at the village level was estimated using data from the 1991/92 Bangladesh Institute of Dev-elopment Studies–World Bank household survey. A village-level regres-sion was fitted (with appropriate weights to adjust for choice-based sam-pling) in which average household consumption was regressed on a number of village-level variables, including the infrastructure variables. The increase in household consumption as a result of better infrastruc-ture is 0.128. Based on average household consumption in villages with-out such infrastructure, an estimate of consumption gains per house-hold can be made.[9]

A recent World Bank study places the per household cost of developing paved roads in an undeveloped village at Tk 2,326 (World Bank 1996c). If the cost of electrifying a village is also assumed to be Tk 2,326 per household, the total per household cost for developing village infrastructure would be Tk 4,652. These cost estimates combined with an estimate of benefits yield a cost-benefit ratio for infrastructure development of 1.38 (table 7.4). That is, it costs society about Tk 1.38 to generate Tk 1 worth of average household consumption through investment in infrastructure development projects. These ratios are lower than those for formal finance, BRAC, and the food intervention programs, indicating that infrastructure investments are more cost-effective than those programs.

## Wage Employment versus Self-Employment for Target Households

If benefits are limited to consumption, Grameen Bank appears to be more cost-effective than other targeted poverty alleviation programs. Grameen Bank also seems to be more cost-effective than nontargeted programs, such as rural-based formal finance or infrastructure development projects. That is, among all the programs considered here, Grameen Bank seems to incur the lowest cost for the same dollar worth of household consumption. (Alternatively, Grameen Bank generates more benefits for the same cost to society.)

Does this mean that resources should be directed away from other programs toward Grameen Bank–type operations? The answer is not obvious. Microcredit programs attract people who self-select into programs because of their innate entrepreneurial ability. All individuals

TABLE 7.4
**Cost-Effectiveness of Infrastructure Development**

| Item | Value |
| --- | --- |
| Annual household consumption in villages without infrastructure (taka) | 25,612 |
| Annual income growth in villages with infrastructure development (percent) | 13.2 |
| Annual income gain per household (taka) | 3,380 |
| Cost of village infrastructure development per household (taka) | 4,652 |
| Cost-benefit ratio | 1.38 |

Note: Presence of electricity and paved roads is used as a proxy for infrastructure development.
Source: BIDS–World Bank 1991/92 survey except infrastructure development data, which are from Ahmed and Hossain 1990, and village infrastructure costs per household, which are estimated from World Bank 1996c.

from target households may not possess this ability. To meet the needs of poor people with different abilities, both self-employment programs (financed by microcredit) and wage employment programs (financed by formal finance or infrastructure development projects that promote broad-based economic growth) should be offered.

Regression of a set of variables—including age, formal education, and indicators of unobserved ability reflected by reading, writing, and numeracy test scores—against program participation confirms the hypothesis that people self-select into different kinds of antipoverty programs: poor people with good oral math skills tend to participate in microcredit programs (table A7.1), while poor people with poor oral math skills are more likely to enter the wage labor market (table A7.2; Greaney, Khandker, and Alam forthcoming). These findings may suggest that individuals' unobserved abilities determine their program participation behavior. The probability of joining a microcredit program is 6 percent higher among those who pass the oral math test, while the probability of taking wage employment is 12 percent higher among those who do not pass the oral math test. Among men the probability of joining a microcredit program is 8.5 percent higher if they pass the oral math test. In contrast, the probability of participating in a microcredit program is insensitive to whether or not women pass the oral math test.[10] Oral math skills reduce participation in wage employment by 9.5 percent for men and 8.3 percent for women. For a man the probability of joining a microcredit program is 7 percent higher if his wife passes the oral math test; for a woman the probability of joining a microcredit program is 7 percent lower if her husband passes the oral math test. These results may indicate that a woman's ability complements her husband's decision to join a microcredit program, while a man's ability is considered a substitute for his wife's participation. Interestingly, both men's and women's abilities deter the spouse from joining wage employment: the probability of not joining wage employment is 12 percent higher for men and 6 percent higher for women if the spouse passed the oral math test.

Among landless people men and women respond differently to wage employment and microfinance program interventions. Landless women participate more (by at least 15 percent) in microcredit programs than in wage employment, while landless men participate more (by at least 61 percent) in wage employment.

Another result worth noting is the importance of microcredit in attracting different types of households with varying sizes of landholding. Even among eligible households, those with larger landholdings are more likely to participate in microcredit programs and less likely to participate in wage employment (see tables A7.1 and A7.2). These findings appear to suggest that the ultrapoor are more likely to use public works programs than credit-based interventions.

## Summary

Grameen Bank and infrastructure development projects appear more cost-effective than other programs at increasing consumption among Bangladesh's rural poor. Among credit programs, microcredit seem to be more cost-effective than formal finance in providing financial services to poor rural clients, with Grameen Bank providing services more cost-effectively than BRAC. Among food intervention and wage employment schemes, Vulnerable Group Development appears to be more cost-effective than Food-for-Work.

Resources would be used more efficiently if the government allocated resources to more cost-effective program interventions. This does not mean that all resources should be rechanneled into the single most cost-effective program or that all people would benefit from a reallocation of resources. People self-select into programs that fit their needs and abilities. Microcredit programs are not a viable option for many people because such programs require skills, such as accounting ability, that many people in the target groups lack. Credit-based interventions are best targeted to those among the poor who can productively use microcredit to become or remain self-employed, while public works programs are best targeted to the ultrapoor who lack the skills to benefit from microcredit.

Microcredit, which finances self-employment activities that are performed at home, is particularly well-suited to the needs of rural women, who are restricted by social custom from working outside the home. Many women lack the entrepreneurial skills to become self-employed, however. For these women—who cannot participate in microcredit programs because they lack skills and cannot participate in the wage market because of social restrictions—literacy promotion and training are necessary so that they can benefit from microcredit.

## Notes

1. A formal analysis of cost-effectiveness appears in appendix C.

2. To the extent that the social costs of formal financial institutions are underestimated because of their underreporting of costs (see chapter 6), the calculated cost-benefit ratios are underestimated.

3. It is difficult to compare microcredit programs and formal credit programs. The loans disbursed by Grameen Bank and BRAC are yearly loans and they have a high recovery rate, yielding low loans outstanding-to-disbursement ratios (69 percent for Grameen Bank in 1991/92). Formal bank disbursements are not limited to yearly loans, and the loan recovery rate is quite low (less than 30 percent), resulting in high loans outstanding-to-disbursement ratios (BKB's loans

outstanding were more than five times loan disbursement in 1991/92). Savings at formal banks are strictly voluntary, while savings at microcredit institutions are usually mandatory.

4. Alternatively, loan disbursements could be used to calculate benefits. However, microcredit and formal lenders extend loans on different terms, making comparison difficult. For this reason it is better to evaluate benefits in terms of loans outstanding. The benefits accrued from loans outstanding are then comparable across programs. Note also that the estimated impact of consumption on cumulative borrowing—that is, the marginal impact of consumption—is the incremental consumption for an additional taka borrowed. Since microcredit loans are extended for one year, the marginal return on loans outstanding should be twice the marginal return on borrowing (disbursement). If it is, the cost-benefit ratios should be almost halved for microcredit loans.

5. Using marginal return to borrowing underestimates the total benefits if average returns are higher than marginal returns (under the assumption of diminishing returns to borrowing).

6. As chapter 3 shows, these programs include about 20 percent nontarget households, giving rise to 20 percent leakage. So actual benefits will be 80 percent of the calculated benefit. For example, they will be Tk 527 million and Tk 324 million for women's and men's borrowing from Grameen Bank, leading to cost-benefit ratios of 1.13 and 1.85, respectively. That is, cost-benefit ratios of the credit programs are underestimated if leakages are not taken into account.

7. These estimates—and the cost-benefit ratios based on them—are presumed to be low, because the reported costs of BKB and RAKUB are underestimated (see chapter 6).

8. The World Food Programme contributes 47 percent of the grain used by the program, and the government of Bangladesh contributes 11 percent. Other contributors are Canada (26 percent), the European Economic Council (8 percent), Australia (5 percent), and Germany (3 percent).

9. Average household consumption in a village after infrastructure development (defined here as electrification and paved roads) can be expressed by the equation $CA = CB(1 + b)$, where $CA$ and $CB$ are average household consumption in a village after and before infrastructure development and $b$ is the percentage gain in consumption (regression coefficient of the infrastructure program dummy, where the dependent variable is the natural logarithm of average household consumption in a village).

10. This suggests that the causality between program participation and oral math skills cannot run from participation to higher math skills. That is, the fact that no association exists between women's math skills and their program participation means that participation in the program cannot itself be improving participants' math skills.

# 8

# Conclusions and Policy Implications: What Have We Learned?

Finance can facilitate economic growth by easing liquidity constraints in production, by providing capital to start up new production or adopt new technology, and by helping producers assume production risk. In recent years finance has also been viewed as an antipoverty tool because it helps the unemployed become employed, thereby increasing their income and consumption and reducing poverty.

For a variety of reasons—including the problems of imperfect information and imperfect enforcement, covariate risks of agricultural production, and political interference—many countries find it difficult to develop sustainable rural financial institutions. However, the recent experience of microcredit and rural credit programs in several countries suggests that sustainable financial institutions may be possible to develop in a rural setting if certain conditions are met:

- The government does not see financial institutions as public transfer mechanisms or interfere with them in any way except to provide prudent regulation and supervision.
- Financial institutions are allowed to set interest rates that reflect market forces and adjust with inflation rates.
- Financial intermediation that includes savings mobilization is an integral part of credit delivery to targeted sectors or groups, so that targeted programs learn to depend on markets rather than solely on donors for funding.
- Loan contracts are enforced through social and economic incentives or other means such as group pressure.
- Grants or subsidized funds are given as seed capital for a limited period of time to support institutional development.

Developing a financial institution for the poor requires that an additional condition be met: the poor need to be targeted with financial services. Providing credit to the poor is often considered risky because the poor have no collateral (land or other physical assets) to offer for bank loans. Moreover, since the poor may not be able to bear the risk of self-employment because they lack entrepreneurial skills, financial institutions serving only the poor may face high default rates. Providing financial services to the poor thus requires an innovative targeting design and a credit delivery mechanism that helps identify and attract only the "able" poor who can initiate and sustain productive use of loans.

This book has evaluated three microcredit programs in Bangladesh that target the poor and women. Funded largely by donors, these programs have attempted to develop sustainable credit delivery mechanisms and savings mobilization schemes that target the poor. The programs use group-based mechanisms to deliver credit and mobilize savings, offer financial intermediation to members, adhere to strict loan recovery mechanisms, and offer noncredit services to augment the effective use of loans. The objective of these programs is to help promote self-employment for the unemployed poor and for women in order to reduce poverty.

## Program Design

Sustained poverty reduction requires actions and policies that help improve both the productive and the human capital of the poor. Policy interventions must be well targeted if benefits are to reach only the poor. In Bangladesh agricultural growth policies, which increased farm production and income, failed to improve either the physical or the human capital of the poor because their growth impact was neither broad-based nor technology neutral. Targeted antipoverty measures without a credit component, such as the Food-for-Work and Vulnerable Group Development programs, have smoothed consumption for the poor who depend on wage income, but they have failed to enhance their human and physical capital.

In contrast, microcredit programs have been able to reach the poor and enhance both their productive and their human capital by generating self-employment. These programs promote human capital development through literacy and social awareness programs and by targeting women. Group-based lending, which minimizes the moral hazard problem of lending by creating social collateral, also reduces the problem of targeting through a group screening mechanism. Group-based lending programs also provide social intermediation and other organizational help, including skills promotion training and marketing, which are essential for sustaining the benefits that accrue to participants and to society. How effective microcredit programs are in reducing poverty and reaching the poor is an important policy question that merits careful program evaluation.

## Program Evaluation

Microcredit programs in many countries use subsidized resources to reach the poor, especially poor women. Since the subsidies allocated to these programs could be used to support noncredit programs, policy-makers must determine whether microfinance is more cost-effective than formal finance and whether it represents the best (or at least an efficient) use of scarce resources with which to reduce poverty.

Two approaches have been taken in evaluating microfinance. The first approach assumes that a cost-effective delivery model yields expected benefits to both program participants and to society as a whole. It thus calculates the net social cost per unit of credit delivered to the target group. The second approach assumes that program placement or program participation is exogenous and that the accrued benefits to participants represent net gains to society at no cost to it. It thus measures the impact on participants only. What is important is identifying the causal impact of program placement and participation and determine whether a program is cost-effective in generating benefits.

Program participation involves both interest and noninterest costs. To be worthwhile to a member, participation must be cost-effective. Participation must also reduce poverty, one of the main objectives of these programs. The literature that attempts to quantify the extent of benefits is methodologically flawed because it does not take into consideration the role of endogeneity of program placement and participation. Program evaluation also fails to quantify cost-effectiveness of programs for both program participants and donors that support these programs. So-called outreach indicators, such as the extent of program coverage, for example, do not reveal whether program participation benefits the poor and, if so, how and at what cost.

Repeated borrowing or high loan recovery rates may not indicate that participants benefit from microcredit programs. In fact, since many microcredit borrowers have no alternative sources of finance, the very low dropout rate among members with a low loan default rate may signal the dependency of participants on the program itself. Even worse, repeated borrowers may use other sources of lending, such as informal lenders, to remain in good standing with a microlender. Evaluation of the impact of borrowing from microcredit programs on household net worth is as important as knowing the extent of loan default among repeated borrowers. The cost-effectiveness of borrowing for borrowers dictates that the return on borrowing is greater than or at least equal to the cost of borrowing. To establish the cost-effectiveness of supporting microcredit programs for donors and governments, research must show that the income and other gains generated by microcredit programs are greater than those generated by alternative uses of the subsidized funds currently allocated to microcredit programs.

A more difficult issue to resolve is whether program participants benefit at the expense of others in society. Because programs create externalities that may hurt or benefit nonparticipants, assessment of a microcredit program must evaluate the benefits to both participants and nonparticipants. Appropriate program evaluation thus requires estimation of cost-effectiveness on both the supply side (whether a microfinance program is cost-effective in delivering program inputs, such as credit) and the demand side (whether a program is cost-effective in generating benefits to participants and nonparticipants).

## Poverty Reduction

Microfinance reduces poverty by increasing per capita consumption among program participants and their families. Annual household consumption expenditure increases Tk 18 for every Tk 100 of additional borrowing by women and Tk 11 for every Tk 100 of additional borrowing by men. With an 18 percent annual increase in consumption, a poor household of six members could be free of poverty by borrowing about Tk 12,000 ($300) a year. Poverty reduction estimates based on consumption impacts of credit show that about 5 percent of program participants can lift their families out of poverty each year by participating in and borrowing from microfinance programs.

Microcredit programs also help smooth consumption, as well as the seasonality of labor supply. Where seasonality has a pronounced impact on labor and consumption patterns of rural households, especially poor households, improved access to borrowing can reduce the impact of seasonality on both consumption and labor supply. Targeted credit also improves the nutritional status of children. The nutritional impact of credit is especially large for girls, and the impact is larger for loans made to women.

The effect of microcredit programs on village-level poverty reduction is somewhat smaller. Overall only 1 percent of rural households can free themselves from poverty each year through microcredit. Moreover, some of this reduction may result from income redistribution rather than income growth. The social cost of supporting microcredit programs is low, however—estimated at $11 per household per year.

Are the poverty alleviation impacts of microcredit sustainable? If poverty reduction is achieved mainly through changes in consumption rather than through changes in income and productivity, poverty reduction impacts are difficult to sustain. Participants in microcredit programs tend to have low levels of skills and knowledge and are therefore limited to borrowing for self-employment in rural nonfarm activities that have low growth potential. Unless activities with high growth potential are supported by microcredit programs, the possibility of long-run poverty reduction through microcredit programs is remote.

Skills development training benefits the poor. For equal capital intensity, the marginal return on capital is higher among BRAC and RD-12 participants, who receive skills development training, than among Grameen Bank participants. But Grameen Bank provides larger loans per borrower than the other two programs. As a result borrowers of Grameen Bank enjoy higher returns to capital than do BRAC and RD-12 borrowers, and the effect of their borrowing on household net worth is higher. These results suggest that loan size matters, and that larger loans are needed to reduce poverty on a sustained basis.

## Growth

Agricultural growth affects the growth of income and productivity in the rural nonfarm sector. However, the fact that the rural nonfarm sector has grown by more than 4 percent a year, while agriculture has grown by less than 2 percent a year, indicates that rural nonfarm growth is affected by other factors as well. The question is how much rural nonfarm growth is possible without agricultural growth.

Because microcredit supports predominantly rural nonfarm activities that may have limited growth potential, it may have a small impact on growth, although its immediate impact on poverty reduction may be substantial. With appropriate skills promotion and market development, however, the rural nonfarm sector can play an active role in increasing overall growth. Two findings are pertinent in this context. First, village-level production gains in manufacturing are higher in BRAC villages than in villages with other microcredit programs or formal finance, even though both formal finance and Grameen Bank provide more credit than BRAC. Second, returns on capital and labor to activities—including manufacturing—are higher in villages with better infrastructure. These findings suggest that rural growth led by nonfarm activities is possible, provided adequate infrastructure investment, including marketing and skills development, is made.

## Women

Microcredit programs are particularly important for rural women, who are excluded by social custom from working outside the home. All three of the main programs in Bangladesh target women, who represent 94 percent of Grameen Bank participants, 88 percent of BRAC participants, and 70 percent of RD-12 participants. Women have proved to be excellent credit risks, with loan default rates of only 3 percent— significantly lower than the 10 percent default rate for men.

Women have clearly benefited from microcredit programs. Program participation has enhanced women's productive means by increasing their access to cash income generation from market-oriented activities and by increasing their ownership of nonland assets. These improvements should enhance women's empowerment within the household, influencing their own and their children's consumption and other measures of welfare (such as schooling). One measure of this increased empowerment is the fact that women's borrowing has an independent effect on household resource allocation, with men investing more in physical capital and women investing more in human capital.[1]

## Rural Financial Markets

The success of microfinance has destroyed three commonly held myths in rural finance: that the poor are not creditworthy, that women represent greater credit risks than men, and that the poor do not save. The large number of beneficiaries of microcredit programs shows how widespread microfinance has become in rural Bangladesh. The impact of microfinance on rural financial markets can be measured by its effect on four indicators of rural finance: the extent of informal lending, the informal lending rate, the extent of interhousehold transfers, and agricultural financing.

Microfinance has reduced the volume of lending from informal sources.[2] Grameen Bank reduced the informal lending rate on loans with terms of more than one year. Grameen Bank also reduced the extent of interhousehold transfers in rural areas. Agricultural financing increased as a result of microfinancing by BRAC and RD-12. Grameen's seasonal and family loans, which support mainly crop production on leased land, also increased agriculture financing in recent years, making agriculture the largest category of loans disbursed by Grameen Bank in 1994.

Microfinance loans are well-targeted. Large farmers (owning more than 2.5 acres of land) received more than 82 percent, small and medium-size farmers (owning more than 0.5 acres but less than 2.5 acres of land) received just 13 percent, and poor and marginal farmers received only 5 percent of total loans disbursed by formal banks. In contrast, landless and marginal farmers received 72 percent, small and medium-size farmers received 24 percent, and large farmers received only 4 percent of microfinance loans.

These findings reveal that small and medium-size farmers, who constitute more than 45 percent of farmers in Bangladesh, have the least access to institutional credit. This lack of adequate access to finance has an adverse impact on both poverty and agricultural productivity. Some commercial banks are pilot testing group-based lending schemes for small and medium-size farmers using donor funds. Even where the loan recovery rate has been high, however, commercial and agricultural development banks have remained reluctant to use their own resources to finance small and medium-size farmers, partly because of the high transactions costs of providing small loans.

## Subsidy Dependence

All three microcredit programs studied are subsidized, although their subsidy dependence has fallen over time. In Bangladesh subsidies are necessary to defray the high costs of social intermediation, the high transactions costs of small loans, the high costs of program placement in poor agroclimatic and risky areas, and the inability to charge interest rates that reflect the full cost of program intervention and inflation.

Subsidy in the form of seed capital or institutional development funds may be required for the institutional development of microcredit programs. But attaining subsidy-free microcredit is possible if it is made a mandate from the outset. Although poverty reduction is the highest priority, the goal of self-sustainability within the shortest possible time should also be incorporated into program design from the beginning. Donors and governments that support subsidized operations of microcredit programs can enforce this by emphasizing that financial sustainability must be attained within a set period and that support is not open-ended. Microcredit programs must deal with this issue if they are to operate with market resources, with less and less dependence on donor funding. But if subsidy is unavoidable to attain the primary objective of poverty reduction and social development, it should be kept to a minimum and used as efficiently as possible.

## Cost-Effectiveness

To allocate resources for poverty reduction efficiently, policymakers must identify the poor and the sources of their poverty. If seasonal unemployment is a source of poverty, then poverty reduction requires targeted measures, such as Food-for-Work, that help smooth consumption. If poverty and unemployment among a segment of the population is permanent, then short-term measures, such as food-for-work, will not be adequate. In Bangladesh, where poverty is rampant and economic growth is too slow to reduce poverty, both targeted measures and broad-based economic growth are essential to combat poverty.

Microcredit reduces poverty, but so do other antipoverty programs, such as targeted food programs and infrastructure development. How do these programs compare with microcredit programs? In terms of their effect on per capita consumption, Grameen Bank and infrastructure development projects appear more cost-effective than other programs, including BRAC, RD-12, agricultural development banks, and targeted food programs. Because different types of programs reach different types of beneficiaries, however, the higher cost-effectiveness of these programs may not indicate that resources should be reallocated from other programs.

Providing access to financial services to small and medium-size farmers who do not have access to such services is required not only to reduce poverty but also to prevent rural landlessness. Donor resources are used largely to develop schemes for the landless; they are not available to develop similar targeted programs to prevent landlessness among small and medium-size farmers. Targeting such farmers with financial services holds the promise of spurring broad-based economic growth and substantially reducing rural poverty in Bangladesh.

## Policy Implications

Microcredit programs in Bangladesh have attracted worldwide attention. The programs have been successful in reaching the targeted poor—especially women, who have not been served by traditional financial institutions—and they have reduced poverty among borrowers. The effect on the economy as a whole has been small, however, because of the nature of the activities microcredit programs support.

These programs have developed a single-product credit delivery mechanism (group-based lending with a weekly repayment schedule) that may be effective in reaching a large number of small producers. But such programs cannot reduce poverty on a large scale. Poverty is caused by many factors, including lack of skills, entrepreneurship, and human capital. Providing credit for generating self-employment cannot solve the multiple causes of poverty.

### Limitations of Microcredit

The sources of the success of microcredit are also the sources of its weakness. Microcredit is self-targeting and hence cost-effective. But not all rural poor are able to benefit from microcredit programs; utilizing loans in productive activities requires entrepreneurial skills that most people lack. Microcredit programs must target only those poor who have some ability to initiate activities with growth potential but lack capital. For the rural poor who are unable to become self-employed, targeted food programs and wage employment may be more appropriate. Microcredit also suffers from its limited ability to increase the size of the loan per borrower because of the limited capacity of borrowers to absorb loans.

Because of the emphasis on outreach, overhead costs are high, and subsidized funds are required over long periods of time. Although group pressure creates incentives to repay loans, enforcing group pressure and discipline involves costs. Microcredit programs must find ways to reduce administrative costs as well as subsidy dependence.

One way of increasing cost efficiency might be to modify the program design. Microcredit programs could increase the size of the group from 5–6 to 10 and the size of the center from 12 to 15–20. They could also relax the landholding criterion to accommodate small and medium-size farmers. Increasing the target base would enable programs to reduce the cost of forming and training groups and lending. At the same time, programs could charge different rates for different types of borrowers and different types of loans and customize loan terms and conditions to meet individual borrowers' needs. By customizing loans, microcredit programs could encourage more successful borrowers to expand their enterprises by offering them larger loans at reduced rates (Khandker 1996). Group-based microcredit programs could also introduce individual rather than group liability for long-term borrowers with excellent repayment records. Moreover, these loans could be repaid on a monthly rather than weekly basis.

In the long run the cost-effectiveness of microcredit depends on how fast it can enhance borrowers' abilities. Microcredit has a market niche because its beneficiaries have no alternatives. Over the long run this dependency could make microcredit vulnerable. Unless borrowers increase their incomes, many will become permanently dependent on microcredit. Loans to individual borrowers should be increased only gradually, so that borrowers are not stretched beyond their means.[3]

The long-run cost-effectiveness of microcredit also depends on the overall growth of the economy, which shapes the nature and extent of borrowers' demand for credit. But relying primarily on the credit demand of poorly educated entrepreneurs may prove too costly for microcredit programs to survive and become cost-effective. As the economy grows, commercial and development banks could finance projects that produce goods similar to those produced by microenterprises on a larger and more profitable scale. Low-cost production by large-scale enterprises would drive down the profit margins of small-scale producers, eventually forcing them out of business. To be able to compete with large-scale enterprises in the future, participants in microcredit programs must become more efficient and they must diversify their activities as the economy expands. Investment in skills development, technology, and market promotion will be necessary to ensure that self-employment in rural nonfarm activities remains viable for the rural poor.

## Replicability

The large number of group-based microcredit programs in Bangladesh proves that the program design is replicable there. Whether such schemes are also replicable outside of Bangladesh has not been formally tested, although the group-based lending model has been used in more than 45 countries, including the United States.

Group-based lending schemes may be unnecessary in an environment in which borrowers are educated and socially and individually accountable and social and government organizations can facilitate the enforcement of loan contracts. When imperfect information and imperfect enforcement make credit transactions risky, however, such schemes may be valuable. Group-based lending is desirable in an economic setting in which the persistence of poverty is rooted in sociopolitical inequity. In such societies individual-based lending rather than group-based lending can reinforce inequity and differentiated access to financial resources. Group-based lending is also preferable if financial intermediation requires social intermediation, which is less expensive to provide to a group than to individuals.

Microcredit may be necessary to provide small loans and promote savings among the poor and women. Microcredit is best targeted to those among the poor who can productively use microcredit to become self-employed. Microcredit, which finances self-employment activities that are performed at home, is well-suited to the needs of women, who are restricted by social custom or other reasons (such as reproductive roles) from working outside the home. However, because of high transactions costs, formal banks are reluctant to use their resources to provide these services to the poor. Subsidized funding may be necessary for institutional development of microfinance.

Before a microcredit program can be replicated, program designers must identify why a group-based scheme is needed, what the credit needs of the poor are and what should determine their participation, whether social and political mechanisms can serve as vehicles for credit delivery, and whether the group-based model is cost-effective. Once the model is replicated, the program's success depends in part on the creativity and commitment of its leadership, its ability to carve out market niches, the availability of subsidized funds for institutional development, an organizational structure that allows for administrative flexibility and decentralized decisionmaking, and intensive training and incentives for a well-motivated staff that is willing to experiment with innovative methods in response to borrower demand.

The chief lesson learned from experience in Bangladesh is that it is necessary to design a system of accountability that works for both program officials and borrowers. Program replication must therefore ensure institution of a socially conscious and transparent system (Yunus 1995). Similarly, although the group-based loan delivery model is replicable in other settings, the optimal basis for replication may be to formulate unique institutions following good foreign examples (Hulme 1990; Thomas 1988, 1993).

The replication of a group-based microcredit program by a commercial bank using its countrywide network may minimize the social cost of banking for the poor and women and obviate the need to establish a new specialized bank for the poor. However, the poor and women need special banking; hence the commercialization of microcredit within a large bureaucracy of a commercial bank should not divert attention from meeting this special need. To meet the needs of the poor, commercial banks could offer loans that do not require physical collateral. Offering such loans could change the relative shares of credit instruments in commercial banks' loan portfolios, but it is not likely to have a significant impact on overall profitability. Moreover, lending to the poor may help cross-subsidize other programs for the poor and reduce the cost of financial intermediation by pooling risk across sectors and borrowers with different wealth endowments. Commercial banks may also work closely with NGOs, supporting their outreach programs. NGOs are better at reaching the poor for on-lending and mobilizing savings in small amounts, which commercial banks find costly. One possible way of reducing the cost of financial intermediation for the poor is forging a relationship between NGOs and commercial banks in which commercial banks provide on-lending funds to NGOs at market rates and NGOs charge a rate that covers their lending cost.

## Future Research

Bangladesh stands out as one of the few countries in which microcredit programs have been replicated successfully. The group-based approach of Grameen Bank has been the force behind the microcredit movement in Bangladesh, where more than 750 small NGOs are applying Grameen's method to extend financial services to the poor, particularly poor women. The group-based microcredit movement is now being adopted in other countries, with the help of both bilateral and multilateral donors, including the World Bank. Future research on microcredit should try to explain why some programs succeed and others fail, using a cost-effectiveness methodology similar to that used here.

Research should also determine the cost-effectiveness of alternative models of rural finance and microcredit. In particular, individual-based and group-based lending programs should be compared. Research should also focus on the role of the group in group-based lending and quantify its impact on loan recovery rates and individual and household welfare.

Research should also try to determine how microcredit can fit into an overall financial framework and how NGO-based microcredit programs can be transformed into specialized financial institutions. Given the array of program interventions for poverty reduction and the need for different programs for various constituents, it is important to determine the optimal use of resources earmarked for poverty reduction. Research on the issue should include panel data analysis, as researchers can handle the endogeneity issues better with panel data than with cross-sectional data. Panel data would also help researchers analyze whether microfinance contributes to growth or merely redistributes income. In particular, future research must determine whether microcredit impacts are sustainable over time. To capture the full impact of credit on an assortment of long-term behaviors, including the value of assets and household consumption, researchers must examine behavioral impacts over a longer period.

Another potential research topic includes examination of possible decreasing marginal returns as microcredit programs expand over time or grant additional loans to long-term borrowers. Because households or villages with the most to gain from access to microcredit are the first to join these programs, early efforts may be more successful than subsequent ones. Later recruits may lack entrepreneurial ability or engage in activities with low returns. Follow-up surveys over a longer period may reveal whether there are decreasing returns to scale as programs expand.

A related long-term issue for future research is the extent of spillover impacts of microcredit programs. The village-level impacts shown here are based on a cross-section of program and nonprogram villages and are likely to misrepresent the true impact of program placement (which also includes the spillover effects) if program placement is not truly exogenous. Village-level follow-up surveys over a longer period are needed to estimate the full extent of spillover effects of microcredit programs.

Many microcredit programs provide noncredit services to their borrowers. Such services may be as important as credit in helping the poor become productively self-employed. Although a large literature suggests that noncredit services are important, no study has successfully demonstrated that noncredit services increase the productivity and income of the poor and are worth supporting. Future research should quantify the impact of noncredit inputs of microcredit programs.

The role of the group in a group-based microcredit program also warrants investigation. Is group-based microcredit necessary, and if so, what is the likely impact on the poor and loan repayment rate? Does it matter that the group is the mechanism through which credit is distributed and monitored, or would credit provided through other mechanisms (such as individual borrowing) achieve essentially the same results? How are groups formed, and how important is the group in facilitating information flows, smoothing consumption, providing insurance, and raising consciousness among borrowers? Such questions are receiving increasing attention from both academics and practitioners. These questions require careful analysis.

## Notes

1. A recent study observes that Grameen Bank and BRAC have influenced social dimensions of women's empowerment in Bangladesh (Hashemi, Schuler, and Riley 1996).

2. A recent study shows that the incidence of informal lending in a Grameen Bank village is possibly correlated with the incidence of repeated borrowing from Grameen. This may indicate that borrowers who lack entrepreneurial skills find it difficult to generate enough income to support weekly loan payments and rely on informal loans to keep up the repayment schedule (Sinha and Matin 1998).

3. A recent study of a northern district of Bangladesh argues that because of widespread delinquency among repeated borrowers, repayment of the previous loan should not be the sole criterion for assessing a borrower's ability and incentive to repay a loan (Sinha and Matin 1998).

# Appendix A:
# Statistical Tables

TABLE A3.1
**Bivariate Tobit Fixed-Effect Estimates of Demand for Credit by Gender**
(log of cumulative credit since 1986, in taka)

| Explanatory variable | Coefficient for women | Coefficient for men |
|---|---|---|
| Brothers of household head own land | 0.036 (0.458) | 0.170 (1.622) |
| Log of household land | 0.026 (0.540) | 0.207 (3.154) |
| Sex of household head | −2.068 (−3.532) | 1.399 (1.551) |
| Age of household head (years) | 0.015 (2.089) | 0.024 (−2.373) |
| Highest grade completed by an adult female in household | −0.074 (−1.754) | −0.026 (−0.458) |
| Highest grade completed by an adult male in household | 0.029 (0.534) | 0.142 (1.802) |
| No adult male in household | −1.257 (−1.923) | |
| No spouse in household | −0.831 (−2.483) | −1.351 (−2.951) |
| Sigma women's credit | 2.083 (33.211) | |
| Sigma men's credit | | 2.312 (26.878) |
| Number of observations | 1,105 | 895 |
| Rho coefficient | −0.075 (−1.313) | |
| Log likelihood | −1,424.393 | |

*Note:* Numbers in parentheses are *t*-statistics.
*Source:* Pitt and Khandker 1996.

TABLE A3.2

## Impact of Credit on Selected Household Outcomes

| Explanatory variable | Log of weekly per capita expenditure in taka (tobit) | Log of women's nonland assets in taka (tobit) | Log of household net worth in taka (tobit) | Log of women's labor hours in past month (tobit) |
|---|---|---|---|---|
| Amount borrowed by women from Grameen Bank | 0.0432 (4.249) | 0.1989 (3.950) | 0.0139 (3.312) | 0.1037 (3.016) |
| Amount borrowed by men from Grameen Bank | 0.0179 (1.431) | −0.0603 (−0.878) | 0.0151 (2.141) | −0.0229 (−0.506) |
| Amount borrowed by women from BRAC | 0.0394 (4.237) | 0.1151 (2.003) | 0.0086 (1.683) | 0.0721 (1.884) |
| Amount borrowed by men from BRAC | 0.0192 (1.593) | 0.0878 (1.007) | 0.0202 (2.544) | −0.0126 (−0.231) |
| Amount borrowed by women from RD-12 | 0.0402 (3.813) | 0.2172 (2.408) | 0.0024 (0.455) | 0.0766 (1.803) |
| Amount borrowed by men from RD-12 | 0.0233 (1.936) | 0.0244 (0.426) | 0.0222 (5.054) | 0.0268 (0.682) |
| Number of participants | 2,696 | 899 | 2,693 | 3,420 |
| Weighted mean and standard deviation of dependent variables | 77.014 (41.496) | 7,399.231 (2,930.02) | 83,474.83 (194,035.5) | 40.328 (70.478) |
| Sample size | 5,218 | 1,757 | 5,218 | 6,602 |

Note: Numbers in parentheses are t-statistics, except for the last column and second to last row, which show standard deviations.
Source: Pitt and Khandker 1996, except for the household net worth estimates, which were calculated separately.

| Log of men's labor hours in past month (tobit) | Girls' current school enrollment (probit) | Boys' current school enrollment (probit) | Contraceptive use of 14- to 50-year-old women (probit) | Recent fertility of 14- to 50-year-old women (probit) | Mean and standard deviation of independent variables |
|---|---|---|---|---|---|
| -0.2189 | 0.0469 | 0.0611 | -0.0905 | -0.0348 | 7,883.985 |
| (-6.734) | (2.919) | (3.644) | (-2.011) | (-0.951) | (9,847.072) |
| -0.1592 | 0.0304 | 0.0072 | 0.4253 | -0.0743 | 2,927.819 |
| (-2.524) | (1.376) | (2.743) | (2.075) | (-2.193) | (7,598.076) |
| -0.1813 | 0.0119 | -0.0028 | -0.0735 | 0.079 | 2,323.055 |
| (-5.884) | (0.682) | (-0.173) | (-1.693) | (2.372) | (3,523.278) |
| -0.1369 | 0.0242 | -0.0076 | 0.0395 | 0.0543 | 1,073.82 |
| (-2.155) | (0.897) | (-0.341) | (0.745) | (1.353) | (3,284.716) |
| -0.2308 | 0.0233 | 0.0793 | -0.1163 | 0.0502 | 1,691.601 |
| (-7.066) | (0.804) | (3.196) | (-2.421) | (1.312) | (2,824.221) |
| -0.1440 | 0.0069 | 0.0293 | 0.0839 | -0.0744 | 3,013.976 |
| (-2.129) | (0.309) | (1.475) | (1.475) | (-1.976) | (5,721.703) |
| 3,534 | 802 | 856 | 902 | 902 | |
| 202.758 | 0.535 | 0.566 | 0.418 | 0.679 | |
| (100.527) | (0.499) | (0.496) | (0.493) | (0.736) | |
| 6,914 | 2,885 | 2,940 | 1,884 | 1,882 | |

TABLE A3.3

## Joint Significance of Various Credit Variables on Socioeconomic Outcomes

($X^2$ statistics)

| Outcome variable | Credit variables $X^2(6)$ | Female credit variables $X^2(3)$ | Male credit variables $X^2(3)$ | Equality of gender-specific credit variables $X^2(3)$ |
|---|---|---|---|---|
| Girls' schooling | 10.04 | 9.28 | 2.66 | 0.92 |
| Boys' schooling | 26.92 | 22.21 | 9.49 | 2.68 |
| Women's labor supply | 16.23 | 14.15 | 0.85 | 8.67 |
| Men's labor supply | 98.66 | 53.11 | 7.65 | 2.26 |
| Household net worth | 43.54 | 13.14 | 34.89 | 9.55 |
| Per capita expenditure | 22.69 | 19.03 | 4.11 | 3.39 |
| Women's nonland assets | 15.95 | 8.39 | 5.12 | 14.27 |
| Contraceptive use | 16.90 | 6.15 | 8.58 | 12.42 |
| Recent fertility | 13.87 | 8.36 | 8.17 | 9.20 |

Note: Critical values are $X^2(3)_{0.10} = 6.25$, $X^2(6)_{0.10} = 10.64$, $X^2(3)_{0.05} = 7.82$, $X^2(6)_{0.05} = 12.59$, $X^2(3)_{0.01} = 11.34$, $X^2(6)_{0.01} = 16.81$.
Source: Pitt and Khandker 1996, except for the household net worth equation, which was estimated separately.

TABLE A3.4

## Thana-Level Fixed-Effect Estimates of Impacts of Credit on Selected Anthropometric Measures of Children

| Variable | Arm circumference (centimeters) Boys | Girls | Body mass index Boys | Girls | Height for age Boys | Girls | Mean and standard deviation of independent variables |
|---|---|---|---|---|---|---|---|
| Amount borrowed by men (taka) | −0.1565 (−0.756) | 0.3017 (1.459) | −0.0594 (−0.251) | 0.2878 (1.745) | −0.2979 (−1.001) | −0.4921 (−1.469) | 9,586.9 (10,182.8) |
| Amount borrowed by women (taka) | 0.4734 (1.534) | 0.6146 (2.519) | −0.2837 (−0.803) | −0.1851 (−0.831) | 1.4185 (2.944) | 1.1627 (2.161) | 9,676.0 (9,712.9) |
| Mean of dependent variables | 14.204 (1.265) | 14.138 (1.511) | 0.001 (0.0001) | 0.001 (0.0002) | 30.768 (19.041) | 31.545 (21.593) | |
| Sample size | 375 | 401 | 375 | 401 | 375 | 401 | |

Note: Numbers in parentheses are t-statistics, except for the last column and second to last row, which show standard deviations.
Source: Pitt and others 1998.

TABLE A3.5A

**Estimates of the Impact of Credit on the Seasonality of Consumption**
(log of weekly per capita expenditure)

| Explanatory variable | Aman season | Boro season | Aus season |
|---|---|---|---|
| Amount borrowed by female x Aman season | 0.0313 (1.206) | | |
| Amount borrowed by female x Boro season | | 0.0339 (1.580) | |
| Amount borrowed by female x Aus season | | | 0.0428 (4.879) |
| Amount borrowed by male x Aman season | 0.00556 (0.238) | | |
| Amount borrowed by male x Boro season | | 0.0143 (1.042) | |
| Amount borrowed by male x Aus season | | | 0.0190 (1.861) |
| Log likelihood | −2,160.34 | −2,191.23 | −1,992.06 |
| Number of observations | 1,757 | 1,735 | 1,726 |

*Note:* Numbers in parentheses are asymptotic *t*-ratios.
*Source:* Pitt and Khandker 1997.

TABLE A3.5B

**Estimates of the Impact of Credit on the Seasonality of Labor Supply**
(log of hours in past month)

| Explanatory variable | Women | | | Men | | |
|---|---|---|---|---|---|---|
| | Aman season | Boro season | Aus season | Aman season | Boro season | Aus season |
| Amount borrowed by female x Aman season | 0.0954 (3.215) | | | −0.196 (−4.047) | | |
| Amount borrowed by female x Boro season | | 0.0951 (3.252) | | | −0.232 (−10.552) | |
| Amount borrowed by female x Aus season | | | .0741 (2.482) | | | −0.0232 (−0.280) |
| Amount borrowed by male x Aman season | −0.00747 (−0.197) | | | −0.171 (−3.953) | | |
| Amount borrowed by male x Boro season | | 0.0209 (0.586) | | | 0.0232 (0.885) | |
| Amount borrowed by male x Aus season | | | −0.00504 (−0.138) | | | 0.0378 (1.096) |
| Log likelihood | −5,054.24 | −4,848.25 | −4,923.42 | −6,145.33 | −6,051.23 | −6,047.89 |
| Number of observations | 2,242 | 2,194 | 2,166 | 2,353 | 2,291 | 2,270 |

*Note:* Numbers in parentheses are asymptotic *t*-ratios.
*Source:* BIDS–World Bank 1991/92 survey.

TABLE A3.6

**Village-Level Impacts of Microcredit Program Intervention**
(weighted generalized least squares estimates)

| Dependent variable | Grameen Bank | BRAC |
|---|---|---|
| Log of total production (taka per year) | 0.559 (2.046) | 0.569 (2.242) |
| Log of farm production | 0.108 (0.321) | 0.346 (0.920) |
| Log of nonfarm production | 0.889 (2.181) | 0.829 (2.237) |
| Log of total net income (taka per year) | 0.294 (1.861) | 0.327 (2.137) |
| Log of farm income | 0.003 (0.017) | −0.068 (−0.354) |
| Log of self-employed farm income | 0.081 (0.185) | 0.211 (0.479) |
| Log of wage farm income | −0.645 (−2.409) | −0.975 (−2.940) |
| Log of nonfarm income | 1.503 (1.592) | 1.786 (1.966) |
| Log of self-employed nonfarm income | 2.419 (2.423) | 0.278 (0.278) |
| Log of wage nonfarm income | 0.374 (0.503) | 2.280 (2.923) |
| Log of total employment (hours per month) | 0.068 (2.387) | −0.112 (−3.439) |
| Log of farm employment | −0.040 (−0.477) | −0.465 (−5.816) |
| Log of self-employed farm employment | 0.109 (1.446) | −0.312 (−3.899) |
| Log of wage farm employment | −0.394 (−2.175) | −0.832 (−4.125) |
| Log of nonfarm employment | 0.197 (2.012) | 0.124 (1.282) |
| Log of self-employed nonfarm employment | 0.511 (2.631) | 0.144 (0.751) |
| Log of wage nonfarm employment | −0.007 (−0.046) | 0.423 (3.312) |
| Total school enrollment rate | 0.017 (0.563) | 0.057 (1.845) |
| Recent fertility | −0.126 (−1.681) | −0.129 (−1.579) |
| Rural male wage (taka per day) | 4.929 (2.091) | 1.949 (0.899) |
| Mean of program placement variables | 0.32 | 0.28 |

*Note:* Numbers in parentheses are *t*-statistics.
*Source:* BIDS–World Bank 1991/92 survey.

| RD-12 | Commercial and agricultural development banks | Mean of dependent variables | |
|---|---|---|---|
| | | All program villages | Nonprogram villages |
| 0.477 (1.954) | 0.622 (2.707) | 102,255 | 46,101 |
| 0.764 (2.065) | 0.188 (0.324) | 10,093 | 7,045 |
| 0.737 (2.192) | 0.920 (2.886) | 92,162 | 46,100 |
| 0.212 (1.266) | 0.447 (3.186) | 32,878 | 22,367 |
| 0.623 (3.060) | 0.300 (1.680) | 12,274 | 9,932 |
| 0.920 (2.038) | 0.459 (0.829) | 9,165 | 6,390 |
| 0.378 (1.657) | 0.472 (1.726) | 3,109 | 3,542 |
| −0.524 (−0.544) | 0.552 (0.561) | 20,605 | 12,705 |
| 0.531 (0.517) | −1.477 (−1.346) | 15,680 | 6,976 |
| −0.907 (−1.189) | 1.372 (1.498) | 4,925 | 5,729 |
| −0.067 (−1.954) | 0.084 (2.792) | 385.4 | 330.9 |
| −0.216 (−3.762) | 0.029 (0.271) | 195.9 | 157.1 |
| 0.225 (2.433) | −0.014 (−0.123) | 115.8 | 78.1 |
| 0.219 (1.232) | 0.155 (0.736) | 80.1 | 78.9 |
| −0.165 (−1.620) | 0.159 (1.421) | 189.5 | 173.8 |
| 0.325 (1.834) | 0.259 (1.409) | 109.6 | 67.2 |
| −0.717 (−4.294) | 0.365 (2.352) | 79.9 | 106.6 |
| 0.002 (0.069) | −0.044 (−1.412) | 50.1 | 48.7 |
| −0.070 (−0.789) | −0.166 (−2.210) | 1.14 | 1.10 |
| −1.134 (−0.496) | −1.869 (−0.652) | 27.63 | 24.23 |
| 0.29 | 0.10 | 0.83 | 0.17 |

TABLE A3.7

**Microcredit Program Impact on Village-Level Poverty**
(weighted generalized least squares estimates)

| Explanatory variable | Moderate poverty | Extreme poverty | Mean and standard deviation of explanatory variables |
|---|---|---|---|
| Village has Grameen Bank | −0.124 (−2.178) | −0.087 (−1.919) | 0.322 (0.468) |
| Village has BRAC | −0.095 (−1.746) | −0.078 (−1.949) | 0.276 (0.448) |
| Village has RD-12 | −0.136 (−2.401) | −0.082 (−1.588) | 0.287 (0.453) |
| Village has paved road | −0.020 (−0.468) | 0.016 (0.751) | 0.28 (0.45) |
| Village has formal commercial bank | 0.006 (0.125) | −0.013 (−0.219) | 0.10 (0.31) |
| Village has electricity | 0.197 (−4.872) | −0.062 (−2.807) | 0.506 (0.501) |
| Distance from thana headquarters (kilometers) | −0.002 (−0.707) | −0.005 (−1.865) | 8.467 (5.787) |
| Village has development program | −0.021 (−0.578) | 0.042 (1.590) | 0.536 (0.500) |
| Proportion of households owning less than half an acre of land | 0.490 (2.276) | 0.325 (3.604) | 0.767 (0.101) |
| Constant | 0.557 (2.723) | −0.056 (−0.105) | |
| Adjusted $R^2$ | 0.316 | 0.201 | |
| Number of observations | 87 | 87 | 87 |
| Mean of dependent variables | 0.626 (0.187) | 0.116 (0.110) | |

*Note:* Numbers in parentheses are *t*-statistics, except for the last column and last row, which show standard deviations.
*Source:* BIDS–World Bank 1991/92 survey.

TABLE A4.1

**Determinants of Participation in Rural Nonfarm Activities**
(probit estimates)

| Explanatory variable | $\partial F/\partial X$ for full-time participants only | $\partial F/\partial X$ for both full- and part-time participants |
|---|---|---|
| Sex of household head (1 = male; 0 = female) | 0.138 (2.938) | 0.196 (3.552) |
| Log of household landholding (decimals) | −0.018 (−2.696) | −0.018 (−2.452) |
| Village price of soybean oil (taka) | 0.006 (0.906) | 0.016 (2.010) |
| Village price of eggs (taka) | −0.042 (−1.937) | −0.055 (−2.498) |
| Village price of milk (taka) | −0.009 (−1.075) | −0.018 (−1.804) |
| Village price of potatoes (taka) | −0.056 (−2.567) | −0.070 (−2.863) |
| Village price of green peppers (taka) | −0.002 (−0.371) | −0.009 (−1.766) |
| Village price of salt (taka) | −0.030 (−1.525) | −0.037 (−2.617) |
| Village price of beef (taka) | 0.006 (2.965) | 0.008 (3.536) |
| Village price of brown sugar (taka) | −0.009 (−1.769) | −0.018 (−3.323) |
| Village female wage rate (taka per day) | −0.002 (−0.557) | 0.008 (1.579) |
| Village child wage rate (taka per day) | 0.010 (2.096) | 0.011 (2.140) |
| No female wage in village | −0.003 (−0.024) | 0.248 (1.991) |
| Percentage of irrigated land in village | −0.100 (−1.918) | −0.157 (−2.678) |
| Village has electricity | 0.157 (5.318) | 0.171 (5.190) |
| Distance from thana headquarters (kilometers) | −0.008 (−3.285) | −0.010 (−3.377) |
| Village has Grameen Bank | 0.056 (1.267) | 0.088 (1.794) |
| Village has BRAC | 0.039 (−0.807) | −0.043 (−0.785) |
| Village has RD-12 | 0.037 (0.778) | 0.041 (0.817) |
| Constant | −0.366 (−0.192) | 0.335 (0.188) |
| Log likelihood | −966.816 | −1,151.453 |
| Number of observations | 1,798 | 1,798 |

*Note:* Numbers in parentheses are $t$-statistics. $\delta F/\delta X$ reports the change (partial) in the probability of the dependent variable ($F$) for changes in any of the independent variables ($X_i$). It is given by the formula, $\delta F/\delta X_i = \beta_i \phi(Z_i)$, where $Z_i = \beta_0 + \Sigma \beta_i X_i$ and $\phi()$ is the density function of the standard normal (Maddala 1988).
*Source:* BIDS–World Bank 1991/92 survey.

TABLE A4.2

## Cobb-Douglas Production Function Estimates for Rural Nonfarm Activities
(ordinary least squares estimates)

| Explanatory variable | Manufacturing Target households | Transport Target households |
|---|---|---|
| Age of household head (years) | 0.044 (2.452) | 0.002 (0.117) |
| Age squared | −0.001 (−2.897) | −0.00004 (−0.151) |
| Education of household head (years) | 0.061 (4.202) | −0.012 (−1.105) |
| Sex of household head (1 = male; 0 = female) | 0.657 (5.393) | −0.146 (−0.555) |
| Log of land value (taka) | 0.006 (0.493) | 0.244 (4.557) |
| Log of capital value (taka) | 0.063 (3.106) | 0.008 (0.974) |
| Log of total labor (hours) | 0.078 (2.932) | 0.095 (2.890) |
| Log of other inputs (taka) | 0.323 (7.375) | 0.030 (1.281) |
| Village has paved roads | −0.163 (−1.473) | −0.061 (−1.085) |
| Village has formal bank | 0.143 (0.821) | −0.085 (−0.771) |
| Village has electricity | 0.090 (0.836) | 0.016 (0.290) |
| Distance from thana headquarters (kilometers) | −0.006 (−0.459) | −0.002 (−0.330) |
| Proportion of households owning less than half an acre of land | −0.093 (−0.592) | 0.328 (2.173) |
| Village has Grameen Bank | 0.331 (2.094) | 0.024 (0.317) |
| Village has BRAC | 0.768 (3.562) | 0.070 (0.766) |
| Village has RD-12 | 0.414 (2.088) | −0.074 (−0.638) |
| Aman season dummy | −0.075 (−0.385) | −0.324 (−1.848) |
| Constant | 4.710 (7.309) | 9.103 (16.671) |
| Adjusted $R^2$ | 0.668 | 0.200 |
| Number of observations | 403 | 407 |

*Note:* Figures shown are coefficients of dependent variables (log of value of production, in taka). Nontarget households are not listed for most activities because there were too few observations to run the regression. Numbers in parentheses are *t*-statistics.
a. Other activities are mainly services.
*Source:* BIDS–World Bank 1991/92 survey.

| | Trading | | Livestock and fisheries | Other activities[a] | All activities | |
|---|---|---|---|---|---|---|
| | Target households | Nontarget households | Target households | Target households | Target households | Nontarget households |
| | 0.022 | −0.006 | −0.002 | −0.014 | 0.026 | −0.109 |
| | (1.463) | (−0.098) | (−0.033) | (−0.397) | (2.689) | (−2.678) |
| | −0.0003 | 0.0002 | −0.0001 | 0.0001 | −0.0003 | 0.001 |
| | (−1.844) | (0.277) | (−0.184) | (0.257) | (−3.283) | (3.674) |
| | 0.026 | 0.069 | −0.059 | −0.005 | 0.030 | 0.052 |
| | (3.314) | (3.173) | (−1.750) | (−0.234) | (3.998) | (2.105) |
| | 0.202 | 1.150 | −0.460 | −0.894 | 0.130 | 0.863 |
| | (1.553) | (3.377) | (−0.886) | (−1.417) | (0.664) | (3.776) |
| | −0.005 | 0.042 | −0.152 | −0.037 | −0.016 | 0.027 |
| | (−0.429) | (1.497) | (−1.829) | (−0.842) | (−1.398) | (1.229) |
| | 0.026 | −0.002 | −0.009 | 0.020 | 0.046 | 0.010 |
| | (3.192) | (−0.058) | (−0.397) | (1.026) | (6.735) | (0.449) |
| | 0.078 | 0.043 | −0.071 | 0.200 | 0.096 | 0.070 |
| | (4.403) | (0.698) | (1.498) | (3.718) | (5.491) | (1.322) |
| | 0.524 | 0.272 | 0.265 | 0.303 | 0.362 | 0.318 |
| | (9.379) | (2.693) | (7.459) | (4.402) | (16.198) | (5.224) |
| | −0.052 | 0.575 | −0.843 | −0.095 | −0.073 | 0.170 |
| | (−0.602) | (1.551) | (−2.396) | (−0.595) | (−1.296) | (0.656) |
| | 0.336 | −0.141 | 0.806 | 0.344 | 0.282 | −0.229 |
| | (2.774) | (−0.414) | (2.468) | (1.764) | (3.883) | (−0.886) |
| | 0.032 | −0.215 | −0.117 | 0.239 | 0.032 | 0.268 |
| | (0.495) | (−1.328) | (−0.478) | (1.519) | (0.650) | (1.917) |
| | 0.009 | −0.019 | 0.026 | −0.013 | 0.002 | −0.013 |
| | (1.674) | (−1.416) | (1.635) | (−0.991) | (0.483) | (−1.065) |
| | −0.109 | 0.105 | 0.280 | 0.174 | −0.007 | −0.129 |
| | (−1.055) | (0.304) | (1.019) | (0.816) | (−0.096) | (−0.309) |
| | 0.135 | 0.529 | 0.275 | −0.226 | 0.237 | 0.074 |
| | (1.534) | (1.892) | (0.633) | (−1.127) | (3.471) | (0.349) |
| | 0.126 | 0.549 | 0.067 | 0.428 | 0.363 | 0.364 |
| | (1.480) | (2.305) | (0.149) | (1.588) | (4.916) | (1.970) |
| | 0.075 | 0.520 | 0.233 | −0.291 | 0.148 | 0.284 |
| | (0.843) | (2.107) | (0.540) | (−1.408) | (2.138) | (1.365) |
| | 0.026 | 0.042 | −0.285 | −0.552 | −0.136 | 0.173 |
| | (0.218) | (0.120) | (−0.853) | (−1.788) | (−1.425) | (0.477) |
| | 4.258 | 6.334 | 8.727 | 7.817 | 5.654 | 8.67 |
| | (6.120) | (4.417) | (6.897) | (5.615) | (13.038) | (6.947) |
| | 0.646 | 0.424 | 0.644 | 0.628 | 0.603 | 0.552 |
| | 969 | 173 | 207 | 200 | 2,186 | 259 |

TABLE A5.1

## Determinants of Branch Manager Salaries at Grameen Bank, BRAC, and RD-12

| Explanatory variable | Coefficients | | | Mean and standard deviation of explanatory variables | | |
|---|---|---|---|---|---|---|
| | Grameen Bank | BRAC | RD-12 | Grameen Bank | BRAC | RD-12 |
| Gender (1 = male; 0 = female) | 0.041 (1.779) | 0.039 (0.881) | –0.012 (–0.192) | 0.962 (0.192) | 0.938 (0.242) | 0.849 (0.360) |
| Education (years) | 0.067 (9.040) | 0.063 (5.909) | 0.064 (2.683) | 15.580 (1.183) | 15.381 (0.918) | 14.977 (1.006) |
| Experience (years) | 0.025 (2.407) | 0.060 (2.736) | 0.068 (2.996) | 4.217 (2.458) | 6.651 (2.589) | 7.965 (4.536) |
| Experience squared | –0.001 (–0.796) | –0.001 (–0.861) | –0.002 (–1.972) | | | |
| Intercept | 6.127 (8.984) | 7.144 (22.776) | 7.207 (6.787) | | | |
| Adjusted $R^2$ | 0.608 | 0.638 | 0.159 | | | |
| $f$-statistics | 34.59 | 29.20 | 3.68 | | | |
| Number of observations | 131 | 97 | 86 | 131 | 97 | 86 |
| Average annual salary of branch managers (taka) | | | | 34,127 | 65,688 | 34,350 |
| Annual salary/GNP per capita | | | | 4.1 | 7.5 | 4.1 |

Note: Estimates for Grameen Bank, BRAC, and RD-12 are based on data from 1991, 1993, and 1989, respectively. Numbers in parentheses in the first three columns are $t$-statistics; numbers in parentheses in the second three columns are standard deviations.
Source: Khandker and Khalily 1996; Khandker, Khalily, and Khan 1995; Khandker, Khan, and Khalily 1995.

TABLE A5.2

**Determinants of Member Dropout Rates for Grameen Bank and BRAC**
(fixed-effect estimates)

| Variable | Grameen Bank | BRAC |
|---|---|---|
| Age of the branch (years) | 0.047 | 0.010 |
| | (5.377) | (1.573) |
| Age squared | −0.002 | −0.0002 |
| | (−1.880) | (−0.678) |
| Log of predicted pay of branch manager (taka) | −0.183 | |
| | (−3.941) | |
| Electrification in villages per square kilometer | 0.239 | 0.102 |
| | (3.527) | (0.816) |
| Road length in villages per square kilometer | 0.042 | −0.608 |
| | (0.264) | (−1.812) |
| Primary schools in villages per square kilometer | 0.202 | 0.500 |
| | (0.484) | (1.633) |
| Secondary schools in villages per square kilometer | −1.641 | −0.260 |
| | (−1.714) | (−0.321) |
| Staff employment and income generation cost (thousands of taka) | | 0.10 |
| | | (3.198) |
| Other skills development costs for staff (thousands of taka) | | −0.10 |
| | | (−2.400) |
| Constant | 1.637 | −0.042 |
| | (3.202) | (−0.210) |
| $R^2$ | 0.715 | 0.268 |
| Number of observations | 357 | 223 |

*Note:* Numbers in parentheses are *t*-statistics.
*Source:* Khandker, Khalily, and Khan 1995; branch-level data of BRAC.

TABLE A5.3

**Determinants of Branch-Level Loan Recovery Rates for Grameen Bank and RD-12**

(fixed-effect estimates)

| Variable | Grameen Bank | RD-12 |
|---|---|---|
| Age of branch (years) | −0.0001 | 0.294 |
| | (−0.026) | (4.407) |
| Age squared | −0.0005 | −0.046 |
| | (−1.292) | (−3.192) |
| Log of predicted pay of branch manager (taka) | 0.0187 | 0.1994 |
| | (1.075) | (0.915) |
| Average training cost (thousands of taka) | 0.047 | −0.001 |
| | (0.984) | (−1.314) |
| Electrication in villages per square kilometer | 0.010 | 0.679 |
| | (0.598) | (1.129) |
| Road length in villages per square kilometer | 0.059 | 0.433 |
| | (1.772) | (1.658) |
| Primary schools in villages per square kilometer | 0.230 | −0.533 |
| | (1.318) | (−0.550) |
| Secondary schools in villages per square kilometer | −0.014 | 6.841 |
| | (−0.051) | (2.288) |
| Average annual rainfall (centimeters) | 0.00003 | −0.0008 |
| | (1.657) | (−2.002) |
| Deviation of rainfall from its mean (centimeters) | −0.00002 | 0.0009 |
| | (−1.251) | (1.628) |
| Commercial banks and Krishi Banks per square kilometer | 0.171 | −7.662 |
| | (1.813) | (−1.791) |
| Constant | 0.637 | 0.030 |
| | (2.894) | (0.072) |
| $R^2$ | 0.551 | 0.381 |
| Number of observations | 357 | 218 |

*Note:* Numbers in parentheses are *t*-statistics.
*Source:* Branch-level data of Grameen Bank and RD-12.

TABLE A5.4

**Estimated Marginal Cost of Membership, Lending, and Savings Mobilization for Grameen Bank, BRAC, and RD-12**

| Item | Grameen Bank | BRAC | RD-12 |
|---|---|---|---|
| Membership (taka) | 138.0 | 39.0 | 5.0 |
| | (5.515) | (1.318) | (0.136) |
| Disbursement per taka | 0.016 | 0.101 | 0.069 |
| | (4.221) | (7.786) | (2.299) |
| Savings per taka | 0.015 | 0.069 | 0.025 |
| | (1.108) | (1.511) | (0.149) |
| Economies of scale | 0.582 | 0.558 | 0.168 |
| | (8.475) | (5.284) | (1.180) |

*Note:* Numbers in parentheses are *t*-statistics.
*Source:* Khandker and Khalily 1996; Khandker, Khalily, and Khan 1995; Khandker, Khan, and Khalily 1995.

TABLE A6.1

## Determinants of Individual Borrowing

| Explanatory variable | Individual borrowing (probit) $\delta F/\delta X^a$ | Log of amount borrowed from formal source (tobit) | Log of amount borrowed from informal source (tobit) | Log of amount borrowed from microcredit institutions (tobit) |
|---|---|---|---|---|
| Age (years) | 0.031 (15.269) | −0.075 (−0.363) | 0.656 (5.763) | −0.120 (−1.414) |
| Age squared | −0.0003 (−13.382) | 0.002 (0.765) | −0.007 (−5.565) | 0.0004 (0.404) |
| Sex (1 = male; 0 = female) | 0.081 (7.274) | 7.877 (5.146) | 9.419 (13.629) | −5.887 (−14.483) |
| Education (years) | 0.005 (2.835) | 0.733 (4.916) | 0.068 (0.932) | −0.250 (−3.953) |
| Log of household landholding (decimals) | −0.021 (−7.270) | 2.013 (5.934) | 0.382 (2.656) | −0.877 (−7.808) |
| Village has paved road | 0.003 (0.220) | −2.862 (−2.076) | 1.864 (3.059) | −0.621 (−1.391) |
| Village has formal bank | −0.021 (−1.153) | 3.362 (1.964) | −4.106 (−4.507) | 1.228 (1.869) |
| Village has electricity | −0.001 (−0.044) | 3.026 (2.553) | −0.664 (−1.271) | −0.094 (−0.235) |
| Proportion of households in village owning less than half an acre of land | −0.209 (−3.357) | −5.083 (−0.880) | 10.311 (3.678) | −12.413 (−6.101) |
| Village has Grameen Bank | 0.016 (0.970) | 2.212 (1.372) | −3.948 (−5.158) | 3.198 (5.485) |
| Village has BRAC | 0.024 (1.498) | −1.226 (−0.768) | −4.482 (−6.323) | 3.554 (6.419) |
| Village has RD-12 | 0.042 (2.578) | −0.184 (−0.128) | −1.162 (−1.839) | 2.444 (4.236) |
| Constant | −2.828 (−9.769) | −24.117 (−3.322) | −28.434 (−7.859) | 19.875 (8.124) |
| Cumulative density function evaluated at mean of explanatory variables (tobit estimates only) | | 0.079 | 0.324 | 0.713 |
| Log likelihood | −2,215.779 | −1,051.652 | −2,034.992 | −2,402.240 |
| Number of observations | 5,499 | 1,283 | 1,283 | 1,283 |
| Mean of dependent variable | 0.17 | 21,536.21 | 5,659.35 | 8,567.46 |

Note: Numbers in parentheses are $t$-statistics.

a. For a probit model, $\delta F/\delta X$ reports the change (partial) in the probability of the dependent variable $(F)$ for changes in any of the independent variables $(X_i)$. It is given by the formula, $\delta F/\delta X_i = \beta_i \phi(Z_i)$, where $Z_i = \beta_0 + \Sigma \beta_i X_i$ and $\phi()$ is the density function of the standard normal (Maddala 1988).

Source: BIDS–World Bank 1991/92 survey.

TABLE A6.2
**Determinants of Informal Interest Rates at Village Level**
(tobit estimates)

| Explanatory variable | Coefficients of interest rates | | | |
|---|---|---|---|---|
| | Less than 3 months | 3–6 months | 6–12 months | More than 12 months |
| Village has formal bank | −3.676 | −1.508 | 1.204 | 1.029 |
| | (−1.638) | (−0.847) | (0.622) | (0.468) |
| Village has electricity | −2.905 | 1.025 | 1.250 | 0.067 |
| | (−2.094) | (0.930) | (1.038) | (0.048) |
| Village has development program | 1.311 | 1.894 | 2.468 | 3.264 |
| | (0.965) | (1.751) | (2.085) | (2.411) |
| Proportion of households owning less than half an acre of land | 20.676 | 8.467 | −0.072 | 1.199 |
| | (2.737) | (1.415) | (−0.011) | (0.161) |
| Village has Grameen Bank | 0.448 | 2.387 | 0.061 | −2.944 |
| | (0.239) | (1.604) | (0.038) | (−1.686) |
| Village has BRAC | 3.604 | 3.078 | 2.774 | 2.731 |
| | (1.935) | (2.077) | (1.716) | (1.484) |
| Village has RD-12 | −0.151 | 2.523 | 0.264 | −0.140 |
| | (−0.079) | (1.650) | (0.159) | (−0.074) |
| Aman season dummy | −0.435 | −2.938 | −1.802 | −2.347 |
| | (−0.269) | (−2.281) | (−1.279) | (−1.453) |
| Constant | −3.412 | 3.080 | 8.971 | 6.477 |
| | (−0.481) | (0.548) | (1.463) | (0.927) |
| Cumulative density function evaluated at mean of explanatory variables | 0.913 | 0.919 | 0.883 | 0.838 |
| Log likelihood | −964.798 | −873.852 | −878.200 | −884.530 |
| Number of observations | 261 | 261 | 261 | 261 |
| Mean of village interest rate in taka per month | 14.03 | 11.60 | 10.92 | 10.56 |

*Note:* Numbers in parentheses are *t*-statistics.
*Source:* BIDS–World Bank 1991/92 survey.

TABLE A6.3
## Determinants of Informal Interest Rates on Individual Loans
(tobit estimates)

| Explanatory variable | Coefficient of interest rate |
|---|---|
| Log of household landholding (decimals) | −0.078 |
| | (−2.532) |
| Village has paved road | −0.415 |
| | (−2.939) |
| Village has electricity | 0.248 |
| | (2.142) |
| Distance from thana headquarters (kilometers) | −0.029 |
| | (−2.760) |
| Village has Grameen Bank | 0.206 |
| | (1.238) |
| Village has BRAC | −0.370 |
| | (−2.281) |
| Village has RD-12 | −0.002 |
| | (−0.015) |
| Village has development program | 0.271 |
| | (2.295) |
| Constant | 1.825 |
| | (2.164) |
| Cumulative density function evaluated at mean of explanatory variables | 0.546 |
| Log likelihood | −503.133 |
| Number of observations | 478 |
| Mean of yearly interest rate (percent) | 44.7 |

Note: Numbers in parentheses are t-statistics.
Source: BIDS–World Bank 1991/92 survey.

TABLE A6.4

**Determinants of Interhousehold Transfers in Taka**
(tobit estimates)

| Explanatory variable | Log of amount transferred to households | Log of amount transferred from households | Log of net transfer to households |
|---|---|---|---|
| Age of household head (years) | −0.276 (−1.707) | −0.170 (−0.924) | −0.175 (−1.006) |
| Age squared | 0.004 (2.100) | 0.003 (1.290) | 0.002 (1.264) |
| Sex of household head (1 = male; 0 = female) | −7.519 (−5.171) | −1.538 (−0.703) | −7.864 (−5.177) |
| Education of household head (years) | 0.525 (4.925) | 0.385 (3.450) | 0.442 (3.902) |
| Log of household landholding (decimals) | 0.130 (0.592) | 2.198 (7.186) | 0.104 (0.448) |
| Village has paved road | −2.500 (−2.516) | −3.016 (−2.636) | −2.216 (−2.124) |
| Village has development program | 0.954 (1.153) | 4.899 (4.423) | 0.671 (0.771) |
| Proportion of households owning less than half an acre of land | 15.012 (3.143) | 7.505 (1.386) | 18.119 (3.548) |
| Village has Grameen Bank | −4.241 (−3.654) | −4.707 (−3.604) | −3.869 (−3.169) |
| Village has BRAC | −2.934 (−2.609) | −0.193 (−0.1590) | −2.211 (−1.874) |
| Village has RD-12 | 0.406 (0.397) | −1.253 (−1.061) | 0.887 (0.820) |
| Constant | −9.775 (−1.658) | −25.983 (−3.549) | −15.006 (−2.370) |
| Cumulative density function evaluated at mean of explanatory variables | 0.125 | 0.048 | 0.118 |
| Log likelihood | −1,368.959 | −910.659 | −1,298.721 |
| Number of observations | 1,769 | 1,769 | 1,769 |
| Mean of dependent variable | 467.990 (2,862.238) | 121.538 (835.639) | 346.45 (2,943.94) |

Note: Numbers in parentheses are t-statistics, except for last row, which shows standard deviations.
Source: BIDS–World Bank 1991/92 survey.

TABLE A6.5

**Determinants of Sources of Borrowing for Agricultural Loans**
(ordinary least squares estimates)

| Explanatory variable | Log of amount borrowed from formal source | Log of amount borrowed from informal source | Log of amount borrowed from microcredit institutions |
|---|---|---|---|
| Sex (1 = male; 0 = female) | 0.648 (4.433) | 0.722 (3.176) | −0.189 (−1.155) |
| Education (years) | 0.081 (1.909) | 0.051 (1.043) | −0.064 (−2.981) |
| Log of household landholding (decimals) | 0.210 (3.993) | 0.283 (3.835) | 0.068 (1.661) |
| Village has paved road | −0.557 (−2.227) | 0.251 (0.774) | 0.027 (0.164) |
| Village has formal bank | 0.140 (0281) | −0.986 (−2.727) | −0.411 (−3.057) |
| Village has electricity | 0.021 (0.092) | −0.390 (1.405) | −0.391 (−2.275) |
| Distance from thana headquarters (kilometers) | 0.001 (0.058) | 0.036 (1.405) | 0.043 (3.188) |
| Proportion of households owning less than half an acre of land | 0.254 (0.2010) | 3.182 (2.163) | 0.392 (0.519) |
| Village has Grameen Bank | 0.362 (1.142) | −0.726 (−1.838) | 0.177 (0.843) |
| Village has BRAC | −0.087 (−0.341) | −0.591 (−1.359) | 0.790 (3.550) |
| Village has RD-12 | 0.045 (0.134) | 0.271 (0.536) | 0.355 (1.692) |
| Constant | −0.581 (−0.488) | −4.260 (−2.508) | −0.638 (−0.673) |
| $R^2$ | 0.115 | 0.143 | 0.046 |
| Number of observations | 1,283 | 1,283 | 1,283 |
| Cumulative amount borrowed (taka) | 5,835 | 4,492 | 4,739 |

*Note:* Numbers in parentheses are *t*-statistics.
*Source:* BIDS–World Bank 1991/92 survey.

TABLE A7.1

## Effects of Education and Test Scores on Individual Participation in Microcredit Programs

(probit estimates)

| Explanatory variable | $\delta F/\delta X$ for whole sample | $\delta F/\delta X$ for men | $\delta F/\delta X$ for women |
|---|---|---|---|
| Age (years) | 0.040 | −0.003 | 0.050 |
| | (11.295) | (−0.460) | (5.026) |
| Age squared | −0.0005 | −0.00002 | −0.001 |
| | (−10.798) | (−0.213) | (−4.671) |
| Sex (1 = male; 0 = female) | −0.151 | n.a. | n.a. |
| | (−8.943) | | |
| Education (years) | 0.002 | 0.012 | −0.012 |
| | (0.357) | (1.619) | (−1.020) |
| Spouse education (years) | n.a. | −0.013 | 0.001 |
| | | (−1.448) | (0.076) |
| Passed reading test | −0.015 | −0.032 | −0.077 |
| | (−0.523) | (−0.725) | (−1.203) |
| Passed writing test | −0.023 | 0.009 | 0.289 |
| | (−0.656) | (0.159) | (2.479) |
| Passed oral math test | 0.061 | 0.085 | 0.071 |
| | (2.876) | (2.926) | (1.272) |
| Passed written math test | −0.033 | −0.041 | −0.113 |
| | (−0.945) | (−0.844) | (−1.072) |
| Spouse passed reading test | n.a. | −0.033 | −0.008 |
| | | (−0.677) | (−0.134) |
| Spouse passed writing test | n.a. | −0.039 | −0.077 |
| | | (0.431) | (−1.188) |
| Spouse passed oral math test | n.a. | 0.074 | −0.070 |
| | | (1.627) | (−1.911) |
| Spouse passed written math test | n.a. | −0.014 | 0.094 |
| | | (−0.157) | (1.373) |
| Log of household landholding | 0.006 | 0.014 | 0.009 |
| | (1.117) | (1.561) | (0.777) |
| Constant | −2.462 | 0.027 | −2.420 |
| | (−6.988) | (0.035) | (3.735) |
| Log likelihood | −1,406.230 | −407.770 | −540.510 |
| Number of observations | 3,153 | 945 | 957 |

n.a. Not applicable.

*Note:* $\delta F/\delta X$ reports the change (partial) in the probability of the dependent variable (*F*) for changes in any of the independent variables ($X_i$). It is given by the formula, $\delta F/\delta X_i = \beta_i \phi(Z_i)$, where $Z_i = \beta_0 + \Sigma \beta_i X_i$ and $\phi()$ is the density function of the standard normal (Maddala 1988). Coefficients of village-level explanatory variables are excluded from the table. Numbers in parentheses are *t*-statistics. Numbers by sex include only household heads or their spouses.

*Source:* BIDS–World Bank 1991/92 survey.

TABLE A7.2

**Effects of Education and Test Scores on Individual Participation in Wage Employment**
(probit estimates)

| Explanatory variable | $\delta F/\delta X$ for whole sample | $\delta F/\delta X$ for men | $\delta F/\delta X$ for women |
|---|---|---|---|
| Age (years) | 0.018 (4.931) | 0.008 (0.919) | 0.035 (3.971) |
| Age squared | −0.0002 (−5.196) | −0.0001 (−1.442) | −0.0004 (−3.438) |
| Sex (1 = male; 0 = female) | 0.610 (27.872) | n.a. | n.a. |
| Education (years) | −0.018 (−2.917) | −0.012 (−1.233) | 0.017 (1.576) |
| Spouse education (years) | n.a. | 0.003 (0.217) | −0.016 (−1.944) |
| Passed reading test | −0.012 (−0.326) | −0.046 (−0.789) | −0.076 (−1.444) |
| Passed writing test | 0.091 (1.890) | 0.159 (2.555) | 0.132 (1.148) |
| Passed oral math test | −0.123 (−4.450) | −0.095 (−2.500) | −0.083 (−1.950) |
| Passed written math test | −0.042 (−0.882) | −0.047 (−0.699) | 0.286 (2.000) |
| Spouse passed reading test | n.a. | 0.043 (0.696) | −0.076 (−1.536) |
| Spouse passed writing test | n.a. | −0.033 (−0.300) | 0.138 (1.624) |
| Spouse passed oral math test | n.a. | −0.119 (−2.109) | −0.062 (−2.175) |
| Spouse passed written math test | n.a. | −0.042 (−0.346) | −0.031 (−0.488) |
| Log of household landholding | −0.086 (−11.537) | −0.073 (−6.010) | −0.060 (−6.113) |
| Constant | −0.943 | 0.937 | −2.407 |
| Log likelihood | −1,437.093 | −541.387 | −302.182 |
| Number of observations | 3,039 | 932 | 945 |

n.a. Not applicable.
*Note:* $\delta F/\delta X$ reports the change (partial) in the probability of the dependent variable ($F$) for changes in any of the independent variables ($X_i$). It is given by the formula, $\delta F/\delta X_i = \beta_i \phi(Z_i)$, where $Z_i = \beta_0 + \Sigma \beta_i X_i$ and $\phi()$ is the density function of the standard normal (Maddala 1988). Coefficients of village-level explanatory variables are excluded from the table. Numbers in parentheses are $t$-statistics. Numbers by sex include only household heads or their spouses.
*Source:* BIDS–World Bank 1991/92 survey.

# Appendix B: Description of the Sample Used in the Bangladesh Institute of Development Studies– World Bank 1991/92 Survey

The sample used in the Bangladesh Institute of Development Studies–World Bank 1991/92 survey consisted of 29 thanas randomly drawn from the 391 thanas in Bangladesh (southern and southeastern thanas that were severely affected by a cyclone in April 1991 were excluded from the sample). Twenty-four thanas in the sample had at least one microcredit program in operation, while five thanas had none. Eight thanas were located in the Khulna region, three in Chittagong, ten in Dhaka, and eight in Rajshahi. Only three thanas were drawn from the Chittagong region because more than a third of the region was affected by the devastating cyclone of 1991. In several thanas more than one of the three credit programs operated. However, although programs overlapped within a thana, an individual did not belong to more than one program concurrently.

Three villages in each program thana were randomly selected from a list of program villages in which a program had been in operation at least three years. Three villages in each nonprogram thana were also randomly picked from the village census conducted by the government of Bangladesh. Villages with an unusually high or low number of households were excluded from the study by sample survey design. Villages with fewer than 51 or more than 600 households were replaced by villages with 51– 600 households. A total of 87 villages were selected.

From the village census list of households, 20 households were drawn from each village, with a ratio of target to nontarget households of 17:3. A random sampling technique was used to pick 17 target households from the nonprogram villages and 3 nontarget households from both program and nonprogram villages. To pick target households from program villages, a stratified random sampling technique was used to ensure that a sufficient number of program participating households were included. The stratified random sampling technique used for program villages was to draw 12 participating households for every 5 nonparticipating households. If 20 households had been drawn from each village, a total of 1,740 households would have been drawn. In fact, 1,798 households were sampled because more than 20 households were sampled in 5 program thanas. In these five thanas, which together covered all three programs, a nutrition survey was conducted. In order to have a large enough sample, a larger number of target households was drawn.

Of the 1,798 households selected, 1,538 were target and 260 were nontarget households. Among the target households, 905 (59 percent) were participating in a credit program. The nutrition study covered 315 households in 15 villages in 5 thanas. Because the distribution of target, nontarget, and participating households in the sample differed from that in the village population, results were adjusted by appropriate household weights to adjust for under- or overrepresentation. All villages surveyed had both male and female credit groups: 15 had no credit program, 40 had credit groups for both men and women, 22 had female-only groups, and 10 had male-only groups. The existence of villages with female-only and male-only groups facilitated estimation of impact by gender.

A detailed household questionnaire was designed to collect information on income, employment, education, consumption, borrowing, asset ownership, savings, children's schooling, fertility behavior, and contraceptive use for households and individuals. For the 315 households included in the nutrition survey, anthropometric data (such as arm circumference, height, and weight) on children under the age of 15 and dietary intake on all individuals were collected.

In addition to the household survey, a village survey questionnaire was administered. This survey collected information about the prices of different crops, fertilizers, wages for men, women, and children, interest rates of informal credit markets, roads, electricity, schools, and distance from thana headquarters. The general household survey was conducted three times during the 1991/92 farming year, based on the three cropping seasons: Aman (November-February), Boro (March-June), and Aus (July-October). Information on village-level prices and wages was collected in the same manner for the three seasons. The nutrition survey was conducted only during the Boro and Aus seasons. People are better-off during the Aman season (hence called the peak season) than during the other two seasons, and worse-off during the Aus season (hence called the lean season).

# Appendix C: Evaluating Microcredit Programs

Although income and employment generation is an explicit objective of all microfinance institutions, poverty reduction may not be a central concern for many of them. For example, village banks supported by Accion International or Women's World Banking in a number of countries are programs for microentrepreneurs where poverty reduction is not a prime concern. In participating countries, such as some in Latin America, microfinance emerged in response to market failures in which formal financial institutions failed to cater their financial services to small- and medium-scale enterprises. In contrast, microcredit programs, such as those in Bangladesh, are poverty alleviation programs, but even if they are instruments for poverty reduction, they nevertheless practice financial intermediation.

Interestingly, some of the poverty alleviation microfinance institutions operate under government regulations, like banks, while some do not. Grameen Bank is an example of the first category, and its performance can be evaluated in terms of whether it is financially self-sustainable. Moreover, since it is a rural bank, its performance must be judged against the performance of traditional rural financial institutions, such as commercial and agricultural development banks. In contrast, programs such as BRAC and RD-12 are not banks and so do not operate under strict banking rules. Being nonbanks, standard financial and economic efficiency criteria may not be strictly applicable. Nevertheless, since they behave like financial intermediaries, they should be subject to conditions similar to those applied to Grameen Bank. The purpose here is to determine whether these bank-like organizations are financially viable and, hence, whether it is possible to transform them into specialized banks.

Because microcredit programs' prime objective is to alleviate poverty, their performance must be judged accordingly. Microcredit programs are often seen as transfer programs; if so, then these programs must be able to transfer resources in a cost-effective way. But targeted microcredit to the poor is one of many instruments for poverty reduction. Broad-based economic growth policies, Food-for-Work, and targeted wage employment schemes are some of the noncredit instruments that also help reduce poverty. Microcredit institutions must thus be evaluated against the performance of alternative instruments for poverty reduction. Often, the poverty impact of these instruments is assessed in terms of the impact of program participation on income, employment, and consumption. While this is a well-established approach, such a method for evaluating Grameen Bank and other microfinance institutions overlooks their financial performance as banks or bank-like organizations delivering financial services to the poor, or as mechanisms for social transfer.

In contrast, the finance literature dwells largely on financial viability of targeted credit programs, as it views them as financial intermediaries. Hence the primary concern of this literature is the cost efficiency of microfinance institutions. That is, it addresses issues such as the amount that it costs to deliver these services and whether the programs providing these services are cost-effective (that is, cover program costs with interest income). But many microfinance institutions address market failures and use grants or soft loans to provide services to target clients. This involves subsidies, and the questions to ask are how much subsidy these programs enjoy, whether they are able to eliminate subsidy, and, if so, how (Yaron 1992b).

Questions are also raised about the distribution of subsidies—that is, who benefits from these programs. Thus identification of beneficiaries is necessary. Program evaluation is then based not only on self-sustainability but also on program outreach, measured by the coverage of target households and the extent of services they receive (Yaron 1992a; Bennett and Cuevas 1996). Outreach indicators are taken as proxies for development impacts of microcredit programs, assuming that self-sustainable financial institutions are likely to contribute to income expansion and poverty reduction—that is, the *output* of efficient rural financial intermediation leads to the desired development *impact* (Yaron, Benjamin, and Piperk 1997). The twin criteria of outreach and self-sustainability become the yardstick of microcredit program evaluation (Yaron 1992a, b; Christen, Rhyne, and Vogel 1994; Chaves and Gonzalez-Vega 1996; Mahajan and Ramola 1996).

The assumption that an efficient financial institution produces a desirable development impact may be questioned. Under certain conditions an inefficient and unsustainable financial system can generate benefits that exceed the costs to the government of sustaining this system. For instance, India's formal financial intermediaries, which are unsustainable without government subsidies, are nevertheless contributing to the growth of the rural economy (Binswanger and Khandker 1995). On the other hand, programs such as microfinance institutions, even if they are effective in reaching target clients and are self-sustainable, may generate benefits that are not sustainable or are so marginal that they do not have an overall impact on growth (Bouman and Hospes 1994). In other words, simple outreach of a self-sustainable financial institution does not guarantee that participants and society benefit from such investments.

Also, even if participants do benefit from an efficient financial institution and, hence, outreach indicators are good measures of a program's success, it is not clear whether program benefits hurt others in society or are costly to policymakers compared with alternative programs. This raises the issues of externalities, income redistribution, and cost-effectiveness of alternative program interventions. Because of program externalities, it is possible that benefits accrued to the poor are generated at the expense of others in society so that the program intervention is not Pareto efficient.[1] Pareto efficiency is more likely to be achieved in a regime in which economic growth permits the expansion of existing activities or the development of new activities that benefit participants without hurting others (Binswanger and Landell-Mills 1995). On the other hand, since subsidized funds have alternative uses through which the poor can also benefit, program evaluation of microfinance institutions must be made on the basis of cost-effectiveness of alternative antipoverty programs.

An ideal method for program evaluation is, therefore, an integrated approach that carries out cost-benefit analyses of alternative programs promoting welfare of both target and nontarget households. Program evaluation is, of course, subject to the social welfare function. If the objective is to promote society's welfare, then the impact must be assessed for both target and nontarget households, as well as participants and nonparticipants. If the social objective function is distributionally neutral, then an evaluation of the target population is sufficient to justify program intervention. But such an evaluation is incomplete, because it ignores program externalities. For example, agricultural development banks, which are subsidized in many countries, are evaluated based on what happens to agricultural growth. Yet a recent evaluation of formal financial institutions in India found that although credit programs were targeted to farmers, agriculture was not the principal beneficiary; the rural nonfarm economy benefited most from targeted agricultural credit programs because credit is fungible across activities and households (Binswanger and Khandker 1995).

## Costs and Benefits of Microfinance

High administrative costs of forming groups and disbursing group-based credit and ancillary inputs make group-based microcredit programs structurally unsustainable. The programs provide small loans to a large number of poor people, who require sustained access to credit to generate employment and income. Although group pressure may promote proper loan use and high loan recovery rates, it is doubtful that these programs could generate sufficient revenue from their operations to support these costs, at least in their early years. It is also unlikely that the rural poor are able to bear the full cost of microcredit, including the start-up cost of program development.

As such, microcredit programs depend to a large extent on the availability of subsidized funds. These funds help promote institutional development. But reliance on subsidized funds forever cannot be justified if these programs aspire to attain sustainability. If subsidies are unavoidable for a credit program catering to the poor, how much subsidies are required to sustain such a banking operation, for how long, and is it worth continuing?

There are two types of subsidies: financial and economic. If a microcredit program is not cost-effective, it will require financial subsidies to continue operating. In addition, if the cost of funding for on-lending is cheaper than the opportunity cost of these funds, the program enjoys an economic subsidy.[2] A microcredit program may receive both types of subsidies, and they are both sources of concern for its long-run viability.

The extent of the subsidies a program requires can be measured using available cost and revenue information and market interest rates. This information would then help determine at what cost the program delivers credit and other inputs to the poor. Four interrelated concepts of sustainability relevant to a program's cost evaluation are financial viability, economic viability, institutional viability, and borrower viability.

A microfinance institution is defined as *financially* viable if it can at least meet the cost per unit of principal lent with the price (that is, the interest rate) it charges its borrowers. It is defined as *economically* viable if it can meet the economic cost of funds (the opportunity cost) used for credit and other operations with the income it generates from lending. And, in order to be *institutionally* viable, it must have effective and well-institutionalized procedures for ensuring administration and management succession, so that it is not dependent on the leadership of a particular person. Moreover, because staff development and incentives contribute to productivity, programs should aim to optimally allocate resources to produce internal and cost efficiency.

But institutional viability cannot be attained unless the benefits from the projects funded by a program meet members' costs of borrowing. This is illustrated by the high collinearity between the *viability of borrowers* and the viability of lenders, which depend on the same environmental and production risks. Whether the benefits from an activity will equal the cost of borrowing depends on borrowers' entrepreneurial abilities, given market and other constraints. The viability of borrowers is therefore crucial to a microcredit program's overall viability. The success or failure of a program should also be judged by how far the program has gone to develop a viable organization for the poor and help borrowers sustain their gains.

To ensure its own financial and economic viability, and that of its borrowers, a microcredit program must become a sustainable institution in terms of program organization and management structure. A sustainable microcredit institution should influence its employees and borrowers to perform efficiently. Given a proper incentive structure, employees will naturally be motivated to improve the organization's delivery and recovery mechanisms. Understanding a microcredit program's institutional development requires examination of its management structure, the incentives for its staff to improve productivity, the structure of the incentive system, and the employee turnover or dropout rate.

Deciding where to open a branch or activity is an important aspect of institutional development cost. A microfinance institution such as Grameen Bank, like other financial institutions seeking to remain financially viable, must avoid, or at least consider, material (agroclimatic and locational) risks in selecting areas for its operation. It is much more difficult to create a viable system of financial intermediation in areas that are flood-prone, areas experiencing pronounced seasonality, and areas that are far from urban centers and that lack the infrastructure to support transportation (Binswanger and Rosenzweig 1986). However, microfinance institutions may need to offer financial services in areas subject to material risk when that risk is a source of poverty. Therefore, by examining program distribution in light of invariant area and agroclimate characteristics, one can infer whether a microcredit program leans toward favorable agroclimate conditions or opts for unfavorable agroclimate conditions that are possible sources of poverty.

Borrower viability can be measured in different ways. One way is to examine whether borrowers have achieved higher income flows over time—and are thus able to repay their loans and possibly accumulate enough capital to no longer require assistance. It may also mean that borrowers have switched to more remunerative sources of income as a result of program participation. Income and occupational mobility of borrowers are therefore important indicators of borrower viability.

Another way to examine the viability of borrowers is to measure how effectively capital is used at the household level. This is done by calculating the rates of return on household investments in order to indicate whether the cost per unit of principal lent is covered by those investments. Cross-sectional household survey data on the net income generated from credit-supported projects would be sufficient to estimate these rates of return across activities and across programs. The average borrower's net increase in income can be compared in absolute terms to a quantitative measure of the expected gain from a targeted credit program. These estimates would provide a uniform assessment of credit use.

A more direct way to assess program impact at the participant level is to examine the effects of borrowing or program participation on observable measures of household welfare such as consumption, savings, asset ownership, net worth, and other socioeconomic indicators (such as contraceptive use, fertility, and school enrollment of children).

Program impacts measured at the participant level do not indicate how society at large has benefited from program inputs. One way to assess this aggregate-level impact is to examine a program's effect on rural wages. Microcredit programs' operations may benefit rural wage workers if their induced benefits make a dent in rural poverty. Microfinanced activities have a positive labor supply effect (because they withdraw labor from the market by enabling workers to employ themselves) and a positive labor demand effect (through an induced income effect) on rural wages. One would therefore expect an increase in rural wages following program placement in an area if the reduction in wage labor supply is not matched by an increase in labor supply from others in the village or if the net increase in labor supply is lower than induced increased demand for labor. The other way to examine overall program impact is to look at the effect of program inputs on community- or village-level income, employment, production, and labor force participation.

## Assessing Financial Efficiency

Financial efficiency can be assessed by determining whether the cost per unit of principal lent by an institution is equal to the rate of interest borrowers are charged, a criterion known as financial efficiency.

If a credit program is to maintain its capital holdings, it must generate sufficient revenue over a given period of time to meet its operating costs. A microcredit program receives revenue from borrowers' interest payments; its costs stem from raising loanable funds, organizing and training borrower groups, administering loans, and covering bad debts. To meet the financial efficiency criterion, a program should charge an interest rate that generates revenue equal to or greater than the cost per unit of principal lent. This can be formally stated as:

$$r \geq \frac{i + \alpha + \rho}{1 - \rho}$$

where $r$ is the interest rate charged per unit of principal lent, $i$ is the cost of raising loanable resources per unit of principal lent, $\alpha$ is the expected cost of administering and supervising a loan per unit of principal lent, and $\rho$ is the expected financial loss per unit of principal lent, or the percentage of principal and interest payments due that is not recovered.[3] Program-level information on operational costs, lending costs, and costs of funds can be used to calculate a program's financial efficiency. Doing so helps determine whether a program requires financial subsidy given its cost of borrowing and, if so, how much.

The financial efficiency criterion does not, however, capture the possibility that the program may fail to satisfy the criterion during a single time period but may still be financially viable over time. It also does not allow the economic subsidy to be estimated or the subsidy recipients to be identified. The success of a microcredit program depends not only on the relationship between the cost per unit of principal lent and the market interest rate but also on the combined successes (or failures) of individual branches. Analysis of the dynamics of sustainability requires examination of the branch-level performance of a program in terms of cost structures, loan recovery, and profits or losses. Both the loan recovery profiles and the percentage of the loan portfolio in arrears are used as proximate measures of a program's economic sustainability.

To capture how a program's cost components and innovative schemes influence its cost structures over time, the cost functions must include all relevant (control and other) variables. Estimating a cost function at the branch level may also help identify whether branch-level operations can break even over the long run and test whether branches are profit-maximizing units. Such branch-level analysis can also identify whether a program is economically viable.

Given its mandate to reach as many rural poor as possible within a designated area, a typical branch aims to expand credit disbursement by expanding membership or increasing the volume of lending per member. A microcredit program can increase individuals' loan absorption capacity through training and other skills development inputs that enhance entrepreneurial skills. Profit-maximizing branches are assumed to minimize the costs of reaching a given level of membership and credit disbursement. Microcredit programs may also seek to minimize the cost of attaining a targeted savings level.

An extensive literature exists on the estimation of cost functions to measure both the operational efficiency and economic viability of a financial program (see Kalari and Zardkoohi 1987; Clark 1984; Benston and Smith 1976; and Srinivasan 1988). A cost function relates the cost of a program to a predetermined quantity of output, the exogenous prices of labor and capital, and a number of control variables that influence cost. The translog specification is a flexible form for estimating a cost function that does not have the restrictive properties of the widely used Cobb-Douglas function. This specification can also help measure a branch's scale and scope economies, as well as the effect of product mix on costs. Economies of scale exist if unit production costs decrease as output expands. Economies of scope exist if joint outputs, such as lending and savings mobilization, are produced at a lower cost than a single output, such as lending. The conditional cost function (conditional on the level of outputs) takes the following form:

$$\ln TC_{jt} = a_0 + a_1 \ln S_{jt} + 1/2[a_2 \ln S_{jt}^2] + a_3 \ln W_{jt} + 1/2[a_4 \ln W_{jt}^2]$$
$$+ a_5 \ln N_{jt} + 1/2[a_6 \ln N_{jt}^2] + 1/2[a_7 \ln S_{jt} \ln W_{jt}]$$
$$+ 1/2[a_8 \ln S_{jt} \ln N_{jt}] + 1/2[a_9 \ln W_{jt} \ln N_{jt}] + IF_{jt} + d_j + e_{jt}$$

where $TC_{jt}$ is the $j$th branch's program costs in period $t$; $S_{jt}$ is a vector of membership, lending, and savings; $W_{jt}$ is the price of labor (defined as the annual average salary plus benefits paid to program workers divided by the total number of workers); $N_{jt}$ is the fixed unit cost of lending (measured by the sum of rents paid and depreciation of equipment divided by the value of all loans); $IF_{jt}$ is a vector of control variables, including infrastructure (roads, schools, commercial banks, and health facilities); $d_j$ is a vector of area-specific fixed endowments, such as flood potential, soil moisture availability, and location; and $e_{jt}$ is the error term.

The cost function can be estimated to determine whether a branch exhibits economies of scale. If economies of scale do exist, membership can be expanded and lending and savings per member can be increased to reduce overhead. An important objective is to find out where existing branches are located along the cost function and whether economies of scale exist and can be captured by intensifying their operations.

The cost function can also identify whether differences in product will influence program cost structures. Branches can be grouped by loan type (for example, technology loans) or by gender composition to examine whether intensifying group interactions with program staff, making smaller loans, or mobilizing individuals or groups perceived to have lower credit risk affects economies of scale. These procedures may increase operating costs. It is thus instructive to analyze how different risk-reducing methods adopted by a program have shaped its cost structures over time and across regions. In particular, this analysis may help explain whether making women its principal beneficiaries reduces costs for a program such as Grameen Bank.

Estimating a conditional cost function requires first estimating a program's output separately in order to use it as a predetermined variable in the cost equation. It is likely that both costs and output are jointly determined (that is, the cost function suffers from a simultaneity bias). The Hausman (1978) endogeneity test is used to test for the existence of simultaneity bias. A two-step procedure is adopted so that instruments that influence only output, not cost, can be identified. First, membership, lending, and savings are estimated as a function of input prices, control variables, and some instruments. Then cost as a function of predetermined output, input prices, and control variables is estimated using the level of output predicted from this first-stage regression.[4]

The financial viability of a credit program can also be measured by estimating a set of reduced-form equations for loan recovery, membership, total lending, input uses, and other indicators of program performance. This helps identify the role of various factors, both at the program and at the area level, in performance over time. Formally,

$$PF_{jt} = b_0 + b_1 PR_{jt} + b_2 IF_{jt} + b_3 S_{jt} + d_j + e_{jt}$$

where $PF_{jt}$ is a vector of performance indicators, $PR_{jt}$ is a vector of input prices, including wages, and $IF_{jt}$, $S_{jt}$ and $d_j$ are defined as before.

Both the cost equation and the performance equation use branch-level panel data and may consequently suffer from bias due to the unobserved heterogeneity of different branches. A fixed-effects technique may be used to control for the unobserved area-specific heterogeneity.[5]

## Measuring Subsidy Dependence and Assessing Economic Viability

Branch-level cost function estimates indicate whether branches of a microcredit program are economically viable. Branch-level economic viability does not imply that the program as a whole is economically viable. Although there is no direct way of estimating total economic viability, it is possible to evaluate whether microcredit programs can operate without low-cost subsidized funds. The extent of economic subsidy —in terms of the opportunity cost of the subsidized funds the program receives—needs to be identified. This will help determine whether a microcredit program can operate without the economic subsidy and, if not, what needs to be done so that it can.

A microcredit program may enjoy two types of subsidies—a financial subsidy, given if the program cannot break even, and an economic subsidy, given if lending is supported by grants or funds obtained at interest rates that are below the market rate. The economic subsidy is defined as the difference between the actual interest rate and the opportunity cost of the subsidized funds and grants received (Yaron 1992b).

The economic subsidy can be separated into three components: the interest (or financial cost) subsidy, the equity subsidy, and the income subsidy. The interest subsidy is defined as the difference between the market interest rate and the concessional interest rate times the amount of the subsidy. Mathematically the interest subsidy is represented as $FCS = A(m - c)$, where $FCS$ is the financial cost subsidy, $A$ is the total annual concessional borrowed funds (outstanding), $m$ is the market interest rate, and $c$ is the concessional interest rate. For grants $c = 0$ and the financial cost subsidy is equal to $Am$. The subsidy on the amount of equity held by a program's group members, the government, and commercial banks is given by $ES = Em$, where $ES$ is the equity subsidy, $E$ is the total amount of equity, and $m$ is the market interest rate.

The income subsidy ($K$) is defined as the amount of grants received as reimbursement for some operating expenses. Sometimes donor agencies reimburse microcredit programs for almost all training expenses. These expenses often appear as revenue on the program's income and expenditure statement. The total subsidy ($SS$) is then given by $SS = FCS + ES + K$.

Net subsidy ($NS$) is the economic subsidy less profit ($P$) and is defined as $NS = A(m - c) + Em + K - P$. Note that the net subsidy can be positive, negative, or zero. If profit is greater than the economic subsidy, the program receives no net subsidy and the net economic cost for continuing operations is zero. In contrast, if the program requires a financial subsidy, its economic subsidy increases. Calculation of the net subsidy depends on how the opportunity cost of the subsidized funds received is defined.

Yaron (1992a) suggests that the fixed-deposit interest rate be used as the reference rate for calculating the subsidy. Because the net subsidy does not provide any information about how dependent a program is on subsidies for its sustainability, Yaron (1992a) compares the subsidy dependence of a program with the interest earned on its loan portfolio (the main activity of a financial development intermediary):

$$SDI = \frac{NS}{LP * i}$$

where $SDI$ is the subsidy dependence index, $NS$ is the annual (net) subsidy received by the institution, $LP$ is the average annual outstanding loan portfolio, and $i$ is the average weighted on-lending interest rate paid on that portfolio.

The subsidy dependence index measures the percentage increase in the average on-lending interest rate required to eliminate the subsidy in a given year while maintaining a return on equity equal to the nonconcessional borrowing cost. A subsidy dependence index of zero implies that profit equals the social cost of operation, meaning that the institution is self-sustainable. A positive subsidy dependence index indicates that the economic cost exceeds profits, in which case the onlending interest rate must be increased by the amount of the subsidy dependence index to eliminate the net subsidy. A subsidy dependence index of 100 percent, for example, indicates the need to double the onlending interest rate to eliminate subsidies.

## Measuring Program Benefits to Participants

The private benefits of microfinance must be evaluated in terms of the program impacts on household behavior and intrahousehold resource allocation. Assume that households consisting of two working-age adults, the male head ($m$) and his wife ($f$), maximize a utility function of the form:

$$U = U(Q, H, l_f, l_m)$$

where $Q$ is the set of market goods consumed by household members, $H$ is the set of nonmarket household-produced goods, and $l_i$ is leisure time consumed by household member $i$ ($i = m, f$). Each of the two adult household members wishes to maximize his or her own utility $u_i$, $u_i = u_i(Q_i, H_i, l_i)$, $i = f, m$, where household social welfare is some function of the individual utility functions $U = U(u_f, u_m)$. A simple form of the function is $U_i = \lambda u_f + (1 - \lambda) u_m$, $0 \leq \lambda \leq 1$, where $\lambda$ is the weight given to the woman's preferences in the household's social welfare function. The parameter $\lambda$ can be thought of as representing the bargaining power of women relative to men in determining the intrahousehold allocation of resources. When $\lambda = 0$ women's preferences are given no weight, and the households' social welfare functions are those of the men (McElroy 1990; McElroy and Horney 1981; Manser and Brown 1980; and Haddad, Hoddinott, and Alderman 1994).[6]

The household-produced goods, $H$, include household care activities, such as food preparation, child care, and the gathering of fuel, some of which cannot be stored for consumption in later periods. This equation can be written as $H = H(L_{mh}, L_{fh}, G; F)$, where $L_{mh}$ is the time devoted to the production of $H$ by men, $L_{fh}$ is the time devoted to the production of $H$ by women, $G$ is a vector of market goods used as inputs in the production of $H$, and $F$ is a vector of technology parameters that affect efficiency in the production of $H$.

Sociocultural factors and the fact that wage employment usually requires a full-time commitment mean that relatively few poor women work in the wage labor market in Bangladesh. If men's time (or that of other household members) is a poor substitute for women's time and important $H$ outputs, such as child care and food preparation, must be produced daily (that is, they cannot be stored), then a woman's working a full day may entail forgoing the production and consumption of highly valued $H$-goods. Women's wage employment outside the home is thus not a viable option for many rural women, who spend most of their time producing $H$. Women's time allocation to $H$ production is more likely if $\lambda$ is small and men's preferences tend to favor certain types of $H$-goods.

But households can produce $Z$-goods—goods for market sale that are not culturally frowned upon. These activities can be produced using part-time labor and do not require production to be done away from the home. Although many of these activities can be performed at low levels of capital intensity, many $Z$-goods require a minimum level of capital.[7] Formally, the production function for $Z$-goods is $Z = Z(K, L_{mz}, L_{fz}^*, A; J)$, $(Z > 0$ if $K \geq K_{min})$, $K$ is capital used in $Z$ production, where $L_{mz}$ is the man's time in $Z$-good production, $L_{fz}^*$ is the efficiency of the woman's labor devoted to the production of $Z$, $A$ is a vector of variable inputs, and $J$ is a vector of technology parameters that affect efficiency in $Z$-good production (information). Positive production requires a minimal level of capital $(K \geq K_{min})$. Production of $Z$-goods and $H$-goods is joint in that $L_{fz}^* = L_{fz} + \omega L_{fh}$ $(0 \leq \omega \leq 1, i = f, m)$, where $L_{iz}$ is the time spent exclusively on the production of $Z$. The jointness of $H$ and $Z$ is shown by the parameter $\omega$. If $\omega = 0$, then $H$ and $Z$ are not subject to joint production and there are no efficiency gains if household members reallocate their time from $H$ to $Z$; instead such allocation involves a loss of $H$ production by the marginal product of labor. If $\omega = 1$, then $H$ and $Z$ are maximally joint in production in that reallocation of time from $H$ to $Z$ production involves no cost and the production of $H$ remains unchanged.

Households maximize utility subject to the budget constraint $P_Q Q + P_A A + P_G G + \varphi L_{fw} = W_m L_{mw} + W_f L_{fw} + P_Z Z + V$, where $P_j$ $(j = Q, A, G, Z)$ is the price of $Q, A, G,$ and $Z$, respectively; $W_m$ is the market wage of men's labor; $L_{mw}$ is men's time devoted to market wage income; $W_f$ is the market wage of women's labor; $L_{fw}$ is women's time devoted to market wage income; $\varphi$ is the transactions cost per unit of labor time of women workers due to socioeconomic constraints; and $V$ is unearned income.

The time constraint for men is captured by $L_m = L_{mw} + L_{mz} + L_{mh} + l_m$, and the time constraints for women is captured by $L_f = L_{fw} + L_{fz} + L_{fh} + l_f$, where $L_m$ is the total time available to men and $L_f$ is the total time available to women.

First-order conditions for maximizing the utility function equation subject to the budget constraint and all other conditions presented here with respect to women's time devoted to $H$ yield:

C.1
$$\left(\frac{\partial U}{\partial H}\right)\left(\frac{\partial H}{\partial L_{fh}}\right) = \tau(W_f - \varphi) - \omega P_Z\left(\frac{\partial Z}{\partial L_{fz}}\right)$$

where $\tau$ is the marginal utility of income. Given the marginal utility of income and the marginal utility of $H$-goods, the marginal product of time devoted to $H$ production depends on three factors: the market wage rate, the transactions cost of market wage employment, and the value of the marginal product of labor in Z-good production.

The first-order conditions for maximizing the utility function with respect to women's time devoted to Z production is:

C.2
$$P_Z\left(\frac{\partial Z}{\partial L_{fz}}\right) = W_f - \varphi,$$

indicating that the marginal product of labor in Z-good production is equal to the market wage less the transactions cost of wage employment. Hence the higher the transactions cost of employment, the greater the allocation of women's time to Z-good production relative to market wage employment. Substituting equation C.2 into equation C.1 yields:

C.3
$$\left(\frac{\partial U}{\partial H}\right)\left(\frac{\partial H}{\partial L_{fh}}\right) = \tau[(W_f - \varphi)(1 - \omega)].$$

Two important implications follow from equations C.1–C.3. The first is that the transactions cost of wage employment for women affects the home production of nonmarket goods. If there is no Z-good production, the third term in the bracket on the right side of equation C.1 is zero and equation C.2 does not exist. Thus the imputed value of nonmarket production is equal to the imputed value of the market wage less the transactions cost of wage employment. That means that women allocate more labor to home production if the transactions cost of wage employment is positive than they do if it is zero. The shadow price of home nonmarket production is thus partially determined by the size of the transactions cost of wage employment.

The second implication is that microcredit enables poor women to engage in Z-good production. The shadow price of home nonmarket production is reduced by the value of the marginal product of time in Z-good production (equivalent to the net market wage) adjusted by the parameter measuring the degree of jointness in $H$ and $Z$ production. If $H$ and $Z$ are not jointly produced (that is, $\omega = 0$), then the shadow price of home production is the net wage from wage employment. This is similar to the case in which no Z-good production takes place because of lack of access to credit to finance $K_{min}$. If $H$ and $Z$ are jointly produced (that is, $\omega = 1$), then the shadow price of home production is reduced by the marginal product of labor of Z-good production. That means an increase in Z-good production can be accompanied by increased production of $H$ without incurring any cost for $Z$ production; all time devoted to producing $H$ also produces $Z$ with the same efficiency because there is no opportunity cost in terms of $Z$ production from the reallocation of time. Because of the jointness of $H$ and $Z$ production, it is possible that households would benefit from withdrawing labor from the wage market when $K_{min}$ is available to support $Z$ production.

For the very poor, especially for women, access to credit may thus alter the optimal time allocation from home production of $H$ to market production of $Z$. If household consumption is at or near the minimal levels necessary for survival, so that saving is almost infinitely costly, even a small quantity of credit for the purchase of $K_{min}$ can have a large impact on household welfare by shifting women's time from the production of $H$, which may have a low shadow value, to the production of $Z$, the marginal product of which is high. In addition, program participation may alter the technology parameters, $F$ and $J$, by providing information and training, which may affect efficiency in $H$- or $Z$-good production and hence income and consumption.

The production of $H$-goods may rise or fall in households that borrow in order to start $Z$-good production. The direction of change in $H$-good production depends on the size of the income effects, the substitutability of market inputs with time inputs, and the degree to which a unit of (women's) time can jointly produce the $Z$-good and the $H$-good. Program participation may also affect household allocations by altering the value of $\lambda$. The value of $\lambda$ may increase with women's greater bargaining power—the resulting of controlling additional resources through targeted credit and consciousness-promoting training.

In the model presented here, the reduced-form determinants of credit program participation include the price of market time (that is, wages); the price of the purchased market good, $Q$; the prices of market inputs into $H$-good production, including the cost of averting a birth and other determinants of fertility; the prices of variable inputs into $Z$-good production; the price of the capital good; age and education levels of the borrower and spouse; and village-level characteristics $(V)$.[8]

Unlike in formal credit institutions, the cost of credit in a group-based credit program includes not only the interest rate but also the timing of repayment and the penalties associated with default. Group-based credit is packaged with responsibilities (meeting attendance, forced saving, shared default risk) and benefits (training, insurance, consciousness-raising). If there were no monitoring of the use of borrowed funds and no group responsibility and decisionmaking in the lending program, individuals would likely want to borrow much more than they actually do in order to capture the premiums associated with the soft terms of the loan. Monitoring credit use makes all program participants "credit constrained" in that the notional demand for credit always falls short of supply. For these reasons all participating households are presumed to be in the same credit demand regime.

## Measuring Benefits to Households

The objective of modeling household behavior when there is an option to participate in a group-based program is to estimate the impact of credit programs on various household outcomes, such as household consumption, time allocation, asset accumulation, contraceptive use, and investments in children.[9] The level of participation in a credit program $(C_{ij})$, measured by the value of program credit, is given by

$$C_{ij} = X_{ij}\beta_c + V_j\gamma_c + Z_{ij}\pi + \varepsilon_{ij}^c$$

where $X_{ij}$ is a vector of household characteristics (such as age and education of household head), $V_j$ is a vector of village characteristics (such as prices and community infrastructure), $Z_{ij}$ is a set of household or village characteristics distinct from $X_{ij}$ and $V_j$ in that they affect $C_{ij}$ but not other household behavior conditional on $C_{ij}$, and $\beta_c$, $\gamma_c$, and $\pi$ are unknown parameters. $\varepsilon_{ij}^c$ is a random error consisting of $\mu_j$, an unobserved village-specific effect; $\eta_{ij}$, an unobserved household-specific effect; and $\varepsilon_{ij}^c$ a nonsystematic error uncorrelated with the other error components or the regressors.

The conditional demand for household outcome, $Y_{ij}$, conditional on the level of program participation $C_{ij}$ is $Y_{ij} = X_{ij}\beta_y + V_j\gamma_y + C_{ij}\delta + \varepsilon_{ij}^y$, where $\beta_y$, $\gamma_y$, and $\delta$ are unknown parameters and $\varepsilon_{ij}^y = (\alpha\mu_j + \mu_j^y) + (\theta\eta_{ij} + \eta_{ij}^y) + e_{ij}^y$, where $\alpha$ and $\theta$ are parameters (corresponding to correlation coefficients), $\mu_i^y$ and $\eta_{ij}^y$ are additional village- and household-specific errors uncorrelated with $\mu_j$ and $\eta_{ij}$, and $\varepsilon_{ij}^y$ is a nonsystematic error uncorrelated with other error components or with the regressors. If $\alpha \neq 0$ or $\theta \neq 0$, the errors $\varepsilon_{ij}^y$ and $\varepsilon_{ij}^c$ are correlated. Econometric estimation that does not take this correlation into account will yield biased estimates of the parameters because of the endogeneity of credit program participation.

The standard approach to the problem of estimating equations with endogenous regressors is to use instrumental variables. In the model presented here, the exogenous regressors, $Z_{ij}$, are the identifying instrumental variables. It is difficult to find any regressors $Z_{ij}$ that can be used as identifying instruments. An approach motivated by demand theory is to use the price of the conditioned upon exogenous variable as an identifying instrument. The most obvious measure of the price of credit is the interest rate charged by the program, but it cannot be used because it does not vary across the sample.

Village fixed-effects estimation, which treats the village-specific error $\mu_i$ as a parameter to be estimated, eliminates the endogeneity caused by unmeasured village attributes, including nonrandom program placement. However, even with village fixed-effects, the endogeneity problem remains if $\theta \neq 0$, (that is, if there are common household-specific unobservable variables affecting credit demand and household outcomes). Lacking identifying instruments $Z_{ij}$, the sample survey was constructed so as to provide identification through a quasi-experimental design.

In the classic program evaluation problem with nonexperimental data, individuals can elect to receive a treatment offered in their village or neighborhood (Moffitt 1991). The difference between the outcome $(Y_{ij})$ of individuals who choose to receive the treatment and that of individuals who do not is not a valid estimate of the treatment's effect if individuals self-select into the treatment group. Lacking any $Z_{ij}$ (or panel data on individuals before and after treatment availability), one method of identifying the effect of the treatment is based upon (presumed) knowledge of the distribution of the errors (Heckman 1976; Lee 1976). If the errors are assumed to be normally distributed, as is common, the treatment effect is implicitly identified from the deviations from normality within the sample of treatment participants. The nonlinearity of the presumed distribution is crucial. If both the treatment and the outcome are measured as binary indicators, identification of the treatment effect is generally not possible even with the specification of an error distribution.

If credit program placement across program villages is not random, using a village fixed-effects estimation technique will remove the source of correlation. However, without further exogenous variation in program availability, the credit-effect parameters $\delta$ (and the parameters $\beta$) are not identifiable from a sample of self-selecting households, as they are "captured" by the village fixed effects. The parameter of interest, $\delta$, the effect of participation in a credit program on the outcome $Y_{ij}$, can be identified if the sample also includes households in program villages that are excluded from making a treatment choice by random assignment or some exogenous rule. In this sample, exogenous rule is the restriction that households must own no more than half an acre of land. Data on the behavior of households that were exogenously denied program choice because they owned too much land are sufficient to identify the credit program effect. A comparison of the outcome $Y_{ij}$ between households with program choice and households without program choice, conditional on all village effects and observed household and individual attributes, is an estimate of the program's effect on that outcome.

To understand the identification strategy, consider a sample drawn from two villages—one with a microcredit program ($j = 1$) and one without ($j = 2$)—and two types of households, landed ($X_{ij} = 1$) and landless ($X_{ij} = 0$). Landed status is assumed to be the only observed household-specific determinant of some behavior $Y_{ij}$ in addition to any treatment effect from the program. The conditional demand equation is $Y_{ij} = C_{ij}\delta + X_{ij}\beta + \mu_j + \varepsilon_{ij}$. The expected value of $Y_{ij}$ for each household type in each village is:

$$E(Y_{ij} \mid j = 1, X_{ij} = 0) = \mu_1$$
$$E(Y_{ij} \mid j = 1, X_{ij} = 1) = \beta + \mu_1$$
$$E(Y_{ij} \mid j = 2, X_{ij} = 1) = \beta + \mu_2$$
$$E(Y_{ij} \mid j = 2, X_{ij} = 0) = \rho\beta + \mu_2$$

where $\rho$ is the proportion of landless households in village 2 who choose to participate in the program. All parameters, including the effect of the credit program $\delta$, are identified from this design.[10]

An underlying assumption of this model is that land ownership is exogenous in this population. Although it is unusual to use program eligibility criteria for purposes of identification in most program evaluations, it seems appropriate to do so here. Unlike evaluation of job training programs, health and nutrition interventions, and many other types of programs in which lack of job skills, poor health, or insufficiency in some other behavior represent both eligibility criteria and the behavior the program directly acts upon, land ownership is used as the eligibility criteria for these credit programs only as a proxy for income, consumption, or total asset wealth. It is a useful indicator because it is simple to quantify, understood within the community, and unlikely to change in the medium term.

Market turnover of land is known to be low in South Asia, and the absence of an active land market is the rationale given for the treatment of land ownership as an exogenous regressor in almost all of the empirical work on household behavior in South Asia.[10] A number of theories have been set forth to explain the infrequency of land sales. Binswanger and Rosenzweig (1986) analyzed the set of material and behavioral factors that are important determinants of production relations in land-scarce settings and concluded that land sales would be few and limited mainly to distress sales, particularly where national credit markets are underdeveloped. Rosenzweig and Wolpin (1985) developed an overlapping generations model that incorporates returns on specific experience and uses low land turnover as an implication. Using data from the Additional Rural Incomes Survey of the National Council of Applied Economic Research (NCAER) of India, they found a very low incidence of land sales.

In the same fashion one can estimate program impacts by the gender of program participants. Introducing gender-specific credit involves a number of estimation problems (Pitt and Khandker 1996; Pitt and others 1995). First, it is likely that the errors of the women's participation equation are correlated with the errors of the men's participation equation; that is, common unobservable variables influence the credit program behavior of both women and men in the household. Second, additional identification restrictions are required when both men's and women's credit programs exist, possibly having different effects on behavior. The first issue is computational—bivariate probability distributions must be evaluated when estimating separate credit or program participation equations. Furthermore, if $Y_{ij}$ is a limited dependent variable, trivariate probability distributions must be evaluated. The second issue—that of identification—can be handled by an extension of the exogenous exclusion restriction. All of these group-based credit programs have single-sex groups. Identification of gender-specific credit is achieved by a survey design that includes some households from villages with only women's credit groups and some households from villages with only men's credit groups.

## Measuring Benefits to Society

The aggregate impact of program intervention is the sum of impacts on both participants and nonparticipants. Resources (both credit and noncredit) provided to the village through program participants can affect the resource allocation and consumption of nonparticipating households through the labor market, through induced income, and through demonstration effects. The immediate impact of borrowing to create self-employment may be a reduction in the labor supply to the wage market. This reduction would employ those who are willing to work for wages at the given demand for wage labor. If the reduction of labor supply is large enough to offset increases in wage employment, wages will rise. Increases in household income may also change other household attributes, such as children's schooling and consumption.

If nonparticipating households are not made worse-off by a program, the program is neutral and the net impact could be positive. If the program displaces existing producers, it has a negative impact on their income. The net impact of the program could be positive or negative, depending on the extent of the positive impacts on participants and the negative impacts on nonparticipants. The net program effect is affected by the economy's growth. If, for example, participating households begin to trade rice, the production and consumption of village rice producers could fall. If income growth induces higher demand for rice, however, the effect on existing producers could be positive.

The other way in which a program can influence behavioral outcomes of nonparticipating households is through demonstration effects. Skills and development training can lead nonparticipating households to adopt similar technology, for example, generating additional income for rural households.

The full benefits of program placement at the society level (the sum of direct and indirect effects of program intervention) must be evaluated to measure the total net effect. Aggregate-level impact is necessary to determine that program interventions contribute to economic growth rather than simply redistribute income (Binswanger and Landell-Mills 1995).

Issues of economic growth are particularly pertinent in the case of Bangladesh, where the economic growth rate has been historically low (4–5 percent a year), suggesting that program participants may have benefited at the expense of nonparticipants. To determine whether this is indeed the case, village-level impact evaluation is necessary.

Aggregate benefits $(B)$ are composed of benefits accrued by participants $(B_p)$, benefits accrued by nonparticipants $(B_{np})$, and costs incurred by nonparticipants $(C_{np})$. Formally, aggregate benefits $(B)$ exceed the sum of participant-level benefits $(B_p)$ if $B_{np} > C_{np}$. $B$ equals the sum of participant-level benefits if $B_{np} = C_{np}$. $B$ falls short of participant-level benefits if $B_{np} < C_{np}$.

The ideal way to evaluate the aggregate effect of a program is to measure village-level impact before and after program placement. When such data are not available, however, it is generally not possible to separately estimate any village net impact from a single cross-section of data. More important, a drawback of estimating program impacts from data on two cohorts (those from villages with and without programs)—in which assignment to cohorts is nonrandom—is the possible misinterpretation of the village fixed effects. Village fixed effects have been treated as time invariant attributes. But it is possible that credit programs can alter village attitudes and other village characteristics, perhaps through demonstration effects. The full effect of the program on behavior must then include any such village "externalities" and not just the direct effect on credit participants.

Consider, for example, the case in which program placement is random but program activities, particularly those aimed at altering attitudes, successfully alter the views of nonparticipants in credit programs on the value of using contraception and limiting family size. In this case, unobserved village contraception propensities would be correlated with program placement, but the causation would not go from village unobserved effects to program placement but from program placement to village unobserved effects. Programs are not placed in villages because of their relative attitudes on contraception; program placement affects the attitudes of credit program nonparticipants in villages. Unfortunately, the only way to measure these external effects is to examine data on villages before and after program introduction.

A more formal statement of this measurement problem explicitly allows for the placement of a credit program to cause a village effect. Rewriting the equation for the conditional demand for household outcome conditional on the level of program participation yields $Y_{ij} = X_{ij}\beta_y + V_j\gamma_y + C_{ij}\delta + \Omega_j + \varepsilon_{ij}^y$, where all terms are defined as before and a new term, $\Omega_j$, is added to the conditional demand equation. This term represents the external effects of a program in a village and has the value zero if no program is located in a village. Whether or not there are nonzero credit program externalities, $\Omega_j$ does not affect the consistency of any estimate of $\delta$, only its interpretation.[12] The program effect parameter, $\delta$, is estimated by the fixed-effects method only if $\Omega_j = 0$ in all villages (that is, none of the village-specific heterogeneity in behavior is caused by programs). If village externalities exist ($\Omega_j \neq 0$), the estimate of $\delta$ represents only the effect of credit on program participants above and beyond its effect on nonparticipants in the village. If program placement is random and $\Omega_j \neq 0$, the nonfixed-effects method is more efficient than the fixed-effects method. If program placement is nonrandom, the nonfixed-effects method is inconsistent. It is generally not possible to estimate the village externality $\Omega_j$ from a single cross-section of data.

The key question in estimating program placement impact that measures both the direct and indirect effects of program placement is the assumption of the randomness of program placement. Programs are not randomly distributed for many interventions (see, for example, Rosenzweig and Wolpin 1982). Microcredit programs may be placed in poorer villages, in which case the unobserved factors that cause poverty may also influence program placement. Identification of program placement independent of village attributes that could affect program placement is critical for estimating village-level program impacts. The village fixed-effects and nonfixed-effects methods to be used to estimate the impact of credit on borrower outcomes would help identify the extent of bias due to program placement endogeneity.

## Cost-Benefit Analysis of Alternative Programs

The incremental output (measured by income) of self-employment-gener-ating schemes must be compared with that of targeted noncredit poverty alleviation schemes, as well as with growth-promoting schemes, such as building rural roads. One way of measuring how efficiently public resources are being allocated is by assessing how equitable the marginal net benefit accruing to society is under each policy intervention. The poli-cy implication is that if, at the current allocation, program A yields a high-er marginal net benefit than program B, society would be better off by reallocating resources from B to A.

Assume that $W_i$ measures for program $i$ the value of the aggregate marginal benefits that society receives per unit of outlay (for food pro-grams) or per unit loaned (for credit programs). This can be written as $W_i = P_i H(P_i) + (NP_i) G(NP_i)$, where $H(P)$ and $G(NP)$ are the incremental benefits per unit of expenditure accruing to program participants ($P$) and program nonparticipants ($NP$), respectively. Aggregate benefits are the sum of the individual benefits weighted by the respective shares of popu-lation by participation status. The aggregate marginal benefits to society are the sum of the direct benefits to participants and the externalities (positive or negative) that the program generates for the local economy.

Incremental gains for participants are expressed in the functional form $H$. Participants draw two kinds of gains from participation: incre-mental consumption in the current period ($y_{i0}$) and the sum of all incre-mental future consumption, $g(y_{i1})$. That is, $H(P_i) = y_{i0} + \delta g(y_{i1})$, $\delta < 1$, where $\delta$ denotes the subjective discount factor.

Incremental current consumption is $y_{i0} = (Y_{i0} - Z)$, where $Y_{i0}$ is actu-al current consumption and $Z$ is preprogram consumption. The stream of future incremental consumption can be approximated by the potential return on the addition to net worth ($DNW$) such that $g(y_{i1}) = \delta(DNW)$, where $\delta$ denotes change in $DNW$. The incremental benefits accruing to the beneficiaries of food programs may be limited to the current period, in which case $DNW$ is negligible or zero.

Benefits for nonparticipants can be measured using the same methodology, although the sources of gain (loss) differ by program intervention and income class. For example, landed household that do not participate in the Food-for-Work program still benefit from the improved road transportation built by the program. Nonparticipants benefit from the induced demand caused by changes in the income and consumption of participants in microcredit programs. The benefit-cost ratio ($B - C$) is defined as the aggregate benefits divided by a measure of the social opportunity cost per unit of outlay in each program ($a_i$), $(B - C)_i = W_i / a_i$. The social cost per unit of outlay for food programs ($a_i$) is greater than 1 if the program cost exceeds the amount received by the beneficiaries. Program costs typically exceed outlays because of over-head and administrative costs. An alternative way of looking at costs is to consider the opportunity cost of not using the funds in some other development activities. The opportunity cost concept is more relevant for the grants and subsidized funds used for the microcredit programs because of their dependence on subsidies.

Benefit-cost ratios can be calculated for participants only (zero weight given to nonparticipants) and for both participants and nonparticipants (with weights given by the distribution of the population at the village level). Alternative programs can then be ranked by their benefit-cost ratios.

## Notes

1. Interventions are Pareto efficient when they benefit at least one person while leaving everyone else at least as well off as before the interventions.

2. This type of subsidy may also be called a social subsidy because the subsidized funds are given to the program to lend to the poor with the objective of reducing poverty.

3. The percentage of financial loss, $\rho$, appears in both the numerator and denominator because the loss involves both the principal and the interest payment. This can be derived as follows. If $X$ is the loan portfolio, then the expected income is $(1 + r)(1 - \rho) X$ and the expected cost is $(1 + \alpha + i) X$. A viable financial institution must ensure that its income exceeds its cost of lending, or $(1 + r)(1 - \rho)X \geq (1 + \alpha + i) X$. After rearranging, $r \geq (i + \alpha + \rho)/(1 - \rho)$.

4. Identifying appropriate instruments is difficult. The availability of credit from other formal sources, such as commercial and other banks, is one set of instruments that may help distinguish membership from the amount of disbursement. Rainfall and other variables may affect the short-run liquidity of borrowers and would thus affect only savings.

5. The problem of area-specific heterogeneity makes ordinary least squares estimates inconsistent (for econometric issues, see Maddala 1988). The problem arises because branches may not be randomly distributed. Area characteristics that are not observable to econometricians may affect placement of branches by Grameen Bank. If these characteristics are time-variant, specific to each branch location, and enter additively into the equation, a fixed-effects estimation technique is appropriate.

6. Borrowing from a microcredit program has no direct bearing on the bargaining framework of household decisionmaking. In the bargaining model literature, both husband and wife have their own unearned income or some bargaining power that can be used to negotiate the marital outcomes, which are then compared with the outcomes available outside marriage. Borrowing from a microcredit program does not imply that income or substitution effects would be different for men and women in the same household. If the effects do differ, it may reflect differences in preferences and substitutability rather than difference in empowerment.

7. This minimum is often the result of the indivisibility of capital. Dairy farming, for example, requires at least one cow; hand-powered looms have a minimum size. For other activities, such as paddy husking, for which the indivisibility of physical capital is not an issue, transactions costs (or the high costs of information) establish a floor on the minimal level of operations. In many countries, including Bangladesh, household income and wealth are so low that the costs of initiating production at minimal economic levels are high.

8. The terms of the loan may affect loan demand, but such effects are not statistically identifiable because all credit program loans carry the same terms. Local credit market conditions, including the informal lending market and the availability of relatives able to transfer funds, affect individual demand for credit.

9. This section is drawn from Pitt and Khandker (1996).

10. A maximum likelihood method is used to estimate the full model incorporating all the regimes: program and nonprogram villages each with two types of households—those that satisfy the eligibility criterion and those that do not. The model could have been estimated using a fixed-effects instrumental variable method with village dummies interacting with land as the instruments for credit received.

11. In a classic paper Rosenzweig (1980) tested the implications of neoclassical theory for the labor market and other behaviors of farm households in India by splitting the sample on the basis of land ownership, treating the sample separation criterion as nonselective.

12. This result relies on the linearity of the conditional demand equation.

# Appendix D: Resolving the Problem of Endogeneity in Estimating the Impact of Credit

To see how endogeneity problems are resolved, assume that male and female borrowing differ by program. In this case the cumulative borrowing $(C)$ from any credit program is written as follows:

(D.1) $$C_{ijf} = X_{ij}\beta_{cf} + V_j\gamma_{cf} + \varepsilon^c_{ijf}$$

(D.2) $$C_{ijm} = X_{ij}\beta_{cm} + V_j\gamma_{cm} + \varepsilon^c_{ijm}$$

where $f$ refers to women, $m$ refers to men, $i$ refers to individual, $j$ refers to village, $X$ refers to the vector of individual and household characteristics, $V$ refers to the vector of village characteristics, and $\varepsilon$ is the error term. The behavioral outcome equation, conditional on the amount of cumulative borrowing, allows not only for gender effects but also for the different effects for each of the three credit programs:

(D.3) $$Y_{ij} = X_{ij}\beta_y + V_j\gamma_y + \sum_k C_{ijf}D_{ijk}\delta_{fk} + \sum_k C_{ijm}D_{ijk}\delta_{mk} + \varepsilon^y_{ij}$$

where $Y_{ij}$ refers to outcomes such as consumption, labor supply, schooling of children, and household net worth of the $i$th household in the $j$th village; $D_{ijk}$ is a dummy value such that $D_{ijk} = 1$ if the individual participates in credit program $k$ and $D_{ijk} = 0$ otherwise; $C_{ijf}$ is the cumulative borrowing by women in household $i$ of village $j$; $C_{ijm}$ is similarly defined for men, and $\delta$ is a program-specific parameter specific to each gender. Note that $D_{ijk}$ may equal 1 even when $C_{ijm}$ or $C_{ijf} = 0$. In that case an individual can participate but does not borrow from a credit program.

The identification in the conditional credit demand evaluation of equation D.3 is essentially done by pooling landless and landed households. The impacts of noncredit variables can be estimated by studying households owning more than half an acre of land, which were disqualified from participating in any of these three programs. Given these estimates, the gender-differentiated credit impacts are estimated by pooling program and nonprogram villages in which not every village has a microcredit program and not every village program is available for each gender.

For continuous outcome equations, such as labor supply, the identifying instrument is landholding interacting with village dummies. However, even if landholding is treated as exogenous and used to identify the credit impact, the quantity of land owned by the household is nevertheless included as one of the regressors ($X_{ij}$) and a dummy variable is included indicating the target/nontarget status of the household, where such status is defined by whether the household owns more than half an acre of land. Village-level fixed effects were used to control for bias due to unobserved village heterogeneity; instrumental-type estimation imposed through parametric restrictions was used to control for unobserved household/individual heterogeneity. (For details on the identification issues, see appendix C).

A maximum likelihood method was used to jointly estimate the demand for credit (equations D.1 and D.2) and the behavioral outcome (equation D.3). Because a choice-based sampling technique was used, weights were used to reflect the approximate distribution of the population in the village. Before the estimates of credit impacts were finalized, however, a series of tests were conducted to determine the most appropriate specification of the equation estimating the impact of credit on household outcomes. Possible specifications tested were whether the credit impact varied by gender of participation and by program. Tests were also done to determine whether borrowing could be treated as exogenous. The tests confirmed that the demand for credit and the impact of credit vary by the gender of the participant and that sample selection bias needs to be controlled for certain outcomes when assessing the impact of participation. As the results show, credit impact estimates were subject to serious sample selection bias in about a third of the outcomes considered (for details see Pitt and Khandker 1996).[1] In addition, although the demand for credit by gender did not vary across programs, the credit impact by gender did vary. (Table A3.3 shows joint significance tests of credit variables for different outcomes of interest.)

Are village-level fixed effects appropriate for estimation? A comparison between fixed-effects and nonfixed-effects estimates shows that the fixed-effects estimation could not be rejected in about two-thirds of the outcomes (Pitt and Khandker 1996).[2]

A fixed-effects instrumental method that controls for both village and household heterogeneity was therefore used to quantify the effect of credit on all socioeconomic outcomes.[3] The results of the estimation of the demand for credit by gender are shown in table A3.1. Because of the use of village-level fixed effects, the estimated equation includes only variables at the individual and household levels. The influence of all the village-level variables is captured through the village fixed effects.

# Notes

1. Sample selection bias was formally tested by determining if the statistical significance of the correlation coefficient of the error terms of the borrowing equation and that of the behavioral outcome equation were statistically significant. Out of 10 outcomes considered here for assessing credit impacts, sample selection bias was found to be significant for 5 outcomes for female borrowing and 4 outcomes for male borrowing when the fixed-effects method was not used for controlling village heterogeneity. However, when village heterogeneity was controlled using a fixed-effects method, sample selection bias was important in only 4 outcomes for female borrowing and only 2 outcomes for male borrowing. Sample selection bias was important for female borrowing in outcomes such as contraceptive use, recent fertility, per capita expenditure, and men's labor supply. For male borrowing sample selection was important only in the case of men's labor supply and recent fertility. Sample selection correction for individual heterogeneity was thus needed in about 40 percent of the outcomes. Sample selection correction was needed more for noneconomic outcomes such as contraceptive use and fertility, and less for economic outcomes such as women's labor supply and nonland assets. Sample selection bias was zero for outcomes such as household net worth.

2. Program placement bias was not significant for a large number of outcomes considered. Ten outcomes were exogenous for each program type and for each gender. Thirty parameters were thus estimated separately for men and women. Out of 30 parameters, program heterogeneity bias was found to be significant for 6 women's credit variables and 12 men's credit variables. The outcomes subject to village heterogeneity bias were labor supply, schooling, women's nonland assets, contraceptive use, and fertility. Interestingly, the impact on per capita expenditure was not biased for program placement heterogeneity. The non-fixed-effects method overestimates the impact of credit on women's labor supply, women's nonland assets, and boys' and girls' schooling. In contrast, the non-fixed-effects method underestimates the impact of credit on men's labor supply, contraceptive use, and fertility. The effect on women's labor supply of female borrowing from RD-12 is overestimated by 13 percent, for example, while the effect on men's labor supply is underestimated by 13 percent.

3. Results thus control for selection bias at the household level. If, for example, more women from less conservative households and fewer women from more conservative households participate, such unobserved characteristics are netted out with this method.

# Bibliography

Abdullah, A., M. Hossain, and R. Nations. 1974. *Report on Integrated Rural Development Programme*. Dhaka: Swedish International Development Authority/International Labour Organization.

Adams, Dale W., and Delbert A. Fitchett, eds. 1992. *Informal Finance in Low-income Countries*. Boulder, Colo.:Westview Press.

Adams, Dale W., and J. D. von Pischke. 1992. "Microenterprise Credit Programs: Déjà Vu." *World Development* 20 (October): 1463–70.

Adams, Dale W., Douglas Graham, and J. D. von Pischke, eds. 1983. *Limitations of Cheap Credit in Promoting Rural Development*. Washington, D.C: World Bank, Economic Development Institute.

———. 1984. *Undermining Rural Development with Cheap Credit*. Boulder, Colo.: Westview Press.

Ahmed, Akhter U. 1993. *Food Consumption and Nutritional Effects of Targeted Food Interventions in Bangladesh*. Dhaka: Bangladesh Food Policy Project, International Food Policy Research Institute.

Ahmed, Akhter U., Sajjad Zohir, Shubh K. Kumar, and Omar Haider Chowdhury. 1995. "Bangladesh's Food-for-Work Program and Alternatives to Improve Food Security." In Joachim von Braun, ed., *Employment for Poverty Reduction and Food Security*. Washington, D.C.: International Food Policy Research Institute.

Ahmed, Raisuddin, and Mahabub Hossain. 1990. "Development Impact of Rural Infrastructure in Bangladesh." *IFPRI Research Report* 83. International Food Policy Research Institute, Washington, D.C.

Ahmed, Zia U. 1989. "Effective Cost of Rural Loans in Bangladesh." *World Development* 17 (March): 357–63.

Alam, Jahangir. 1988. "Rural Poor Programme in Bangladesh: Experience of NGOs, GB, and BRDB." Working paper prepared for the Study on Cooperatives in Bangladesh, Dhaka.

Alam, Mustafa. 1989. "Special Employment Programs in Bangladesh: An Evaluation of Major Schemes." In M. Muqtada, ed., *The Elusive Target: An Evaluation of Targeted-Group Approaches to Employment Creation in Rural Asia*. New Delhi: International Labour Office, Asian Regional Team for Employment Promotion.

Alamgir, M. 1983. "Review of the Public Rural Works Program of Bangladesh 1960–78." *Bangladesh Development Studies* 11 (1,2): 13–40.

Amin, Ruhul, M. Kabir, J. Chowdhury, A. U. Ahmed, and R. B. Hill. 1994. "Poor Women's Participation in Income-Generating Projects and Their Fertility Regulation in Bangladesh: Evidence from a Recent Survey." *World Development* 22 (April): 555–65.

Amin, Sajeda, and Anne R. Pebley. 1990. "Gender Inequality within Households: The Impact of a Women's Development Program in 36 Bangladesh Villages." *Bangladesh Development Studies* 22 (June–September): 12–54.

Asaduzzaman, Muhammad, and Barbara Huddleston. 1983. "Evaluation of Management of Food-for-Work Programme." *Bangladesh Development Studies* 11 (March–June): 41–96.

AST-MOA (Agricultural Sector Team for the Ministry of Agriculture). 1991. *1991 Census of Life Irrigation.* Dhaka.

Bangladesh Bureau of Statistics. 1989. *Rural Credit Survey in Bangladesh 1987.* Dhaka: Ministry of Planning.

Bennett, Lynn, and Carlos E. Cuevas. 1996. "Sustainable Banking with the Poor." *Journal of International Development* 8 (March–April): 145–52.

Bennett, Lynn, Mike Goldberg, and Pamela Hunte. 1996. "Ownership and Sustainability: Lessons on Group-Based Financial Services from Five NGOs in South Asia." World Bank, Washington, DC.

Benston, George J., and Clifford W. Smith, Jr. 1976. "A Transaction Cost Approach to the Theory of Financial Intermediation." *Journal of Finance* 31 (May): 215–31.

Besley, Timothy, and Stephen Coate. 1995. "Group Lending, Repayment Incentives and Social Collateral." *Journal of Development Economics* 46 (1): 1–18.

BIDS (Bangladesh Institute of Development Studies). 1990. "Evaluation of Poverty Alleviation Programs." Dhaka.

Binswanger, Hans P. 1983. "Agricultural Growth and Rural Nonfarm Activities." *Finance and Development* 20 (2): 38–40.

Binswanger, Hans P., and Shahidur R. Khandker. 1995. "The Impact of Formal Finance on the Rural Economy of India." *The Journal of Development Studies* 32 (2): 234–62.

Binswanger, Hans P., and Pierre Landell-Mills. 1995. *The World Bank's Strategy for Reducing Poverty and Hunger: A Report to the Development Community.* Environmentally Sustainable Development Studies and Monograph 4. Washington, D.C: World Bank.

Binswanger, Hans P., and Mark R. Rosenzweig. 1986. "The Behavioral and Material Determinants of Production Relations in Agriculture." *The Journal of Development Studies* 32 (October): 503–39.

Binswanger, Hans P., Shahidur R. Khandker, and Mark R. Rosenzweig. 1993. "How Infrastructure and Financial Institutions Affect Agricultural Output and Investment in India." *Journal of Development Economics* 41 (August): 337–66.

Bouman, F. J. A., and Otto Hospes, eds. 1994. *Financial Landscapes Reconstructed: The Fine Art of Mapping.* Boulder, Colo.: Westview Press.

BRAC (Bangladesh Rural Advancement Committee). 1984. *Peasant Perceptions: Famine, Credit Needs, Sanitation.* Rural Studies Series 1. Dhaka.

Braverman, Avishay, and J. Luis Guasch. 1986. "Rural Credit Markets and Institutions in Developing Countries: Lessons for Policy Analysis from Practice and Modern Theory." *World Development* 14 (October/November): 1253–67.

———. 1989. "Rural Credit in LDCs: Issues and Evidence." *Journal of Economic Development* (Korea) 14 (June): 7–34.

CGAP (Consultative Group to Assist the Poorest). 1997. "A Review of the World Bank's Microfinance Portfolio FY91–FY96." World Bank, Washington, D.C.

Chadha, G. K. 1986. "Agricultural Growth and Rural Non-Farm Activities: An Analysis of Indian Experience." In Yang-Boo Choe and Fu-Chen Lo, eds., *Rural Industrialization and Non-Farm Activities of Asian Farmers*. Seoul: Korea Rural Economics Institute/Asian and Pacific Development Center.

Chaves, Rodrigo A., and C. Gonzalez-Vega. 1996. "The Design of Successful Rural Financial Intermediaries: Evidence from Indonesia." *World Development* 24 (January): 65–78.

Cho, Yoon-Je, and Deena R. Khatkhate. 1989. *Lessons of Financial Liberalization in Asia: A Comparative Study*. World Bank Discussion Paper 50. Washington, D.C.

Chowdhury, Anwarullah. 1982. *Agrarian Social Relations and Rural Development in Bangladesh*. Totowa, N.J.: Allanheld, Osmun Publishers.

Chowdhury, Omar Haider. 1983. "Profile of Workers in the Food-for-Work Programme in Bangladesh." *Bangladesh Development Studies* 11 (March–June): 111–34.

Christen, R., E. Rhyne, and R. Vogel. 1994. "Maximizing the Outreach of Microenterprise Finance: The Emerging Lessons of Successful Programs." International Management Communications Corporation, Arlington, Va.

Clark, Jeffrey A. 1984. "Estimation of Economies of Scale in Banking Using a Generalized Functional Form." *Journal of Money, Credit and Banking* 16 (February): 53–68.

Datt, Gaurav, and Martin Ravallion. 1995. "Growth and Poverty in Rural India." World Bank, Office of the Vice President, Development Economics, Washington, D.C.

———. 1996. "Why Have Some Indian States Done Better than Others at Reducing Rural Poverty?" Policy Research Working Paper 1594. World Bank, Policy Research Department, Washington, D.C.

Dessing, Maryke. 1990. *Support for Microenterprises: Lessons for Sub-Saharan Africa*. World Bank Technical Paper 122. Washington, D.C.

Feder, Gershon, Monika Huppi, and Jacob Yaron. 1989. "Agricultural Credit: Experience and Implications for Future Projects." World Bank, Agricultural and Rural Development Department, Washington, D.C.

Feder, Gershon, Tongroj Onchan, Yongyuth Chalamwong, and Chira Hongladarom. 1988. *Land Policies and Farm Productivity in Thailand*. Baltimore, Md.: The Johns Hopkins University Press.

Foster, Andrew D. 1995. "Prices, Credit Markets and Child Growth in Low-Income Rural Areas." *The Economic Journal: The Journal of the Royal Economic Society* 105 (May): 551–70.

Foster, James, Joel Greer, and Erik Thorbecke. 1984. "A Class of Decomposable Poverty Measures." *Econometrica* 52 (May): 761–66.

Fuglesang, Andreas, and Dale Chandler. 1988. "Participation as Process: What We Can Learn from Grameen Bank, Bangladesh." Oslo: Norwegian Agency for Development Cooperation.

Ghate, Prabhu. 1992. *Informal Finance: Some Findings from Asia*. London: Oxford University Press.

Goetz, Anne Marie, and Rina Sen Gupta. 1996. "Who Takes the Credit? Gender, Power, and Control Over Loan Use in Rural Credit Programs in Bangladesh." *World Development* 24 (1): 45–63.

Greaney, Vincent, Shahidur R. Khandker, and Mahmudul Alam. Forthcoming. *Bangladesh: Assessing Basic Learning Skills.* Dhaka: University Press Limited.

Gurgand, Marc, Glenn Pederson, and Jacob Yaron. 1994. *Outreach and Sustainability of Six Rural Finance Institutions in Sub-Saharan Africa.* World Bank Discussion Paper 248. Washington, D.C.

Haddad, Lawrence, John Hoddinott, and Harold Alderman. 1994. "Intrahousehold Resources Allocation: An Overview." Policy Research Working Paper 1255. World Bank, Policy Research Department, Washington, D.C.

Hashemi, Syed M., Sidney Ruth Schuler, and Ann P. Riley. 1996. "Rural Credit Programs and Women's Empowerment in Bangladesh." *World Development* 24 (April): 635–53.

Hausman, Jerry A. 1978. "Specification Test in Econometrics." *Econometrica* 46 (November): 1251–71.

Hazell, Peter B. R., and Steven Haggblade. 1991. "Rural Urban Growth Linkages in India." *Indian Journal of Agricultural Economics* 46 (4): 515–29.

Hazell, Peter B. R., and C. Ramasamy. 1991. *The Green Revolution Reconsidered: The Impact of the High-Yielding Rice Varieties in South India.* Baltimore, Md.: The Johns Hopkins University Press.

Hazell, Peter B. R., and Alisa Roell. 1983. "Rural Growth Linkages: Household Expenditure Patterns in Malaysia and Nigeria." IFPRI Research Report 46. International Food Policy Research Institute, Washington, D.C.

Heckman, James J. 1976. "The Common Structure of Statistical Models of Truncation, Sample Selection and Limited Dependent Variables and a Simple Estimator for Such Models." *Annals of Economic and Social Measurement* 5 (4): 475–92.

Hoff, Karla, and Joseph E. Stiglitz. 1990. "Introduction: Imperfect Information and Rural Credit Market: Puzzles and Policy Perspectives." *The World Bank Economic Review* 4 (3): 235–51.

———. 1997. "Moneylenders and Bankers: Price-Increasing Subsidies in a Monopolistically Competitive Market." *Journal of Development Economics* 52 (April): 429–62.

Holt, Sharon L., and Helena Ribe. 1991. *Developing Financial Institutions for the Poor and Reducing Barriers to Access for Women.* World Bank Discussion Papers 117. Washington, D.C.

Holtsberg, Christer. 1990. *Evolution of Selected Rural Development Policies and Projects.* Vol. 6 of *Evolution of Poverty Alleviation Programmes.* Dhaka: Bangladesh Institute of Development Studies.

Hossain, Mahabub. 1984. "Productivity and Profitability in Bangladesh Rural Industries." *Bangladesh Development Studies* 12 (1–2): 127–61.

———. 1988. "Credit for Alleviation of Rural Poverty: The Grameen Bank in Bangladesh." IFPRI Research Report 65. International Food Policy Research Institute, Washington, D.C.

Hossain, Mahabub, and M. Mokaddem Akash. 1993. "Public Rural Works for Relief and Development: A Review of the Bangladesh Experience." IFRPI Working Paper 7. International Food Policy Research Institute, Washington, D.C.

Hossain, Mahabub, and M. Asaduzzaman. 1983. "An Evaluation of the Special Public Works Program in Bangladesh." *Bangladesh Development Studies* 11 (1, 2): 191–226.

Hossain, Mahabub, and S. Rashid. 1991. *Labor Force, Employment, and Access to Income Earning Opportunities in Bangladesh*. Dhaka: Bangladesh Institute of Development Studies.

Hossain, Mahabub, and Binayak Sen. 1992. "Rural Poverty in Bangladesh: Trends and Determinants." *Asian Development Review* 10 (1): 1–34.

Hulme, David. 1990. "Can the Grameen Bank Be Replicated? Recent Experiments in Malaysia, Malawi and Sri Lanka." *Development Policy Review* 8: 287–300.

Hulme, David, and Paul Mosley. 1996. *Finance against Poverty*. New York: Routledge Publishing.

Huppi, Monika, and Gershon Feder. 1990. "The Role of Groups and Credit Cooperatives in Rural Lending." *The World Bank Research Observer* 5 (July): 187–204.

Hymer, Stephen, and Stephen A. Resnick. 1969. "A Model of an Agrarian Economy with Non-agricultural Activities." *American Economic Review* 59 (September): 493–506.

IIMI/BSERT (International Irrigation Management Institute/Bureau of Socio-Economic Research and Training). 1995. *Workshop on the Study on Privatization of Minor Irrigation in Bangladesh*. Paper and proceedings volumes 1 and 2. Dhaka: Asian Development Bank and Ministry of Agriculture.

Islam, A. K. M. A. 1974. *A Bangladesh Village: Conflict and Cohesion*. Boston: Schenensman Publishing Co.

Jain, Pankaj S. 1996. "Managing Credit for the Rural Poor: Lessons from Grameen Bank." *World Development* 24 (January): 79–89.

Jones, Steve. 1979. "An Evaluation of Rural Development Programmes in Bangladesh." *Journal of Social Studies* (University of Dhaka, Bangladesh) 6: 51–92.

Kalari, James W., and Asghar Zardkoohi. 1987. *Bank Cost, Structure and Performance*. Lexington, Mass.: Lexington Books.

Khan, A. A. 1971. "Rural Credit Programme of Agricultural Cooperative Federation." Comilla: Bangladesh Academy for Rural Development.

Khandker, Shahidur R. 1996. "Grameen Bank: Impact, Costs and Program Sustainability." *Asian Development Review* 14 (1): 97–130.

Khandker, Shahidur R., and Osman H. Chowdhury. 1996. *Targeted Credit Programs and Rural Poverty in Bangladesh*. World Bank Discussion Paper 336. Washington, D.C.

Khandker, Shahidur R., and Baqui Khalily. 1996. *The Bangladesh Rural Advancement Committee's Credit Programs: Performance and Sustainability*. World Bank Discussion Paper 324. Washington, D.C.

Khandker, Shahidur R., Baqui Khalily, and Zahed Khan. 1995. *Grameen Bank: Performance and Sustainability*. World Bank Discussion Paper 306. Washington, D.C.

Khandker, Shahidur R., Zahed Khan, and Baqui Khalily. 1995. *Sustainability of a Government Targeted Credit Program: Evidence from Bangladesh*. World Bank Discussion Paper 316. Washington, D.C.

Lee, L. F. 1976. "Estimation of Limited Dependent Variable Model by Two-Stage Methods." Ph.D. dissertation. University of Rochester, Department of Economics, Rochester, N.Y.

Lovell, Catherine H. 1992. *Breaking the Cycle of Poverty: The BRAC Strategy*. West Hartford, Conn.: Kumarian Press.

Maddala, G. S. 1988. *Introduction to Econometrics*. New York: Macmillan.

Mahajan, Vijay B., and Bharti Gupta Ramola. 1996. "Financial Services for the Rural Poor and Women in India: Access and Sustainability." *Journal of International Development* 8 (March): 211–24.

Management Systems International. 1987. "Institutional Assessment of Food-for-Work and Feeder Road Programmes in Bangladesh." Washington, D.C.

Manser, M., and M. Brown. 1980. "Marriage and Household Decision-making: A Bargain Analysis." *International Economic Review* 21 (February): 31–44.

McDonald, John F., and Robert A. Moffitt. 1980. "The Uses of Tobit Analysis." *Review of Economics and Statistics* 62 (2): 318–21.

McElroy, Marjorie B. 1990. "The Empirical Content of Nash-Bargained Household Behavior." *The Journal of Human Resources* 25 (4): 559–83.

McElroy, Marjorie B., and Mary Jean Horney. 1981. "Nash-Bargained Household Decisions: Towards a Generalization of the Theory of Demand." *International Economic Review* 22 (June): 333–49.

Mitra and Associates. 1991. *Integrated Food-for-Work Project: Labor Survey 1991*. Dhaka.

Moffitt, Robert A. 1991. "Program Evaluation with Nonexperimental Data." *Evaluation Review* 15 (3): 291–314.

Morduch, Jonathan. 1998. "The Microfinance Schism." Harvard University, Department of Economics, Cambridge, Mass.

Murshid, K. A. S., and Atiq Rahman. 1990. "Rural Informal Finance Markets in Bangladesh: An Overview." Research Report 126. Bangladesh Institute of Development Studies, Dhaka.

Nishat, A., and M. S. K. Chowdhury. 1983. "Engineering Survey of WFP-Aided Food-for-Work Programme in Bangladesh." *Bangladesh Development Studies* 11 (1, 2): 97–110.

Osmani, Siddiqur Rahman, and Omar Haider Chowdhury. 1983. "Short Run Impacts of Food-for-Work Programme in Bangladesh." *Bangladesh Development Studies* 11 (March–June): 135–90.

Otero, Maria, and Elizabeth Rhyne, eds. 1994. *The New World of Micro-Enterprise Reform: Building Healthy Institutions for the Poor*. West Hartford, Conn.: Kumarian Press.

Patten, Richard H., and Jay K. Rosengard. 1991. *Progress with Profits: The Development of Rural Banking in Indonesia*. San Francisco: Institute of Contemporary Studies Press.

Pitt, Mark M., and Shahidur R. Khandker. 1996. *Household and Intrahousehold Impact of the Grameen Bank and Similar Targeted Credit Programs in Bangladesh*. World Bank Discussion Paper 320. Washington, D.C.

———. 1997. "Credit Programs for the Poor and Seasonality in Rural Bangladesh." World Bank, Poverty Reduction and Economic Management Network, Washington, D.C.

Pitt, Mark M., Shahidur R. Khandker, Omar H. Chowdhury, and Daniel Millimet. 1998. "Credit Programs for the Poor and Nutritional Status of Children in Rural Bangladesh." PSTC Working Paper 98–01. Brown University, Population Studies and Training Center, Providence, R.I.

Pitt, Mark M., Shahidur R. Khandker, Signe-Mary McKernan, and M. Abdul Latif. 1995. "Credit Programs for the Poor and Reproductive Behavior in

Low Income Countries: Are the Reported Causal Relationships the Result of Heterogeneity Bias?" PSTC Working Paper 95–04. Brown University, Population Studies and Training Center, Providence, R.I.

Quasem, M. A., and Mahabub Hossain. 1985. "Impact of Agricultural Policies and Programmes on Small Farmers in Bangladesh." Report prepared for the Food and Agricultural Organization of the United Nations, Rome.

Rahman, Rushidan I. 1996. "Impact of Grameen Krishi Foundation on the Socio-Economic Condition of Rural Households." Working Paper 17. Bangladesh Institute of Development Studies, Dhaka.

Rahman, Zillur, and Mahabub Hossain, eds. 1995. *Rethinking Poverty: Bangladesh as a Case Study*. New Delhi: Sage Publications.

Rashid, Mansoora, and Robert M. Townsend. 1994. *Targeting Credit and Insurance: Efficiency, Mechanism Design and Program Evaluation*. ESP Discussion Paper. 47. World Bank, Education and Social Policy Department, Washington, D.C.

Ravallion, Martin. 1991. "Reaching the Rural Poor through Public Employment: Argument, Evidence, and Lessons from South Asia." *The World Bank Research Observer* 6 (July): 153–75.

———. 1994. *Poverty Comparisons*. Vol. 56 of *Fundamentals of Pure and Applied Economics*. Chur, Switzerland: Harwood Academic Press.

Ravallion, Martin, and Binayak Sen. 1995. "When Methods Matter: Towards a Resolution of the Debate about Bangladesh's Poverty Measures." Policy Research Working Paper 1259. World Bank, Washington D.C.

Riedinger, Jeffrey M. 1994. "Innovation in Rural Finance: Indonesia's Baden Kredit Kecamatan Program." *World Development* 22 (3): 301–13.

Rosenzweig, Mark R. 1980. "Neo-classical Theory and Optimizing Peasant: An Econometric Analysis of Market Family Labor Supply in a Developing Country." *Quarterly Journal of Economics*. 94 (1): 31–55.

Rosenzweig, Mark R., and Oded Stark. 1989. "Consumption Smoothing, Migration and Marriage Evidence from Rural India." *Journal of Political Economy* 97 (August): 905–26.

Rosenzweig, Mark R., and Kenneth I. Wolpin. 1982. "Government Interventions and Household Behavior in a Developing Country: Anticipating the Unanticipated Consequences of Social Programs." *Journal of Development Economics* 10 (April): 209–25.

———. 1985. "Specific Experience, Household Structure, and Intergenerational Transfers: Farm Family Land and Labor Arrangements in Developing Countries." *Quarterly Journal of Economics* 100 (supplement): 961–87.

———. 1993. "Credit Market Constraints, Consumption Smoothing and the Accumulation of Durable Production Assets in Low-Income Countries: Investments in Bullocks in India." *Journal of Political Economy* 101 (2): 223–44.

Sacay, Orlando J., and Bikki K. Randhawa. 1995. *Design Issues in Rural Finance*. World Bank Discussion Paper 293. Washington, D.C.

Schuler, Sidney Ruth, and Syed M. Hashemi. 1994. "Credit Programs, Women's Empowerment, and Contraceptive Use in Rural Bangladesh." *Studies in Family Planning* (International) 25 (March–April): 65–76.

Sinha, Saurabh, and Imran Matin. 1998. "Informal Credit Transactions of Microcredit Borrowers of Rural Bangladesh." University of Sussex, Poverty Research Unit, Brighton, U.K.

Srinivasan, Aruna. 1988. "A Multiproduct Cost Study of Rural Bank Branches in Bangladesh." Ph.D. dissertation. Ohio State University, Department of Agricultural Economics and Rural Sociology, Columbus, Oh.

Stiglitz, Joseph E. 1990. "Peer Monitoring and Credit Markets." *The World Bank Economic Review* 4 (3): 351–66.

Stiglitz, Joseph E., and Andrew Weiss. 1981. "Credit Rationing in Markets with Imperfect Information." *American Economic Review* 71 (3): 393–410.

———. 1983. "Incentive Effects of Termination: Applications to the Credit and Labor Markets." *American Economic Review* 73 (5): 912–27.

Subbarao, K., Aniruddha Bonnerjee, Jeanine Braithwaite, Soniya Carvalho, Kene Ezemenari, Carol Graham, and Alan Thompson. 1997. *Safety Net Programs and Poverty Reduction: Lessons from Cross-Country Experience*. A Directions in Development book. Washington, D.C.: World Bank.

Thomas, J. 1988. *Credit Programs for the Informal Sector in Peru*. London: London School of Economics.

———. 1993. *Replicating the Grameen Bank: The Latin American Experience*. London: London School of Economics.

Townsend, Robert M. 1994. "Risk and Insurance in Village India." *Econometrica* 62 (3): 539–91.

USAID (U.S. Agency for International Development). 1973. *AID Spring Review on Small Farm Credit*. Washington, D.C.

———. 1991. *Mobilizing Savings and Rural Finance: The AID Experience*. AID Science and Technology Series. Washington, D.C.

Varian, Hal R. 1990. "Monitoring Agents with Other Agents." *Journal of Institutional and Theoretical Economics* 146 (March):153–74.

von Pischke, J. D., Dale W. Adams, and Gordon Donald, eds. 1983. *Rural Financial Markets in Developing Countries: Their Use and Abuse*. Baltimore, Md.: The Johns Hopkins University Press.

Webster, Leila, and Peter Fidler, eds. 1995. *The Informal Sector and Microfinance Institutions in West Africa*. A World Bank Regional and Sectoral Study. Washington, D.C.

WGTFI (Working Group on Targeted Food Interventions in Bangladesh). 1994. *Options for Targeting Food Interventions in Bangladesh*. Report prepared by International Food Policy Research Institute, Academy for Planning and Development, Bangladesh Rural Advancement Committee, Cooperative for American Relief Everywhere, Food Planning and Monitoring Unit, Institute of Nutrition and Food Services, and U.S. Agency for International Development.

World Bank. 1975. *Agricultural Credit*. A World Bank Paper. Washington, D.C.

———. 1987. "Bangladesh: A Program for Financial Sector Reform." Sector Report. South Asia Region, Country Department I, Industry and Energy Division, Washington, D.C.

———. 1990. *World Development Report 1990: Poverty*. New York: Oxford University Press.

———. 1993. *A Review of Bank Lending for Agricultural Credit and Rural Finance, 1948–1992*. Washington, D.C.

———. 1996a. "Bangladesh: Poverty Alleviation Microfinance Project." Staff Appraisal Report. South Asia Region, Country Department I, Private Sector Development and Finance Division, Washington, D.C.

———. 1996b. "Bangladesh: Rural Finance." Report 15484-BD. South Asia Region, Country Department I, Agriculture and Natural Resources Division. Washington, D.C.

———. 1996c. "Bangladesh: Second Rural Roads and Markets Improvement Project." Staff Appraisal Report. South Asia Region, Country Department I, Infrastructure Operations Division, Washington, D.C.

———. 1996d. "A Worldwide Inventory of Microfinance Institutions." Sustainable Banking with the Poor, Washington, D.C.

———. 1997. "Bangladesh: The Non-Farm Sector in a Diversifying Rural Economy." Report 16740-BD. South Asia Region, Country Department I. Washington, D.C.

Yaron, Jacob. 1992a. *Assessing Development Finance Institutions*. World Bank Discussion Paper 174. Washington, D.C.

———. 1992b. *Successful Rural Finance Institutions*. World Bank Discussion Paper 150. Washington, D.C.

———. 1994. "What Makes Rural Finance Institutions Successful?" *The World Bank Research Observer* 9 (1): 49–70.

Yaron, Jacob, McDonald P. Benjamin, and Gerda L. Piperk. 1997. *Rural Finance: Issues, Design and Best Practices*. Environmentally Sustainable Development Studies and Monograph 14. Washington, D.C.: World Bank.

Yunus, Muhammad. 1983. "Group-based Savings and Credit for the Rural Poor: Grameen Bank in Bangladesh." Paper presented at the Inter-Country Workshop on Group-based Savings and Credit for the Rural Poor sponsored by the International Labour Organization UN Inter-agency Panel on People's Participation, Bogra, Colombia, November 6–13, 1983.

———. 1995. "Towards Creating a Poverty-Free World." Paper presented at the Annual Meeting of the U.S. Committee for World Food Day, January 25, Washington, D.C.

Zohir, S. 1990. *Rural Roads and Poverty Alleviation*. Dhaka: Bangladesh Institute of Development Studies.

# Index

Abdullah, A., 20

Abed, F. H., 16, 90–91

Adams, Dale W., 1, 2, 5, 110

Agricultural development banks; cost-effectiveness of, 13–14; lending practices, 113–16, 125–28; performance compared to microcredit institutions, 116–21

Agricultural sector; borrowing and lending in, 111–16; crop cycle, 50–51; employment in, 18; Green Revolution technology, 19–20; land ownership, 18–21; linkages to rural nonfarm sector, 63; low growth of, 19, 63, 149; small and medium-size farmers in, 128–31

Ahmed, Akhter U., 23, 30, 138, 139, 140

Ahmed, Raisuddin, 30, 63, 138

Ahmed, Z. U., 111

Akash, M. Mokaddem, 23

Alam, Jahangir, 9

Alam, Mahmudul, 142

Alam, Mustafa, 9

Alamgir, M., 137

Alderman, Harold, 192

Amin, Ruhul, 9

Amin, Sajeda, 9

Antipoverty programs; Food-for-Work, 137; recommended design of targeted, 146; self-selection into, 142; Vulnerable Group Development, 137

Asaduzzaman, Muhammad, 21, 137

Bangladesh Institute of Development Studies–World Bank household survey, 38, 112, 140, 180–81

Bangladesh Krishi Bank (BKB); cost of outstanding loan from, 134–35; lending policies, 113

Bangladesh Rural Advancement Committee (BRAC), 3, 12; cost-benefit ratios, 136; cost of outstanding loan, 134–35; decentralization of, 91; financing the rural nonfarm sector (1990–94), 69–72; group-based approach, 23–32; group viability and member dropout (1986–94), 95–97, 171t; institutional structure, 90–95; intent and approach, 16–17; loans and member savings (1990–94), 89–90; marginal returns to capital and labor, 75–76; members and borrowers (1989–94), 88–89; microcredit program of, 23–29; noncredit services and training, 32–34; primary education program, 33; profitability, 97–102; Rural Credit Program, 98–99; sectoral distribution of loans,

68–72; sources of interest, income, and equity subsidies (1990–94), 102–6; staff size, retention, productivity, and pay structure (1990–94), 93–95; village-level organizations operated by (1989–94), 87–88

Bangladesh Rural Development Board (BRDB) replaces IRDP, 17–18; Rural Development Project-12 of, 3, 90–91

Banking system: agricultural development banks, 113–16, 125–28; Grameen Bank in context of, 88; nationalized commercial banks, 113–16, 125–28; targeting of loans, 150

Benefits: identification of, 133–34; of microcredit programs, 9–10, 199–201; of Work-for-Food and Vulnerable Group Development, 138

Benjamin, McDonald P., 183

Bennett, Lynn, 6, 8, 183

Benston, George J., 189

Besley, Timothy, 6, 28, 31, 100

Binswanger, Hans P., 1, 3, 4, 5, 8, 10, 63, 65, 106, 123, 125, 140, 183, 184, 186, 198, 200

BKB: *See* Bangladesh Krishi Bank (BKB).

Borrowers: credit constraints among, 76–77

Borrowing: benefits to society of microcredit, 199–201; controlling for endogenous, 43–45; determinants of household, 122–23, 173t; differences in impact on household of male or female, 46–51; effect on per capita expenditure, 46–47; impact by gender of cumulative, 46; impact of men's and women's, 60–61; patterns of household, 112, 122–28; sources of agriculture-

related, 125–28, 177t. *See also* Lending, informal; Lending programs, group-based; Loan recovery

Bouman, F. J. A., 2, 183–84

BRAC: *See* Bangladesh Rural Advancement Committee (BRAC).

Braverman, Avishay, 1, 29, 111

Brown, M., 192

Canadian International Development Agency (CIDA), 4

Capital: capital intensity, 72–80; marginal returns to, 72–80; sources of start-up, 77–78;

CARE, 22t, 137

Chadha, G. K., 63

Chandler, Dale, 29, 92

Chaves, Rodrigo A., 6, 108, 183

Children: microcredit impact on nutritional well-being, 49, 162t; microcredit impact on schooling, 49, 162t

Cho, Yoon-Je, 5

Chowdhury, Anwarullah, 17

Chowdhury, M. S. K., 139

Chowdhury, Omar H., 21, 138, 139

Chowdhury, Osman H., 55

Christen, R., 3–4, 6, 8, 183

Clark, Jeffrey A., 189

Coate, Stephen, 6, 28, 31, 100

Comilla model of rural development, 17

Commercial banks, nationalized: lending practices, 125–28; performance of, 113–16;

Consultative Group to Assist the Poorest (CGAP), 4

Consumption: marginal return to, 135–37; as measure of poverty, 55–60; as measure of program benefits, 134; by microfinance program participants, 148; effect of microcredit borrowing on the seasonality of, 50–51, 163t; related to microcredit borrowing, 45–51

Contraception: use related to micro-credit borrowing, 50, 160t

Cooperatives: of farmers in Comilla model, 17, 20; structure in RD-12 project, 18;

Cost-benefit analysis: of credit program instruments, 134–37; of infrastructure projects, 139–41; measuring cost-benefit ratios, 133; of noncredit poverty alleviation plans, 202–3

Cost-effectiveness: of alternative credit programs, 110, 133, 134, 135–36, 184; of Food-for-Work and Vulnerable Group Development programs, 138–39, 151; of Grameen Bank, 151–52; of infrastructure development, 139–41, 151; measurement of, 135; of microcredit, 147–48, 151–52, 153, 155

Costs: of infrastructure development, 141; of Food-for-Work and Vulnerable Group Development programs, 137–38

Credit: Financial sector; endogeneity in estimating impact of, 205–6; extension of formal, 112, 136; gender-differentiated, 205–6; impact on selected households, 47, 160–61t. See also Banking system

Credit market, rural: with lack of development, 110–11; segmentation in, 111–13

Credit programs: cost-benefit analysis of instruments, 134–37; costs of services from Grameen, BRAC, BKB, and RAKUB, 134–35; government, 20–21, 29; support provided by targeted, 133

Cuevas, Carlos E., 8, 183

Data sources: for analysis of program sustainability, 86; for assessment of microcredit program benefits,

38; Bangladesh Institute of Development Studies–World Bank household survey, 140; used by microcredit institutions, 91–92

Datt, Gaurav, 30, 137

Dessing, Maryke, 6

Donald, Gordon, 1, 5

Economic growth: agricultural sector, 19, 149; constraints in rural non-farm sector on, 79–81, 149; financial sector, 112–16; infrastructure development as tool for, 140

Education: BRAC primary education program, 33; relation to incidence of borrowing, 123; World Bank funded project, 33. See also School enrollment; Training

Employment: creating sustainable, 2; labor force participation in Bangladesh, 19; in microcredit program villages, 53–54; opportunities in rural areas, 63; options in rural areas, 63; in rural non-farm sector, 65–67. See also Labor force; Self-employment; Wage employment

Endogeneity, 133, 147, 156, 196, 197, 201, 205–7; controlling for, 43–5, 52, 67; test, 190

Farmers, small and medium-size: improving access to credit, 128–30; microcredit loans to, 150–51; as share of rural households, 131; subsistence level functioning, 128

Feder, Gershon, 1, 2–3, 5, 42, 65

Fertility: effect related to microcredit program participation, 50

Fidler, Peter, 2, 3, 6, 8

Financial institutions: conditions for sustainable rural, 145; for the poor, 145–46

Financial institutions, formal: financing of rural nonfarm sector, 81; lending to rural nonfarm sector, 68, 70–71; in rural credit market, 111–13; share of rural credit provided by, 130; subsidy dependence, 120–21. *See also* Banking system

Financial sector: formal growth and performance in Bangladesh, 112–16; targeting of rural loans, 150. *See also* Banking system; Commercial banks, nationalized; Financial institutions

Fitchett, Delbert A., 2, 110

Food-for-Work program: costs and benefits of, 137–39; objectives, 21–23; self-targeting, 30; services of, 137; targeted groups, 11

Food programs: social cost of, 202–3; targeted, 133

Foster, Andrew D., 3, 5

Foster, James, 56

Fuglesang, Andreas, 29, 92

Funding: for Grameen, BRAC, and RD-12, 90; sources for NGOs, 4

Ghate, Prabhu, 2, 110

Goetz, Anne Marie, 7

Goldberg, Mike, 6

Gonzalez-Vega, C., 6, 108, 183

Government role: Subsidies in development of rural infrastructure, 140; in funding microcredit institutions, 90; proposed for rural finance, 130; in regulation of microcredit institutions, 182. *See also* Commercial banks, nationalized

Graham, Douglas, 1, 5

Grameen Bank: access to foreign donor funds, 29; cost-benefit ratios, 136; cost-effectiveness of, 141; cost of outstanding loan, 134–35; decentralization of, 91; financing for rural nonfarm sector

(1990–94), 68–72; group-based lending scheme, 3, 23–32, 155; group viability and member dropouts (1986–94), 95–97, 171t; institutional structure, 91–95; loans and member savings (1990–94), 89–90; marginal returns to capital and labor, 75–76; members and borrowers (1989–94), 3, 88–89; microcredit program, 23–29; profitability, 97–102; sectoral distribution of loans, 68–72; sources of interest, income, and equity subsidies (1990–94), 102–6; staff size, retention, productivity, and pay structure (1990–94), 93–95; village-level organizations operated by (1989–94), 87–88

Greaney, Vincent, 142

Greer, Joel, 56

Groups: group-based formation restricted by gender, 45; role as intermediaries, 86; viability and member dropout rates, 95–97, 171t. *See also* Lending programs

Guasch, J. Luis, 1, 29, 111

Gupta, Rina Sen, 7

Gurgand, Marc, 6

Haddad, Lawrence, 192

Haggblade, Steven, 63

Hashemi, Syed M., 9, 157

Hausman, Jerry A., 190

Hazell, Peter B. R., 63

Health program: provided by BRAC, 32–33

Heckman, James J., 197

Hoddinott, John, 192

Hoff, Karla, 1, 5, 110, 124

Holt, Sharon L., 1

Holtsberg, Christer, 23

Horney, Mary Jean, 192

Hospes, Otto, 2, 183–84

Hossain, Mahabub, 6, 9, 18, 19, 20, 21, 23, 30, 55, 57, 63, 75, 106, 111, 137, 138, 139, 140

Households: benefits of microcredit borrowing to, 196–99; consumption of microfinance program participants, 148; differences in impact of male or female borrowing, 46–51; effect of institutional lending on borrowing of, 121–28; impact of microcredit programs on nonparticipatng, 51–55, 164–66t; interhousehold transfers, 124–25, 150, 176t; landless, 107–8; net worth of borrowers, 47, 160–61t; reduction of poverty at level of, 56–57

Huddleston, Barbara, 21

Hulme, David, 6, 9, 154

Human capital: development of, 1; investment of rural women in, 150

Hunte, Pamela, 6

Huppi, Monika, 1, 5

Hymer, Stephen, 63

Impact: gender differentiated, 42, 44–46, 60, 129, 136, 159t, 181, 199, 205–6

Income: effect of rural infrastructure on rural, 140; microcredit institution staff, 93–95, 170t; in microcredit program villages, 53; rural nonfarm sector as source of, 65–67; sources in rural nonfarm sector, 65–67. See also Wage income

Industrial sector modernization, 19

Infrastructure, rural: combating poverty with investment in, 133; construction through Food-for-Work program, 21–23, 137; cost-benefit analysis of projects, 139–41

Integrated Rural Development Program (IRDP), Bangladesh, 17

Interest rates: break-even rate for

Grameen and BRAC, 97–98; charged by Grameen and BRAC, 97–99; charged by microcredit instituitons, 106–8, 110; determinants of informal village-level, 124, 174t, 175t; effect of raising, 13; informal, 110; proposed policy to eliminate subsidies, 104–8

International Fund for Agricultural Development (IFAD), 4, 16

Investment: by men and women in human and physical, 150; in rural infrastructure, 133

Islam, A. K. M. A., 17

Jain, Pankaj S., 100

Jones, Steve, 20

Kalari, James W., 189

Khalily, Baqui, 3, 6, 99, 100, 102, 107, 108, 109

Khan, A. A., 20

Khan, Akhter Hamid, 17

Khan, Zahed, 3, 6, 99, 100, 102, 107

Khandker, Shadihur R., 3, 5, 6, 8, 10, 50, 55, 65, 99, 100, 102, 107, 123, 140, 142, 153, 183, 184, 199, 206

Khatkhate, Deena R., 5

Labor: marginal returns to, 72–80

Labor force: effect of microcredit borrowing on the seasonality of, 50–51, 163t; impact on supply at village level of microcredit programs, 51–55, 164–66; sectoral allocation, 18

Landell-Mills, Pierre, 1, 3, 4, 184, 200

Landlessness: effect of, 18–19, 107–8; methods to reduce rural, 152; of rural households, 63

Land ownership: employment opportunities with, 64–65; lacking in rural areas, 18–19; participation in microcredit programs based on,

32, 40–43, 123; preferred lending
to entities having large, 129; relation to levels of microcredit borrowing, 11, 123; of rural households, 17, 63. *See also*
Landlessness; Poverty
Leakage: in Food-for-Work and
Vulnerable Group Development
programs, 22t; in microcredit programs, 144
Lee, L. F., 197
Lending, marginal cost of, 100–2
Lending, informal: borrowing rate in
relation to formal sources of credit, 124; to finance agriculture,
126–27; lack of regulation of, 111;
loan contracts enforced by
lenders, 110; reduction in rural,
150; role in low-income countries,
2; in rural credit market, 111–13;
to rural nonfarm sector, 70–72;
targeting and monitoring, 30–31
Lending programs, group-based,
23–32, 36, 86, 146; BRAC as, 12;
conditions for successful, 153–55;
credit-constrained borrowers, 42;
microcredit programs, 5–6, 31–32;
moral hazard in, 30; peer monitoring, 29; RD-12 as, 12; two-tier
cooperatives, 17–18, 20. *See also*
Interest rates; Loan recovery
Literacy program: provided by BRAC,
32–33
Loan, 30, 48, 71–72, 98, 101–02, 112,
134–35, 147, 185; default cost, 3, 5,
28, 84, 120, 121; disbursements, 89,
92, 94, 112, 117; enforcement, 6,
29, 31, 110; portfolio(s), 34, 70,
115, 120, 125–26, 129, 188, 191;
recovery rate, 3, 5–8, 28, 100, 106,
110, 115–16, 129, 131, 147, 150,
185; repayment, 6–7, 15, 24, 47,
84–85, 96, 106, 123, 129; sizes, 41,
89, 149

Loan recovery, 110, 113, 116, 146,
188, 190; determinants of, 84–85;
by formal lenders (1981–93),
115–16; from group-based women
compared to men, 28; rates for
Grameen and RD-12 branch-level,
100, 116, 172t; related to agrocli-
mate risk, 106–7; risk factors in,
8–9, 84–85
Lovell, Catherine H., 17, 92
Maddala, G. S., 122
Mahajan, Vijay B., 183
Management: Grameen, BRAC, and
RD-12, 92–93; microcredit institutions, 35
Management Systems International,
23
Manser, M., 192
Manufacturing sector, rural: marginal
return to capital, 79; production
gains at village level, 149; share of
rural nonfarm business, 81
Matin, Imran, 157
McDonald, John F., 122
McElroy, Marjorie B., 192
Membership: marginal cost of, 100–2
Men: borrowing patterns of, 45–51,
159t; credit demands of, 123, 173t;
impact of borrowing by, 60–61;
investment in physical capital,
150; landless, 142; participation in
microcredit programs, 23, 43,
173t; program benefits to, 192–96
Microcredit: critics of, 2; proponents
of, 2–3
Microcredit institutions: decentralized, 34–35, 91; development in
many countries, 3–4; financial viability and profitability, 97–102;
financing of rural nonfarm sector,
81; performance compared to agricultural credit banks, 116–21; in
rural credit market, 111–13; subsidy dependence, 7–9, 120–21

Microcredit programs: advocates of, 2–3; analysis of cost-effectiveness, 101–2, 172t; benefits, 9–10; codes of conduct for members of, 26–27t; credit delivery mechanism, 5–6, 24–25t; defining participation in, 40–43; effect on poverty, 55–60; eligibility in Bangladesh for, 60; evaluation of, 147; features of BRAC, Grameen, and RD-12, 23–29; financial and economic subsidies, 185, 190–91; financial efficiency of, 187–90; future research, 155–57; group-based lending, 31–32, 36, 86; group features, 24–25t; institutional hierarchy, 91–92; land ownership eligibility criterion, 23, 32, 40; lending to rural nonfarm sector, 70–72; loans outstanding, 89; loan recovery, 8–9, 28, 47, 84–85, 100, 106, 115–16, 172t; membership criteria, 24–25t; membership growth in, 88; member savings, 89; for men and women, 23–29; noncredit services, 32–34; outreach and loan recovery, 6–7; outreach evaluation, 87–90; participation levels, 60–61; program design, 146; proposal to modify, 153; replicable, 153–55; rural credit market, 112–13; savings mobilization, 24–25t; small and large, 3; social development, 24–5t; socioeconomic effects, 61, 162t; subsidies for, 7–9; targeting of loan recipients, 150, 152–53; World Bank financing of, 4. See also Noncredit programs; Program participation; Program sustainability

Microfinance: costs and benefits of, 184–87; in response to market failure, 182; role in agriculture, 112–13

Mitra and Associates, 21, 23

Moffitt, Robert A., 122, 197
Morduch, Jonathan, 8
Mosley, Paul, 6, 9
Murshid, K. A. S., 110

Nations, R., 20
Nishat, A., 139
Noncredit programs: cost-benefit analysis of, 202–03; helping to reduce poverty, 182, 202–03; NGO instruments of, 23; services and training, 32–34

Nonfarm sector, rural: capital intensity of microcredit-financed activities, 72–80; categories of activities in, 65–66; Cobb-Douglas production function, 67–68, 168–69t, 189; components of, 64; constraints on growth of, 79–81; determinants of participation in, 64–65, 167t; financing of, 69–72; growth of, 149; linkages to agricultural sector, 63 marginal rates of return to capital, 72–73, 74t, 79–80; marginal returns to capital and labor of microcredit financed activities, 72–80; source of productivity in the, 65–69; sources of start-up capital for, 77, 78t

Nongovernmental organizations (NGOs): BRAC as, 12; noncredit targeted programs, 23; in rural credit market, 112–13; small-scale microcredit programs, 3, 155; sources of funding, 4

Norwegian Agency for International Development (NORAD), 4

Nutritional well-being of children, 49, 162t

Osmani, Siddiqur Rahman, 138, 139
Otero, Maria, 3
Outreach, microcredit programs, 87–90

Pareto efficiency, 184

Patten, Richard H., 6
Pebley, Anne R., 9
Pederson, Glenn, 6
Peer pressure, 3, 6, 28, 100
Piperk, Gerda L., 183
Pitt, Mark M., 50, 199, 206
Poverty: attempts to alleviate, 19–23;
    determinants of and methods to
    reduce, 1; effect of microcredit at
    national level on, 59–60; effect of
    microcredit on, 55–60; as factor in
    subsidy dependence, 106–07; mea-
    sured in terms of consumption,
    55–60; reduced by microfinance
    programs, 148–49; sources in
    Bangladesh, 18–19
Production, village-level, 53, 164–66t;
    See also Manufacturing sector,
    rural
Productivity: increasing, 1–2; in rural
    nonfarm sector, 65–69
Program participation: benefits of,
    147–48; cost-effectiveness of, 147;
    defining, 40; factors influencing,
    40–43; of households headed by
    women and men, 43; individual
    decision, 38; microcredit programs,
    60–61; per capita consumption
    related to, 148; survey design, 44–45
Program sustainability: analysis of,
    86; condition for, 84

Quasem, M. A., 138, 139
Quasi-experimental survey design,
    38, 44–45, 197

Rahman, Atiq, 110
Rahman, Rushidan I., 130
Rahman, Zillur, 18
Rajshashi Krishi Unnayan Bank
    (RAKUB): cost of outstanding loan
    from, 134–35; lending policies, 113
RAKUB See Rajshashi Krishi
    Unnayan Bank (RAKUB).

Ramasamy, C., 63
Ramola, Bharti Gupta, 183
Randhawa, Bikki, K., 5
Rashid, Mansoora, 100
Rashid, S., 19
Ravallion, Martin, 2, 18, 30, 137
RD-12 See Rural Development
    Project-12 (RD-12).
Resnick, Stephen A., 63
Rhyne, Elizabeth, 3, 4, 6, 8, 183
Ribe, Helena, 1
Riedinger, Jeffrey M., 6
Riley, Ann P., 157
Risk: crop compared to rural non-
    farm production, 125–27; lowering
    loan default risk, 29; related to
    loan recovery, 8–9, 84–85, 106–7
Risk, agroclimate: for microcredit
    institutions, 106–7; relation to
    subsidy dependence, 8–9
Roell, Alisa, 63
Rosengard, Jay K., 6
Rosenzweig, Mark R., 3, 8, 106, 111,
    125, 140, 186, 198, 199, 201
Rural credit delivery mechanism, 5
Rural development, Comilla model,
    17
Rural Development Project-12 (RD-
    12), 3, 12; financing for rural non-
    farm sector (1990–94), 69–72;
    group-based approach, 23–32;
    group viability and member
    dropouts (1986–94), 95–97; loans
    and member savings (1990–94),
    89–90; marginal returns to capital
    and labor, 75–76; members and
    borrowers (1989–94), 88–89;
    microcredit program of, 24–29;
    noncredit services and training,
    32–34; profitability, 101–2; sec-
    toral distribution of loans, 68–72;
    staff size, retention, productivity,
    and pay structure (1990–94),
    93–95; village-level organizations

operated by (1989–94), 87–88
Rural Works program: objectives of, 21–23; self-targeting, 30

Sacay, Orlando J., 5
Savings: marginal cost of, 100–2; in microcredit program banks, 89–90; as part of microcredit programs, 29
School enrollment: impact of microcredit on children's, 49, 162t; village-level with microcredit program, 54–55, 160–161t
Schuler, Sidney Ruth, 9, 157
Self-employment: effect at village level, 51; facilitated by microcredit programs, 47–48; as focus of Vulnerable Group Development, 137; loans for, 7; in microcredit program villages, 53–54; offering of programs for, 142; providing credit for, 2; in rural areas, 63. *See also* Women
Self-selection: into antipoverty programs, 142–43; effect of targeting on, 29–32; group lending as aid to, 6; into microcredit programs, 141–42
Sen, Binayak, 18, 55, 57
Sinha, Saurabh, 157
Skills development training, 12, 17, 33–34, 149
Smith, Clifford W., Jr., 189
Social cost: measurement of, 134; or net subsidy of lending, 135–37
Srinivasan, Aruna, 189
Stark, Oded, 111
Stiglitz, Joseph E., ix, 1, 5, 6, 28, 100, 110, 124
Subbarao, K., 137
Subsidies: for credit programs in many countries, 5; dependence, 7–9, 151; dependence by Grameen and BRAC (1990–94), 104–6; dis-

tribution of, 183; factors in reducing dependence on, 13; for microcredit programs, 7–9, 11, 102–8; sources of Grameen and BRAC (1990–94), 102–6; used by microcredit programs, 146–47
Subsidy dependence index, 120–21, 191–92
Swedish International Development Authority (SIDA), 4

Thana, definition of, 17
Thomas, J., 154
Thorbecke, Erik, 56
Townsend, Robert M., 5, 100
Training: for Grameen Bank, BRAC, and RD-12 managers, 35; for microcredit institution staff, 92–93; as precondition for microcredit programs, 28; provided by BRAC and RD-12, 32–34, 149; provided by Grameen Bank, 33; for skills development, 12, 17, 33–34, 149
Transactions costs: of microcredit programs, 7, 21, 30, 47, 101, 129, 151, 154

U.S. Agency for International Development, 5, 22t, 137

Varian, Hal R., 1, 6
Village level: borrowing in Grameen, BRAC, and RD-12 villages, 123; effect of differences in, 44; effect of microcredit on poverty at, 57–59; gains in manufacturing, 149; impact of microcredit programs on, 51–55, 164–66t; impact of program placement on, 37; organizations operated by Grameen, BRAC, and RD-12, 87; reduction of poverty at, 57, 148; rural nonfarm participation at, 65,

167t; socioeconomic effects of microcredit at, 61

Vogel, R., 4, 6, 8, 183

von Pischke, J. D., 1, 2, 5

Vulnerable Group Development program: costs and benefits of, 137–39; objectives of, 21–23

Wage employment: offering of programs for, 142; self-selection into, 142; targeted, 2

Wage income: impact of village-level microcredit programs on, 54, 164–65t; for unskilled labor, 19

Webster, Leila, 2, 3, 6, 8

Weiss, Andrew, 5

Wolpin, Kenneth I., 3, 199, 201

Women: assistance through Vulnerable Group Development, 21–23; borrowing patterns of, 123, 173t; credit demands of, 45–51, 159t; effect of *purdah* system for, 28, 44; gains from program participation, 6–7, 12, 28, 43, 47–49, 160–62t; impact of borrowing by, 61; importance of microcredit programs for rural, 149–50; landless, 142; microcredit programs for, 23; program benefits to, 192–96; served by Grameen, BRAC, and RD-12, 88

World Bank: contribution to microfinance growth, 4; financing of microcredit programs, 4; help in infrastructure development, 140

World Food Programme, 22t, 137

Yaron, Jacob, 1, 5, 6, 8, 105, 183, 191

Yunus, Muhammad, 2, 16, 90–91, 154

Zardkoohi, Asghar, 189

Zohir, S., 23